Teaching Writing in K–8 Classrooms

Iris M. Tiedt

Director, South Bay Writing Project
San Jose State University

S. SuzAnne Bruemmer
Sheilah Lane
Patricia Stelwagon
Kathleen Oda Watanabe
Mary Young Williams

Teacher Consultants
South Bay Writing Project

Teaching Writing in K–8 Classrooms

THE TIME HAS COME

PRENTICE-HALL, INC., Englewood Cliffs, New Jersey 07632

Library of Congress Cataloging in Publication Data
Main entry under title:

Teaching writing in K–8 classrooms.

Bibliography: p.
Includes index.
1. English language—Study and teaching (Elementary) 2. English language—Writing—Study and teaching (Elementary) I. Tiedt, Iris M.
II. Title: Teaching writing in K-eight classrooms.
LB1576.T43 1983 372.6'23 82–10231
ISBN 0–13–896290–1

Printed in the United States of America

10 9 8 7 6 5 4 3

Editorial/production supervision and interior design by Joan L. Stone
Cover design by Judith Winthrop
Manufacturing buyer: Ron Chapman

ISBN 0-13-896290-1

Prentice-Hall International, Inc., *London*
Prentice-Hall of Australia Pty. Limited, *Sydney*
Prentice-Hall do Brasil Ltda., *Rio de Janeiro*
Prentice-Hall Canada, Inc., *Toronto*
Prentice-Hall of India Private Limited, *New Delhi*
Prentice-Hall of Japan, Inc., *Tokyo*
Prentice-Hall of Southeast Asia Pte. Ltd., *Singapore*
Whitehall Books Limited, *Wellington, New Zealand*

Contents

To the Reader, ix

1

Exploring the Writing Process, 1

A Philosophy of Writing Instruction, 2
Bridging Language Development, 6
Focusing Instruction, 10
Recommended Instructional Strategies, 13
Teacher Attitudes, 18

2

Using Oral Language, 22

Using Children's Literature, 23
Dramatic Activities, 28
Using the Listening Center, 33

3

Developing Fluency, 39

Word Play Activities, 40
Parallel Stories, Poems, and Lists, 53
Poetic Forms, 63

4

Narrative Writing, 74

Simple Narrative Forms, 75
Elements of a Story, 83
Paragraph Development, 91

5

Expository Writing, 100

Categorizing, 102
Observation, 105
Report Writing, 109
Letter Writing, 118

6

Writing Effective Sentences, 122

Transcribing and Expanding, 123
Sentence Building, 130
Sentence Modeling, 138
Using Punctuation, 140

7

Making Effective Word Choices, 143

Word Structure, 144
Word Meanings, 147
Word Play, 154
Figurative Language, 162

8

Editing
revising, rewriting, and proofreading, 167

Editing Aids and Exercises, 169
Group Editing, 177
Peer Editing, 182
Self-editing, 187
The Follow-up, 194

9

Evaluating Student Work, 203

Evaluation Strategies, 204
Peer and Self Evaluation, 215
Management System, 221

APPENDIX

Resources, 228

Alphabet Books, 229
Books about Language, 229
Films and Writing, 232
Multicultural Books for Children, 233
Picture Books, 236
Poetry Resources for Teachers, 236
Self-awareness, 237
Stimulating Writing, 238
Children's Books with Themes, 240
Wordless Books, 244
Writing across the Curriculum, 246
The Writing Process, 248
Recommended Reading List for Students, 249

Index, 253

To the Reader

"If you want to write, write," wrote an ancient Greek philosopher. This sagacious advice bears repeating; we encourage you to have students write every day. We also recognize that teachers need help in carrying out this goal.

Teaching Writing in K–8 Classrooms was compiled by a team of teacher-authors who are excited about teaching writing. They share ideas designed to help you stimulate elementary school students to write and to love it! They describe effective teaching methods in clear, well-organized steps that make it easy for you to present successful composition lessons.

This textbook, moreover, solves the perennial problem of language arts instruction: focus. Based on a sequential holistic model that centers language arts instruction on composition, this strong writing program integrates listening, speaking, reading, and writing.

If you hesitate to teach writing because of the heavy paperload, furthermore, here are specific suggestions for relieving your anxiety. You will learn how and why to teach students to edit their own work independently, with their peers, or with your personal assistance.

We recommend that you read the first chapter carefully, for it describes the model on which the writing program presented in this book is based. It explains the assumptions on which the program is grounded—for example, the emphasis on oral language as a foundation for successful composition.

The program can be followed at any level for a full year. The activities are adaptable to fit the learning needs and abilities of children of all ages. Here is a curriculum that will surely lead to improved writing for children who follow the activities for at least a year. The returns will be even greater, of course, for children who work with the program for longer periods of time.

Children can write. We invite you to explore the possibilities of working with young authors. It is a challenge and a joy to help them discover the exciting ideas they have to share.

San Jose, California
September, 1982

Iris M. Tiedt, Director
South Bay Writing Project

Teaching Writing in K–8 Classrooms

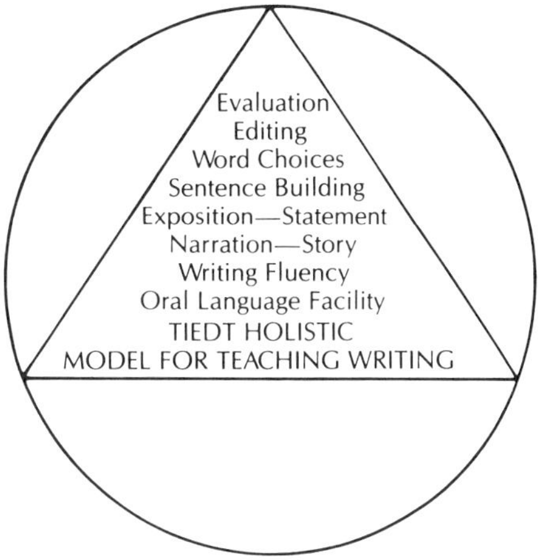

1

Exploring the Writing Process

A successful writing program begins when children speak their first words. The child who moves readily into written composition is the one who has been talking easily for years, trying out language patterns, asking for information, developing and expanding vocabulary. As children learn how English speakers string words together, they develop an "ear" for language that enables them to speak and write effectively.

As an informed classroom teacher, you can facilitate this natural development by providing an environment in which growth can take place. By encouraging children to use language in varied ways, creative oral language activities set the stage for working with written language. Composition evolves naturally when students talk about common experiences, begin writing as a group process, and then write individually with adult assistance. This oral language foundation is prerequisite for developing both writing and reading abilities. A strong writing program integrates all of language arts instruction around the center core of composition.

This book describes a holistic approach to composition instruction that focuses on writing but includes development of listening, speaking, thinking, and reading skills. Prepared by experienced teachers, the activities in this text provide a natural sequence that can be adapted to any grade level. Because the authors believe that teaching writing is exciting, they recommend activities that are not only purposeful but also enjoyable. They have tried to make your job easier by providing clear, step-by-step instructions as well as suggestions for follow-up activities and variations that you might wish to try.

In this introductory chapter you will find a framework for teaching writing that is both theoretically sound and practical. After reading the chapter, you should be able to

1. Write your own definition of the writing process
2. List a number of basic assumptions about writing instruction
3. Describe a holistic approach to teaching composition
4. Define your role in working with young writers
5. Answer basic questions that parents ask.

As you read each section of the chapter, you may find it helpful to form small groups for discussing the ideas presented and asking questions about writing instruction.

A PHILOSOPHY OF WRITING INSTRUCTION

In order to teach effectively, you need to know, first of all, what you believe about what, how, and why you teach. In order to be an effective teacher of writing, you need to clarify your thinking about writing and the process of teaching young people to write. You need to develop a personal philosophy of writing instruction.

The word *writing* is ambiguous: Does it mean practicing penmanship, composing a sonnet, or simply putting words on paper? You may think of the labored efforts of your students or the polished professional work that stands on library shelves. Writing is all of these.

In the classroom, however, teachers usually focus on writing as a process that involves thinking and ultimately produces a product. Moffett summarizes the developmental stages of writing:

- Drawing and handwriting—starts with imagery for sensory-motor activities.
- Transcribing and copying—starts verbatim with others' speech and texts.
- Paraphrasing, summarizing, plagiarizing—starts with other writers' material and ideas.

• Crafting conventional or given subject matter—starts with topics and language forms.

• Revising inner speech—starts with inchoate thought.[1]

The young child must, of course deal initially with the physical act of forming letters on paper as he or she struggles to transfer ideas from the brain to a sheet of paper. The young writer will be aided in learning to compose his or her thoughts appropriately by talking aloud and perhaps dictating to an aide. Knowledge about writing will grow through transcribing the speech of others or restating what others have said. Soon even the youngest child begins working with the craft of writing, composing original compositions. A writer, at any age or level, uses all aspects of the writing process, for inner speech or thought is present even for the young child struggling to master the letter symbols needed for putting words on paper.

In planning learning experiences for children, it is important to consider three *C's:* child, cognition, and craft. Evaluation of these variables is essential in designing curricula at any level and working with any subject matter. Examine the implications of focusing on these components as you plan a writing program.

Child

The primary consideration in planning a writing curriculum and the activities to be included is the child who will be directly involved. Consider the child's needs at each stage of development. A major concern, for instance, is the development of self-esteem. Children engaged in writing must feel that they can succeed, and a writing program must be designed with that need in mind. By beginning with oral language activities and fluency exercises, you can make certain that all children start the writing program with a positive attitude.

Writing is a difficult task that requires the child to synthesize many abilities. You need to support the child's efforts through instructional strategies that remove obstacles to successful writing. You can provide security for the beginner by using prewriting techniques such as brainstorming ideas that might be used in the writing activity or trying a new kind of writing as a group composition.

Teaching children how to edit first drafts before they make their writing public helps them to assume pride as well as responsibility for their work. When you have removed yourself from the position of wielder of the red pencil, you can offer more positive reinforcement, and the student can develop self-confidence. Working with each child in individual conferences gives you an opportunity to provide formative evaluation as the student develops a piece of writ-

[1]James Moffett, "Integrity in Teaching of Writing," *Phi Delta Kappan*, December 1979, pp. 276–79.

ing. Evaluation, too, becomes more positive and more beneficial, an integral part of the learning process.

As you plan your writing program, remember that students come from different backgrounds and have varied personal attributes. Moffett and Wagner summarize this variation:

> Different individuals have dominances toward the physical, the emotional, the intellectual, or the intuitive. Some gravitate toward visual media, some toward auditory, some toward manipulatory, and some toward the kinesthetic (the body itself as medium). Some learn better from peers, some from elders, some from the same sex, some from the other sex, some from certain personality types, and so on. Each has learned the same words in different connections and has private as well as public meanings for them. Each has a different notion about what language, especially written language, is worth and what it can do for him. Youngsters the same age want to read very different things, and any one class may have a spread of reading maturity ranging over six to ten grades as measured by standardized reading tests.[2]

Planning a writing program for such diverse individuals calls for an individualized approach. Individualized instruction means that even group activities should be planned with concern for individual needs. An individualized program includes open activities to which any student can respond, opportunities for each child to interact with other students, and activities that guarantee success for everyone.

Cognition

The second concern in developing a writing program focuses on the child's thinking process. The writing program should promote language growth and concept development, for no student can write effectively without developing cognitive ability to support that effort. In order to write, children need a subject to talk about, something to say about it, and the words and syntactic structures with which to express their ideas. Closely intertwined, concept development and language grow together.

Research on the functions of the right and left hemispheres of the brain has increased the teacher's understanding of cognition. The left side of the brain handles linear thinking, which is logical and easily codified. The right side of the brain, which works with holistic thinking, can deal with multiple stimuli, see interrelationships, and make creative leaps. By emphasizing the linear thinking associated with the left hemisphere, education has almost totally neglected

[2] James Moffett and Betty Jane Wagner, *Student-centered Language Arts and Reading, K-13*, 2nd ed. (Boston: Houghton Mifflin, 1976), p.26.

the thinking processes of the right hemisphere. Compare these types of thinking:

Linear, logical	Holistic, creative
Categorizing	Inferring
Sequencing	Associating
Defining	Synthesizing
Analyzing	Evaluating
Summarizing	Composing

In writing, students use a complexity of linear and holistic skills. They use linear processes to organize information, and holistic processes to generate original thoughts, draw conclusions, and integrate operations. Consider, for example, the processes involved as students write a research report:

Selecting a topic	Writing the first draft
Researching the subject	Judging the written composition
Taking notes	Making revisions
Sorting and organizing the findings	Final editing and proofreading
Planning the presentation	Making the writing public in some way[3]
Considering the audience	

Iris Tiedt points out that the students' handling of such operations depends on their mental maturity as well as their experience in problem solving and decision making. "A third factor in determinig success with the complex processes involved," she notes, "is the instructor, for the teacher's positive attitude and ability to teach thinking skills within a well-structured curriculum enable the student to learn."[4]

Craft

Young writers need information about the writing process itself, the craft. They need to learn the various forms of writing and the conventions that aid readers—punctuation, capitalization, spelling, paragraphing. They will learn this craft best through experience in writing and by reading the writing of others.

Students begin writing by talking and thinking about ideas—factual observation or creative fantasy—to be expressed in poetry or prose. They select a method of organization, such as chronology, and then put their ideas in order. Students need guidance as they work. They need to hear and read "book lan-

[3]Iris M. Tiedt, *The Language Arts Handbook* (Englewood Cliffs, N.J.: Prentice-Hall, 1983).
[4]Ibid.

guage," the standardized, more formal English that they are trying to write. Teachers can support their efforts with liberal but genuine praise, and by serving as resource persons and trusted co-workers.

The craft of writing involves the knowledge of grammatical structures and the ability to check grammaticality against a developing "ear for language" to see if a sentence "sounds right." The craft involves familiarity with concepts that you may take for granted:

- We leave spaces between words. (As we speak, words run together so that it's difficult for children to know when one word stops and another begins.)
- We begin the first word of a sentence with a capital letter and end the sentence with a mark of punctuation. (These conventions benefit the reader.)

As children mature, they learn to work with more advanced concepts in the writing process:

- Don't repeat the same word too frequently. Substitute a synonym to avoid monotony.
- Every time a new person speaks in a story, you must indent for a new paragraph and use quotation marks.
- The period or comma goes inside the final quotation mark, not outside.

As you develop a writing program, remind yourself of these three components: child, cognition, and craft. Emphasizing one over the others causes a serious imbalance. A good writing program enables children to succeed, to develop their thinking processes, and to communicate effectively.

BRIDGING LANGUAGE DEVELOPMENT

Listening and speaking comprise the primary methods of learning and using language. Both involve the spoken language, the development of language abilities that begins as infants hear family members talking and singing to them. At this time the child can learn any language—German, English, Japanese, Yupuk, Tagalog.

Experiences with the written language usually begin incidentally as children read their names, road signs that they see repeatedly, and other words that they encounter. Certainly most children are aware of words and letters although the extent of their experiences with written language differs widely during the preschool years. Children are eager to learn how to work with written language as they begin to relate words and sentences that they can say to those they can write and read.

The acquisition of speech occurs in a natural setting. Children learn from their peers and family without formal instruction. They feel a need to communicate; intrinsic rewards motivate them to work hard at this task, which remains highly individualized. Reading and writing instruction are much more structured, less closely tied to the individual needs of each child, and controlled by the teacher, textbook, and curriculum guide. The following diagram demonstrates the interrelationships among the language arts—listening, speaking, reading, and writing—and the role that thinking plays in language growth.

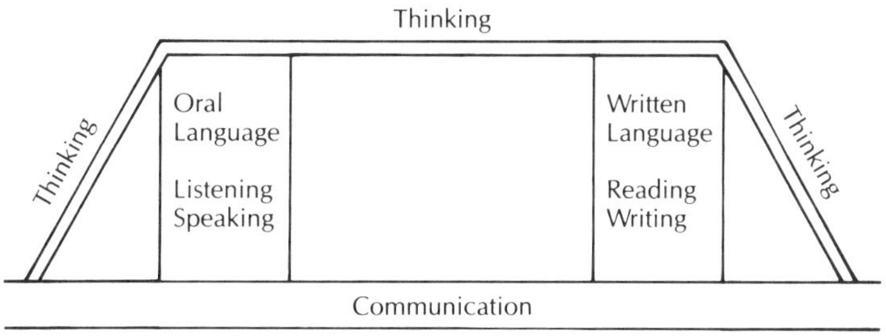

A model for bridging language development. From *The Language Arts Handbook* by Iris Tiedt. Copyright 1983 by Prentice-Hall.

Of all the language skills, writing is the most difficult to acquire. The physical act of handwriting, which requires muscle coordination, is a slow, laborious act compared to instant thought and spontaneous speech. In addition, the child is soon exposed to the complex conventions of written language—punctuation, capitalization, and perhaps the biggest bugaboo, spelling. While reading is a receptive skill, writing requires the child to produce the thoughts, words, syntax, and sequence of the story to be written. Writing involves creative production, an active process that researchers are just beginning to understand.

Because writing is the most complex of the language arts, it needs to be taught within a strongly supportive structure. The holistic model presents writing as a language art, beginning with a strong oral language foundation. Intended as a year-long curriculum framework for any level, this model begins with the student's oral language, moves into personal writing experiences that involve each student, then into longer forms of writing, and finally focuses on more specific studies of grammar, style, usage, conventions, and the precise choice of language. Each level of the model delineates the primary focus of the writing program at that stage. This text spells out activities that focus appropriately on necessary developmental skills for each stage.

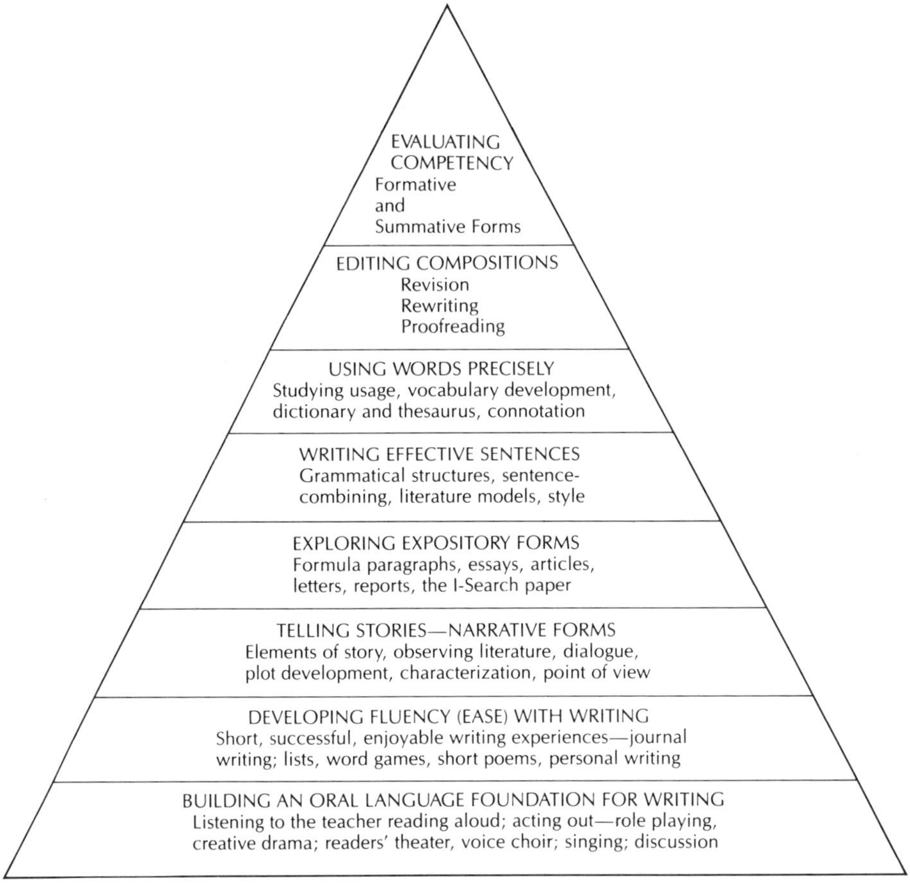

The Tiedt holistic model for teaching writing: A sequential framework for focusing group instruction during a one-year period.

The holistic model has been used widely in curriculum development. It provided the basis for a study, Plan Write, which involved an entire junior high school faculty in creating a writing program that crossed the entire curriculum. This highly successful project brought teachers together, furthermore, to discuss the teaching of writing. Teachers across the curriculum decided how and what to teach that would improve student writing.[5]

The South Bay Writing Project has trained consultants in the use of this holistic model so that they can implement it in their classrooms and evaluate the results at all levels. Research findings reveal that following the model effects a change in student attitude toward writing; it creates an "I can" attitude that

[5]San Mateo County, California, Superintendent of Schools, *Plan Write* (ESEA, Title IVC Project, 1979).

results in greater quantities of writing and improved quality. Student writing is assessed both holistically and analytically.[6]

The holistic model described in this book is based on the following assumptions:

1. Children learn to write by writing.
2. Emphasis should be placed first on gaining fluency (ease) in writing, writing quantity rather than being overly concerned about "correctness."
3. Writing is best taught as one of the language arts with strong emphasis on oral language as both a foundation and a continuing support to writing activities.
4. The writing process is as important as the written products students create.
5. Students improve their writing abilities by listening to and reading the writing of other students as well as that of published authors.
6. Students are gradually developing an "ear for language," an internalized knowledge of grammar, against which they can test their sentences.
7. As students prepare to make selected pieces of writing "public," to publish their writing in some way, they improve their writing abilities by editing (revising and polishing) their own writing independently or by working with their peers or the instructor.
8. Student writers need positive formative and summative evaluation of their work, appreciation for what they have accomplished.

Although this holistic model is presented in a triangle that connotes a hierarchy, the model should be used flexibly. Focuses for the stages of development are sequential and depend on increasing maturity as the student grows through the writing process. Oral language, although it is the foundation for writing, is never dropped from the writing program, but remains as an essential component of every writing experience. Although editing and evaluation are placed at the top of the pyramid, students may edit work that is to be published during the first months of the year. These aspects of the writing process, however, are not emphasized during the first writing experiences. The model is not meant to be rigid.

In order to implement this holistic model flexibly, you need to be familiar with the total program. As you plan for the year, you must feel comfortable with its goals and objectives and understand its intent. You need to read ahead to become aware of editing and evaluation techniques that you can introduce as soon as they are appropriate. You need to understand why emphasis on sentence structure and word choice is delayed until students are writing with a certain amount of fluency and can study these aspects of grammar and usage within the context of their own writing. You can develop your writing program for the year by following this curriculum framework, including your own cre-

[6]South Bay Writing Project, *Annual Report* (San Jose State University, 1981).

ative activities, feeling free to talk about aspects of writing that occur as students try writing experiments. If you understand the model, you will not begin the year with a traditional grammar approach that kills student interest in writing or waste time red-penciling student errors instead of providing support for student editing, a valuable learning experience for young writers.

The holistic model is designed as a year-long writing program that begins ideally in September. Useful at any grade level, this curriculum framework can be adjusted to the needs of a particular group of students. Students who need more time for developing oral language abilities—primary grade students, those learning English as a second language, handicapped students including those who are retarded—will spend more time on the foundation for writing. More able students will move quickly through oral language into fluency and into writing narrative and expository forms. It is important, however, not to omit any of the stages because the attitudes and values that develop in each stage help to increase an individual's competence as a writer.

FOCUSING INSTRUCTION

To understand the rationale behind this curriculum framework, you should become acquainted with the eight focuses of the holistic model, including the activities used and attitudes developed at each stage. The eight focuses are described briefly below, and then each one is developed in detail in one of the subsequent chapters. You are encouraged to add your own favorite writing ideas as appropriate.

Oral Language

Without a strong oral language foundation, no student will write well. At any grade level, therefore, you should begin instruction orally. Students need to hear language, particularly "book language," for that is the kind of language they will eventually write. This formal language may be foreign to many of your students. Although avid readers provide this input for themselves, you must build it into the writing program for those who are less able. Focusing on oral language builds vocabulary and knowledge of sentence syntax, exposes students to new concepts, and develops self-esteem. You cannot afford to ignore the oral foundation for a writing program.

Writing Fluency

Your aim should be to help students begin writing easily and with pleasure. First experiences must be designed so that all students can succeed; for example, plan group compositions that begin orally. Young students and those who need remedial assistance benefit from dictating to the teacher or an aide. To support early experiences, you may want to provide models, or language patterns, that help less skillful writers get started. At this stage, students are directed to write about what they know—themselves, their common knowledge, and students' universal concerns. Journal writing is a popular teaching strategy that promotes fluency. At this stage writing experiences must be short, within the ability of the student, and rewarded by a sense of satisfaction and accomplishment.

Narrative Writing

A natural step beyond the first attempts at writing is the telling of stories, beginning orally. Sharing stories the students have heard—jokes, anecdotes, nursery tales—is the foundation for writing narrative forms of literature, an important prewriting activity that prepares students to write. Role playing and acting out stories help youngsters think about dialogue. Talking about the sequence of events in a story you have read aloud develops awareness of plot. Thus, oral language continues to support the composition process.

As young children begin writing "sentence stories," supported through dictation, they learn to read what they dictated, the language experience method of teaching reading and writing. Beginning with these prewriting activities, children soon develop more complicated stories. They learn to handle the capitalization and punctuation required in dialogue as the need arises. Emphasis at this stage remains on developing fluency and helping each student to feel successful in communicating to an audience. Students speak and write sentences intuitively without analysis and drill on grammar. Even the youngest writers can discuss mood, theme, setting, and point of view as they experiment with the elements of story. Through these experiences they begin to think of themselves as authors who create literature, and they enjoy publishing some of their work.

Expository Writing

Writing explanations, directions, and business letters introduces young writers to the writing of nonfiction. At this stage they can easily learn to write a "formula" paragraph that answers a question or explains a process. Once they have mastered this formal paragraph, they can focus on ways of writing nonfiction creatively following models taken from magazine articles or advertising. In the elementary school, functional research shows students how to find the answers they need rather than how to research assigned topics. This approach eliminates purposeless copying and plagiarizing to produce lengthy papers that impress parents and teacher. Engaging students in writing for a purpose encourages clarity and persuasiveness as they strive to communicate to a specific audience.

Educators who plan writing assessments often require students to write an essay and expect that they will develop paragraphs according to the traditional formula: a topic sentence, three substantiating sentences, and one concluding sentence. This form can be applied to all writing, and consequently, the ability to write an expository paragraph has become a measure of writing competency. While recognizing that teaching students to follow any kind of pattern helps them to develop skills, we should also be aware that few writers of nonfiction are guided by rigid rules that limit forms of self-expression.

Writing Effective Sentences

Developed intuitively, students' first sentences are based on the knowledge of grammatical structures they have acquired from listening to language. After students are writing fluently, focus on sentence building. Show students how to write more mature, more effective sentences. Through examining the writing in books that they read or papers other students have written, they can observe the need for sentence variety. Show students how to expand or combine sentences in their work to make the writing more varied. Discuss the flow of language, the idiom, and the use of descriptive phrases. Focusing on the students' own sentences provides an opportunity to discuss both grammar and style at a time when they are motivated to study this aspect of writing.

Using Words Precisely

Another focus for fluent writers is word choice. Within the context of student writing you can focus on the conventions of usage. Students develop vocabularies as they discuss the denotations and connotations of the words they encounter. Show young writers how to use more precise language and how to manipulate words to create an effect. At this stage students will be stimulated to pore over dictionaries and the thesaurus as they seek out more interesting words. This focus enables students to polish their use of language and leads to working with idioms, examining models from literature, and reading their own writing more critically.

Editing: Revising and Polishing

Learning to edit one's own writing is an ability that grows slowly. Students require specific instruction on editing as they develop their writing abilities. Editing focuses attention on the conventions—capitalization, punctuation, and spelling—but it must also utilize concepts that have developed throughout the various stages of the writing program. Students can learn to watch for repetition of one word or lack of clarity. They can help each other determine whether their writing is logical and communication is clear. Editing is a challenging process that includes reviewing the first draft, revising the content, checking mechanics or conventions, rewriting, and at last, proofreading. Editing prepares a piece of writing to be made public, to go out into the world alone.

Not everything a student writes will be revised, but periodically the teachers should provide a purpose for polishing: some type of publication that motivates each student to perfect a selection of his or her work. Publication can be on the bulletin board, in a newsletter sent home to parents, or in a school paper. Be sure to let students do their own editing, working alone or in small groups, supported by your guidance. Students will not learn how to edit their writing if you assume all the responsibility and do all the work. This approach to teaching reduces the paperwork that overwhelms many teachers.

Evaluating Student Writing

The student must be directly involved in evaluating his or her own writing and that of others in the class. Through reading the writing of other students and scoring the papers holistically, even young writers learn what makes some papers better than others. Help students develop a list of criteria for writing that is weak, good, or outstanding so that students are aware of how others judge their work.

Working directly with an individual child in a scheduled conference, you can examine the student's work together as the student revises it or makes notes. Taking samples of student writing as a benchmark at the beginning of the year and as a posttest at the end of the year provides a valid method of assessing student growth. Holistic assessment is an excellent way of ranking student writing in a large group as well as identifying students who write adequately for their grade level and those who require additional supportive instruction. Analytical assessment of student writing, a more time-consuming method of evaluation, provides diagnostic information to guide instruction for individual students.

The holistic model integrates the language arts curriculum around a strong writing focus. Oral language activities are used as prewriting experiences throughout the program, and a reading-writing approach provides the bridge between the encoding and decoding levels of written language and the more advanced thinking abilities involved in comprehension and composition. Working through the activities described in the chapters of this book will enable you to develop a strong writing program for children of all ages and abilities.

RECOMMENDED INSTRUCTIONAL STRATEGIES

A number of teaching strategies are subsumed within the holistic model for instruction. These basic strategies are essential to the success of the writing program described in this text. The strategies reflect a concerned and informed attitude toward writing and toward the student who is learning to write. Be aware, for example, of how difficult the writing process is and how important it is to give students as much positive support as possible. Individualizing the writing experience, grouping for sharing and evaluation, and taking time for the prewriting warm-up session are suggestions that you will find effective.

Individualizing the Writing Program

Writing is inherently an individualized process. Even if you give all students in your classroom the same topic and the same directions, the results of their writing will differ widely. Students write out of their personal experiences and according to their abilities . They have different perceptions of the world and various motives and needs. The writing that is produced reveals a person. Talk with students about developing an individual voice as they speak to the world.

Recognize that your students are not all beginning from the same starting place. Collect a sample of each student's writing to help you assess each one's writing abilities, diagnose student needs, and plan further instuction.

Continue the individualized approach by conferring individually with each student about once a month. Have students keep individual folders of their work so that you have a record of their progress. See that every student gets some affirmation of his or her efforts through your oral comments or positive, interested notes that you write on a page of a journal or the back of a poem.

Response Groups for Sharing, Editing, and Evaluation

An individualized program gives students time to work with other students and with the instructor. After every writing assignment has been completed, plan time for sharing in small groups of five or six. Never plan to have an entire class read their stories aloud to the whole class as that requires too much time and becomes boring after the first 15 minutes. Working in response groups permits each student to read his or her work to an audience and to hear what five other students wrote. Students enjoy hearing what fellow students have done, and they often make helpful suggestions to improve communication and effectiveness. Working with response groups establishes an audience, as students write for each other, not just for the teacher.

When peer pairs work together at the editing stage, each helps the other revise a piece of writing. Reading the first draft aloud to a buddy is an effective way for children to determine if they have written what they intended to say. A pair of students can present their writing together by taking the roles of characters or by reading alternate paragraphs. Working in dyads, both students try to underwrite the success of the team. As in a doubles tennis match, both players contribute to its success.

Prewriting Warm-up Sessions

Students should never be expected to begin writing without warming up. This prewriting experience could be a discussion about a topic the group will write on. One effective method of warming up is group or individual brainstorming, sometimes called "clustering." Words and phrases are clustered around a central subject, as shown here.

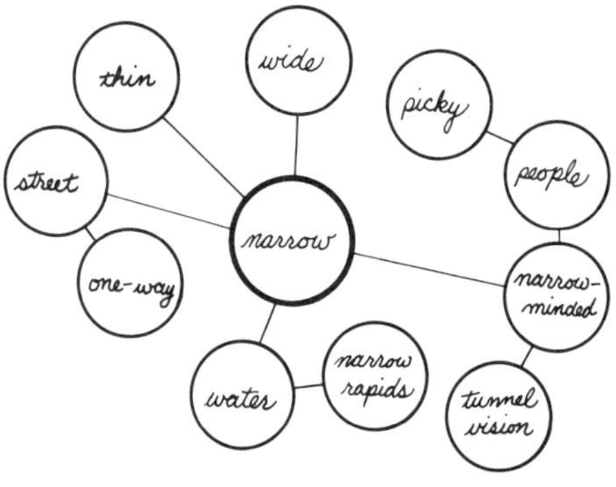

After clustering, each writer can compose a paragraph or more about some appealing aspect of the topic. After clustering around the word *narrow,* for example, a student wrote this paragraph.

> When I first thought about the word narrow, nothing came to my mind. After I started jotting down words, however, I could think of a lot of things to say. I could write a book, for instance, about narrow-minded people. I hate people who always think the worst about what you have done without giving you time to explain. Like the time I hit a ball through my neighbor's window. He came running out yelling as if I had done it on purpose. I didn't have a chance!

Primary children can use the clustering technique, too. They simply adjust it to their abilities.

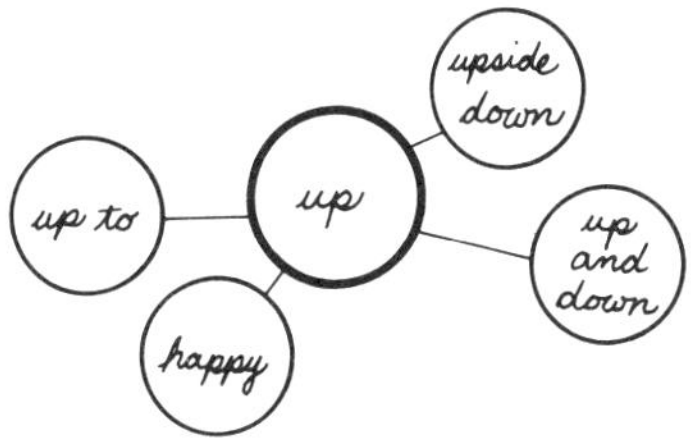

> Mom always asks me what I am up to. On a sunny day I feel up like a balloon or a kite. I go up and down on the teeter-totter. Up is fun. Down is plop!

Prewriting experiences can take many different forms. After watching the wordless film *Clown,* for example, students could talk about the film and then write the story or their impressions of how the main character felt when he lost his dog. A large poster can stimulate discussion that leads into writing. Role playing a situation that students identify with involves them in a problem that all can respond to. Reading a short book aloud is yet another stimulus for talking followed by writing.

Prewriting warm-up sessions prevent the "blank page syndrome" that plagues writers by providing vocabulary and ideas so that every student has something to say.

Dictation in the Classroom

Two kinds of dictation are appropriate for use in your classroom, and both are effective. The first kind is dictation by students who cannot write independently: first grade children, a handicapped student, or an upper-grade student who needs remedial aid. The other kind is dictation by the teacher with students acting as scribes—a highly successful technique that can serve many purposes at all grade levels.

Dictating to the teacher or an aid permits students to "write" stories even if they have not yet learned to write or cannot manage the physical act of writing. Students can dictate into a recorder or directly to someone who prints or types what is dictated. Because students have spoken the sentences, they can read what is printed. This method is called the "language experience approach" to reading. Dictation is an outstanding example of teaching that integrates the language arts.

When the teacher dictates sentences to a group of students, he or she has selected sentences designed to teach specific concepts. Sentences may be composed by the teacher or selected from a library book or a reading text. A teacher who wants to help fourth grade students learn to punctuate quotations correctly might use these sentences:

1. "Where are you going today, Mark?" asked Mrs. Martin.
2. Mark replied, "I'm going to the store for Mother."
3. "Do you need anything?" he added. "I can put everything in my basket."

Using this method, the teacher asks students first to listen to the sentence. As the sentence is repeated slowly, the students write it as well as they can. Then four or five students write the sentence on the chalkboard, and the class corrects the sentences aloud, while all children correct the sentences they have written on their papers. The process is repeated for each sentence. The dictation is done again the next day so that children can see how much better they are at "taking dictation."

Teacher dictation is an effective method of providing increasingly sophisticated grammatical structures for students learning English as a second language, or of presenting the standard English dialect to students who speak another dialect. As sentences are written on the board, teacher and students can discuss the meaning of terms used and any grammatical structures that are not familiar to students. Concepts selected for instruction are presented in the context of writing, which should aid transfer to students' original compositions.

Selecting a dictation passage from multicultural literature serves additional purposes. A book such as *Dragonwings* by Laurence Yep or *Sound of Sunshine, Sound of Rain* by Florence Heide introduces children to different ethnic groups within the structure of the basic curriculum. Telling older students of Yep's historical novel about Chinese Americans and then dictating from the book will stimulate their interest in reading the book. Heide's book could be read aloud to children in any elementary or junior high school classroom because all of them will empathize with the blind black boy who narrates the story. After discussing the ideas and the writing, students will be interested in trying to write some of the author's sentences as you dictate.

The instructional strategies presented in this section can be used at all levels to involve students in writing. Although designed as methods of teaching writing, they all include listening, speaking, and reading. The holistic approach to teaching composition is stimulating because it engages students in thinking as part of the writing process.

Guidelines for a Strong Writing Program

How do you begin a writing program? In September, or whenever you begin working with a new group of students, follow these procedures to ensure the success of your composition curriculum:

1. Have each student decorate a manila file folder in which to collect writing over a period of time. Place the folders in a cardboard box or file that is accessible to the students. All writing is placed in these folders so that students can review their work and select something they wish to revise or to discuss in an individual conference.

2. Conduct a writing assessment for all students in your class. (The whole school or the entire district also may be assessed.) Have students write about a carefully selected topic, often called a *prompt:*

> Write three paragraphs about a pet or toy that you especially like. Tell who gave you the pet or toy, what it looks like, and where it is now.

Tell the students that this piece of writing will be their "benchmark," to show how much they grow as writers during the year. Compare this "benchmark" to recording their heights on the wall to measure their growth.

3. Have each student begin writing a personal journal. These journals should be kept in student folders so they are available for writing at the designated time.

4. Show students how to make a personal dictionary in which to record words that each one needs to learn how to spell. Words are entered at any time during writing sessions. The dictionaries are kept in student folders.

5. Read chapters 2 and 3 and begin using the activities each day. After about a month, depending on the abilities of the group, move into chapter 4. About a month later, begin work from chapter 5, and so on. (You do not have to use every activity described in the book. You may want to add some of your own favorite activities.) Read chapters 8 and 9 so that these ideas can be used as appropriate during the year.

6. Have students write every day. Adjust the quantity of writing and the length of time to the needs of the group. Bring writing into other areas of the curriculum, too. Display student work and provide positive reinforcement for every child.

7. Introduce response groups so that students become accustomed to sharing their writing with each other before they begin editing experiences. Talk about these groups as an audience. Stress writing to communicate to this audience as students begin a new composition.

8. Schedule reading aloud every day to provide input for language and concept development. As you read, guide students to observe the author's writing style, interesting words and images, a character description, or an effective bit of dialogue. Select different forms of writing—poetry and prose, narrative and expository styles, short books or stories and longer works that continue over a period of time.

9. Refuse to do copy editing for students. Don't worry unduly about errors that are made as beginning students engage in free writing and pleasurable fluency activities. About once a month, publish student writing in some way—a showcase on the bulletin board, a writing selection mounted on colored paper to share with their parents, a simple booklet of student writing. Each student will then select writing to revise and polish from the first draft stage using self-editing, peer editing, or teacher conferences as described in Chapter 8. Editing is a vital part of the learning process for students and should be done in the classroom as an essential part of the writing program.

10. Evaluate student writing positively, appreciating whatever the child achieves. Assess the individual child's growth by comparing his or her benchmark writing sample with subsequent samples taken just prior to grading periods. Prepare a set of coded writing samples to show parents how their child's writing compares to that of others in the room. Discuss appropriate expectations with parents for the individual child's achievement and what measures can be taken to promote growth.

A strong writing program provides a focus for language arts instruction. Listening, speaking, the use of literature—all support composition. The holistic approach to writing is a stimulating process, a positive shared experience that is self-motivating for your students.

TEACHER ATTITUDES

As you think about writing, you can begin to sort out the understandings about the writing process that affect the way you will teach. What attitudes and concepts will you share with the young people in your classroom? Here are several that you might consider:

1. You learn to write by writing. The more you write the better you write.

2. Writing is a craft that you can learn. You can try different forms and learn how to construct more effective sentences and paragraphs.

3. As you read a book, observe the author's writing. You can learn how writing is done by reading the work of skilled writers.

Can you think of additional concepts that you would like to share with student writers?

The following comments about writing were made by classroom teachers who work with K-8 children.

Teachers Comment on Teaching Writing

There are few cooks who never experience disaster, but the good cook views each mistake as a chance to learn, experiment, or know what not to do next time. Mistakes in writing, likewise, need to be viewed as chances to learn.—Roberta Neakrans

As a teacher I attempt to facilitate my students' growth to their fullest potential, both physically and mentally. For them to grow, they need to learn to communicate . . . to read, to speak, and to write in such a fashion that they may understand others and be understood in turn.—Bob Long

I believe in the positive effects a person can receive from participating in the writing process. I write and share along with the children on our various assignments. In our classroom writing is fun, a successful experience for everyone.—Cheryl Wierwille

If children learn the process of writing, find each stage rich and rewarding, and are taught skills as they recognize the need for them, they bring to the writing experience many ideas that can be communicated clearly and interestingly. They begin to value written ideas and become knowledgeable, skillful, and appreciative of the writing process.—Gwen Freeman

I respect what students are trying to say and the efforts, however contorted the results, they have made in attempting written communication. My goal is to allow students to experience a feeling of success and to perceive writing as a positive form of self-expression. I use positive, rather than negative reinforcement, therefore, that allows children to enjoy writing, thus encouraging them to write and to grow in their ability to write.—Elaine Messick

Listening, speaking, reading, and writing are part of the process of learning and growing. It is possible to express ideas and thoughts orally, but some thoughts and ideas are better expressed in writing. What happens to us while we are writing and as a result of writing, causes us to change. Our writing may be read, discussed, laughed at, or ignored. Whatever happens, we will feel or express some response. We will bring to our next experience of listening, reading, speaking or writing, new ideas, and so the process continues.—Ruth Gibbs

Learning to write takes time and effort. Writing is a difficult process, but all students can learn to write clearly and concisely if they have consistent, daily practice, and receive support and encouragement. Teachers must assume the role of motivators rather than editors. If teachers can make writing pleasurable, students will want to write, and their quality of writing will improve. Students can write, but they need the guidance of teachers.—Sandra Way

My students write about topics which have meaning, importance, and significance for them. They express in writing in all academic areas. They not only write reports, but choose from a variety of divergent topics. expose my students to many styles of writing, and I give them the opportunity to reflect or to imitate these styles.—Linda Gonzales

It is clear that these teachers are excited about teaching writing. Is their excitement contagious? You will discover how enjoyable the teaching of writing can be as you help students discover that they *can* write, and as you begin to overcome such pitfalls as "paper overload" and confusion about teaching the mechanics of writing. Teaching writing could be the most exciting experience in your teaching career.

CHALLENGE

1. Discuss the following assumptions:[7]
   a. The teacher is the key to the improvement of student writing.
   b. Most teachers have not been prepared to teach writing effectively.
   c. Successful teachers of writing can share their expertise with other teachers.
   d. Teachers of writing should write.
   e. Current research provides some information about writing instruction, but these findings are not widely known.
   f. Writing is best taught as one of the language arts with strong emphasis on oral language.
   g. The writing process is as important as the written products students produce.
   h. Responsibility for teaching writing is shared by teachers of all subjects.
2. Write a one-page statement of your philosophy of writing instruction. Keep this statement in your notebook. At the end of the course, read it again to see if you still agree with what you have written.
3. Organize a writer's notebook in which to keep your notes, original writing, and information about composition. Identify a section for each chapter of this book. Create a sample of your own writing to use as a benchmark for your personal growth as a writer.

RECOMMENDED RESOURCES

Clapp, Ouida, and the Committee on Classroom Practices. *Teaching the Basics—Really!* Urbana, Ill.: National Council of Teachers of English, 1977.

[7]South Bay Writing Project, "Programs and Services, 1981–1982," p. 2.

Hailey, Jack. *Teaching Writing.* Berkeley, Calif.: University of California Instructional Laboratory, 1978.

Hennings, Dorothy G., and Barbara M. Grant. *Written Expression in the Language Arts.* New York: Teachers College Press, 1981.

Lundsteen, Sara W., ed. *Help for the Teacher of Written Composition, K-9.* Urbana, Ill.: NCRE and ERIC, 1976.

Maxwell, Rhoda J., and Stephen Judy, eds. *Composing: The 1979 Yearbook of the Michigan Council of Teachers of English.* Lansing, Mich.: MCTE, 1979.

Moffett, James, and Mary Jane Wagner. *Student-centered Language Arts and Reading, K-13.* Boston: Houghton Mifflin, 1976.

Neman, Beth. *Teaching Students to Write.* Columbus, Ohio: Merrill, 1980.

Nilsen, Don L. F., and Alleen Pace Nilsen. *Language Play: An Introduction to Linguistics.* Rowley, Mass.: Newbury House, 1978.

Tiedt, Iris M. *Exploring Books with Children.* Boston: Houghton Mifflin, 1979.

Tiedt, Iris M. *The Language Arts Handbook.* Englewood Cliffs, N.J.: Prentice-Hall, 1983.

Tiedt, Sidney W., and Iris M. Tiedt. *Language Arts Activities for the Classroom.* Boston: Allyn & Bacon, 1978.

Wolf, Maryanne, and others. *Thought & Language/Language & Reading.* Cambridge, Mass.: Harvard Educational Review, Reprint Series no. 14, 1980.

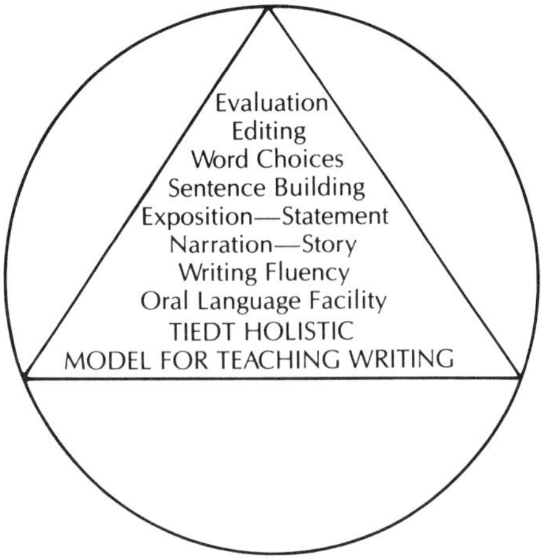

2

Using Oral Language

Oral language is the foundation of all language development. It is essential for readiness in reading and writing skills. The child who has a strong oral language facility becomes a good reader and has a greater potential for writing well. Oral language is the primary source of all other language forms; therefore emphasis on speaking and listening should not be limited to the education of the very young child. Instead it should be carried throughout the child's school development.

Young children learn language gradually by listening to language spoken around them. Soon they learn to connect individual words with objects, ideas, and actions. Gradually, increasingly effective use of listening and speaking skills supports the students as they move toward the more complex reading and writing skills. Oral language skills are essential for several reasons:

1. Oral language is the most common mode of expression.
2. Oral language is the first form a child learns.

3. For many children oral language remains the mode in which he or she feels most secure.

Oral language experiences should challenge children to extend, enrich, and elaborate the language patterns they already know. Include strategies involving listening and speaking skills, such as reading aloud to students and providing experiences with readers' theater, puppetry, and choral speaking.

This chapter is divided into three parts: Using Children's Literature, Dramatic Activities, and Using the Listening Center. The study of literature reaffirms the importance of the student's own experiences and opens them to images, ideas, and events that enrich their lives. Children need to hear literature as they learn to use language more effectively. Through drama, you can help your students improve social attitudes and relationships, gain greater self-confidence and emotional stability, and develop independent thinking and personal creativity. Using the listening center will enable you to provide guided experiences designed to improve student listening abilities. The sample lessons provided in each section show you how to promote oral language as part of a strong writing program.

After working through the activities in this chapter you will be able to

1. Introduce children to different modes of expression
2. Provide a developmental sequence of oral language experiences
3. Teach children specific speaking and listening skills

USING CHILDREN'S LITERATURE

Reading aloud to children exposes them to the full beauty and flavor of the English language. It also helps to improve their writing style when children hear forms of literature they might not ordinarily read. Children need to hear "book language," the kind of language they will be expected to write. Children need help to observe the authors' writing style. Include different forms of writing such as poetry, prose, narrative, and exposition, when reading to children.

In this section students work with literature orally through using pattern books, focusing on a theme, exploring nursery rhymes, and experimenting with choral speaking.

USING PATTERN BOOKS

Objectives:

Students will be able to

1. Listen to a repeatable pattern throughout a book
2. Use the same pattern in telling a short story of their own in sequential order

Description:

After reading aloud the story *Fortunately, Unfortunately* by Remy Charlip, students will follow the pattern to create a story of their own. Other pattern books can be used in a similar manner.

Organization:

Large group, 20 minutes; Small group, 15 minutes

Procedure:

1. Write the words *fortunately* and *unfortunately* on the board and give the meaning of each.
2. As you read the story about Ned who was both fortunate and unfortunate, have the students listen carefully for these two words until they have found the pattern.
3. As you read the story, pause when you come to the words *fortunately* and *unfortunately*. Have the children join in by saying these words with you.
4. After reading the story, have students tell you the fortunate and unfortunate things that happened to Ned.
5. Make up a pattern story and have the students fill in the missing parts. Let the story be about you, the teacher, or ask if any student wants to volunteer a story.

> *Fortunately*, our teacher, Mrs. Lane, was so tired last night, she went to bed very early.
> *Unfortunately*, the alarm did not go off, and she woke up very late.

6. Continue to invent these stories until most class members have had a chance to supply the missing endings.

Follow-up:

- Have students work in groups of four or five to create stories using this pattern. Let each group share their story by telling it to the class.
- Have students form small groups and make books using their *fortunately, unfortunately* stories.
- Other pattern books that can be used are:

Viorst, Judith. *Alexander and the Terrible, Horrible, No Good, Very Bad Day*. New York: Atheneum, 1972.

Zindel, Paul. *I Love My Mother*. New York: Harper & Row, Pub., 1975.

Zolotow, Charlotte. *Do You Know What I'll Do?* New York: Harper & Row, Pub., 1958.

Zolotow, Charlotte. *If It Weren't for You.* New York: Harper & Row, Pub., 1966.

See page 63 for additional suggestions for using pattern books.

FOCUSING ON A THEME (LOVE)

Objectives:

Students will be able to

1. Listen to a story about love
2. Tell ten things that they love about a person

Description:

After the teacher reads aloud the story entitled *I Love My Mother* by Paul Zindel, students will write ten special feelings about their parents.

Organization:

Large group, 20 minutes; individual, 15 minutes

Procedure:

1. Write the word love on the board and give the meaning.
2. Tell students that you are going to read a story about a boy and his feelings about his mother.
3. Begin reading the story and pause to show the illustrations.
4. After reading the story, ask questions:

   Name some things this boy loved about his mother.
   Is there a father in the house? Where could he be?

5. Tell students that you would like them to think quietly about a loved one—a parent, a grandparent, or other special person. Have them write ten reasons why they love this person.
6. After two or three minutes, have students share one thought about that special person. (Example: I love the way my mother gave me a hug whenever I woke up from a bad dream.)
7. Now, call on each student to read one thing they love about their special person.

Follow-up:

- Have the students make a greeting card showing drawings about the person on the card.

• Have students write their special feelings in a poem and then read it aloud to the class.

• Other books on the theme of love are:

Silverstein, Shel. *The Giving Tree.* New York: Harper & Row, Pub., 1964.

Viorst, Judith. *The Tenth Good Thing about Barney.* New York: Atheneum, 1971.

Williams, Margery. *The Velveteen Rabbit.* Garden City, N.Y.: Doubleday, 1926.

CHORAL SPEAKING

Objectives:

Students will be able to

1. Interpret poetry orally in a group
2. Follow markings on a poem

Description:

After listening to the poem "Poor Old Lady," students will be able to say the poem in unison, creating several gestures of their own.

Organization:

Large group, 35 minutes

Copies of poem "Poor Old Lady"

Procedure:

1. Tell students that you are going to read a poem entitled "Poor Old Lady." They are to tell you what problems this woman had.

2. Read the poem aloud to students, interpreting the markings as indicated.

Poor Old Lady

Unknown

— Poor old lady,/she swallowed a fly.
? I don't know why she swallowed a fly.
— Poor old lady,/I think she'll die.

— Poor old lady,/she swallowed a spider.
• It squirmed and wriggled and turned inside her.
✓✓ She swallowed the spider to catch the fly.
? I don't know why she swallowed a fly.
— Poor old lady,/I think she'll die.

— Poor old lady,/she swallowed a bird.
! How absurd! She swallowed a bird.
✓✓ She swallowed the bird to catch the spider.
✓✓ She swallowed the spider to catch the fly,
? I don't know why she swallowed a fly,
— Poor old lady,/I think she'll die.

— Poor old lady,/she swallowed a cat.
! Think of that!/She swallowed a cat.
✓✓ She swallowed the cat to catch the bird.
✓✓ She swallowed the bird to catch the spider.
✓✓ She swallowed the spider to catch the fly,
? I don't know why/she swallowed a fly.
— Poor old lady/I think she'll die.

— Poor old lady, she swallowed a horse.
! She died, of course!

Markings:

— Read slowly
/ Slight pause
? Sounding like a question
• Make movement
✓✓ Read faster
! With excitement

3. Place markings on the board and go over them with the students. Pass out a copy of the poem to each student and review each marking line by line, having students repeat each line after you.

4. Have students read the poem several times making changes in markings where they feel there should be special emphasis.

Follow-up:

- Divide the class into several groups, including a separate group for each marking on the poem. Allow students time in their groups to prepare how they are going to read and act out their parts.
- Have students form groups to create short stories about this old lady, and read their stories to the group.
- Have students do choral speaking of Martin Luther King's speech, "I Have A Dream."

NURSERY RHYME CHARACTERS

Objectives:

Students will be able to retell nursery rhymes using new characters.

Description:

After hearing several Mother Goose nursery rhymes, students will retell nursery rhymes with their own characters.

Organization:

Large group, 15 minutes; partners, 25 minutes

Procedure:

1. Read several nursery rhymes with students and have students share some of their favorites with the class.

2. Have students change characters in nursery rhymes to a famous hero, TV personality, or movie star. Example:

Old Mother Hubbard went to the cupboard to fetch her poor dog a bone. But when she got there the cupboard was bare, and so the poor dog had none.	Darth Vader went to the shuttle to get R2-D2 his gun. But when he got there the shuttle was bare, and so R2-D2 had none.

3. Have students work in pairs. Each pair will rewrite three nursery rhymes.

4. Provide several books on nursery rhymes for students, or make copies of nursery rhymes for students to work with. Have students share their nursery rhymes orally with the rest of the class.

Follow-up:

- Have students put their new nursery rhymes on tape.
- Have students make a bulletin board displaying their retold nursery rhymes.
- Have students pick persons out of history to use in their nursery rhymes.

DRAMATIC ACTIVITIES

Children are potentially creative. Drama gives them a chance to express themselves creatively and behave in a spontaneous manner. Children need to experiment with using their bodies and voices.

In this section students have experiences in puppetry, developing character sketches, role playing news items, and applying readers' theater techniques.

FOLKTALE PUPPETRY

Objectives:

Students will be able to

1. Create their own folktales using stick puppets
2. Act out their own newly-created folktale by using stick puppets

Description:

After listening to a folktale, for example, *Why the Sun and the Moon Live in the Sky* by Elphinstone Dayrell (Houghton Mifflin, 1968), students put on a puppet show telling the story in their own words.

Organization:

Large group, three days, 35 minutes each day

Procedure:

1. Tell students that a folktale is a story or legend handed down among the common people. Read them any interesting folktale (possibly one suggested by a social studies unit).

2. Tell students that they will do a puppet show using the characters in the story.

3. After reading the story, have the students name the main characters. Have them retell the story.

4. Brainstorm other possible ideas for folktales. Give the following examples and have students provide more:

   Why is there thunder in the sky?
   Why do the stars twinkle at night?
   Why does a cow give milk?

5. Divide the class into groups of five or six students and have them write their own short folktales.

6. Demonstrate how to make stick puppets using tongue depressors. Children can glue a head to the stick or draw other figures to glue on the sticks.

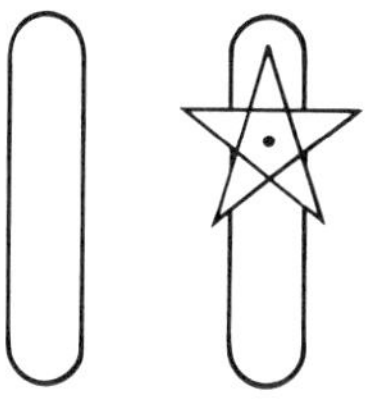

7. Remind each group that they will need:

   A narrator
   People to make characters
   People to decorate the stage (cardboard box)

8. Allow time for children to make their presentation on the third day.

Follow-up:

- Have students record their folktales on a cassette tape to be used in a listening center.
- Have children create folktales about historical events, such as how the West was won or how states were named.

SPONTANEOUS DRAMATICS

Objectives:

Students will be able to

1. Use pictures to improvise dialogue for a variety of people
2. Create voices for persons unknown to them, suggested by pictures

Description:

After choosing distinctive faces from magazines, students create voices for unknown persons.

Organization:

Large group, 35 minutes; small group, 10 minutes

Procedure:

1. Have students create voices for pictures of people who are unknown to them.
2. Tell students that, when they are creating voices, they need to consider several things:

   Pitch—high or low sound
   Stress—the accent on a word
   Juncture—the stops or pauses between words

3. Encourage students to find pictures that show an emotion or form of expression, such as anger, excitement, sadness. Locate pictures of people of various ages and share them with the class.
4. Have students try expressing emotion through their faces.
5. Call students up to select a picture and match a voice to that person.

Follow-up:

- Have students use several pictures to create a skit by role playing a situation.
- Have students select famous historical persons and create voices for them.

ROLE PLAYING NEWS ITEMS

Objectives:

Students will be able to

1. Act out headlines found in the daily newspaper
2. Work in small groups effectively

Description:

Students will work in groups to role play headlines found in local newspapers.

Organization:

Large group, 10 minutes; small group, 25 minutes

Procedure:

1. Tell students that they will be role playing stories based on headlines from the local newspaper. They will work in groups of 3–5 students.
2. Tell students that you will read the headlines to them and they are to act them out. Older students may read and choose their own headlines.
3. Give students three minutes to act out their headlines. Ask each group to make a headline for the class to see, or put headlines on oaktag.
4. Give them an example: Fireman Receives Award for Saving Children. Choose several students to role play this headline.
5. Divide the class into smaller groups and pass out a headline to each group. Allow students ten minutes to plan their role playing.
6. Have the class act out their role-playing skits.

Follow-up:

- Place several headlines on the chalkboard. Have the groups play charades while class members guess what title is being acted out.
- Have students bring in positive articles about their community to share with the class through role playing.

READERS' THEATER

Objectives:

Students will be able to

1. Take turns reading folktales with expression
2. Brainstorm ideas on how they would like to do a readers' theater presentation

Description:

Students take turns reading aloud short literature selections using readers' theater techniques.

Organization:

Large group, 45 minutes

Procedure:

1. Write the term *readers' theater* on the board and tell students that in readers' theater, students are involved in exploring literature and improving reading skills by

Planning a presentation
Selecting and preparing material to be presented
Rehearsing the production
Making a readers' theater presentation before an audience.

2. Tell students that you are going to read them a folktale prepared for performance by a readers' theater group. Read the folktale entitled "The Wind is from the North" as retold by Iris Tiedt (which follows).

3. Pass out copies of this folktale to students. Remind students of different forms of intonation such as surprise, indignation, and anger. Demonstrate the pacing of significant lines. Have different students read the parts.

4. Divide the class into four groups. Give each group a folktale to prepare as a readers' theater presentation.

5. Call on each group to read in front of the class.

The Wind Is from the North

A Folktale from Finland

N_1 Osmo, the slow and lumbering bear, one day surprised himself by catching a plump grouse. He was so proud that he went marching back and forth through the forest holding the grouse carefully between his teeth.

O "They'll all be jealous, and they'll see that I am rather quick on my feet despite my great weight."

N_2 Mikko, a clever fox, seeing Osmo carrying the handsome grouse, determined to get the bird away from the bear. He pretended not to see the grouse as he intently sniffed the wind.

M "I'm trying to decide from which direction the wind is blowing."

O "Hm, hm."

N_1 The bear replied without opening his mouth.

M "What's that you say, friend? It's coming from the South?"

N_2 The bear muttered something again.

O "Hm, hm."

N_1 The fox continued to tease the old bear until Osmo could stand it no longer. Anyone could see that the wind was blowing strongly from the North.

O "North!"

N_2 As he opened his mouth to say "North," of course, the grouse flew off, much to rascally Mikko's delight.

M "Oh, Osmo, you should never have said, 'North.' If someone had asked me, I would have said 'East'."

Retold by Iris Tiedt[1]

Follow-up:

- Have students brainstorm ideas for a presentation the whole class can do, for example, a program for parents or stories to share with younger students.
- Provide many books from different subjects in helping students select materials for their readers' theater presentation.
- Give children experiences in preparing scripts of short stories before choosing the actual one they want to perform.
- Plan a presentation on a holiday theme.
- Have students use the readers' theater technique in preparing a script from literature about a part of history they are studying now.

USING THE LISTENING CENTER

To understand why listening is important, children need to learn the purpose of listening. A brief introduction by the teacher puts listening into a practical framework by showing children that unless they listen carefully, they will be unable to accomplish what you want them to do.

In this section there are four listening center activities: using art materials to follow directions, identifying objects in the classroom from descriptions, recognizing different types of sentences by playing a game, and putting a story in the correct order using comic strips. Although each activity has been structured to stand alone, you may decide to use only part of the activity or parts of several activities. Thus, the material allows a wide range of choices in selection and presentation.

You can arrange a listening center for small groups by bringing desks together to form a corner, or use a study carrel, desk, or table for individual listening. In all of these activities you will need a blank tape, cassette recorder, and earphones. Before beginning any activity in the center, instruct students on the purpose of the activity and show them how to use the equipment properly. Have a response card for each activity so that students can correct their work. You can vary the amount of time spent on each activity. An activity could be ten minutes or a half-hour at your convenience.

[1]Iris Tiedt, *Reading Strategies* (San Jose, Calif.: Contemporary Press, 1976).

FOLLOWING DIRECTIONS

Objectives:

Students will be able to

1. Listen to directions given on a tape
2. Draw a picture by following the directions

Description:

Students draw a picture after listening to directions given to them on a tape.

Organization:

Small group, 10 minutes

Procedure:

1. Prepare a cassette tape and an answer sheet (the picture to be drawn).
2. Tell students that they are going to draw a picture after they listen to your directions on the tape. They should be cautioned to listen very carefully and to have their paper and crayons in front of them when the tape begins.
3. Tell students:

> In the middle of the paper you are to draw a lake. Around the lake, and to the bottom of the paper, you are to color green grass. Next, you will make the sky light blue, and it should touch the grass. Next; make three birds flying in the sky. Now, draw four children around the lake. One of them must be you.

(Give the students plenty of time to draw by pausing after each instruction.)

4. Tell students to compare their drawing to the picture on your sheet.
5. Have students listen to the tape again if the drawing is incorrect.

Follow-up:

- On another listening tape, give instructions on how to make a paper airplane or snowflake.
- Have students make their own tape giving directions for an exercise in physical education.
- Have students record tapes giving directions on how to play a game they know.

DESCRIPTIONS

Objectives:

Students will be able to

1. Listen to descriptions given on tape

2. Choose the correct words from descriptions of familiar objects in their classrooms

Descriptions:

Students listen to descriptions on tape and identify objects in the classroom.

Organization:

Small group 20 minutes; individuals 10 minutes

Procedure:

1. Make copies of this word list for students:

windows ______	desk ______
chalkboard ______	paper ______
pencil ______	book ______

2. On the tape, describe objects to students. They are to see if they can find the object on the word list. Students are to number each object in the order in which they heard it. Examples:

a. Most of the time I am white and I have lines on me. I wish students wouldn't press so hard on me because it hurts. What am I?
b. Some children have no respect. They just slam me on their desk and turn my pages so fast that I sometimes get dizzy. What am I?
c. I am long and thin and everyone squeezes me too tight. I should have a sharp point on one end and a soft spot on the other. What am I?

3. Make up several descriptions following the same pattern. Pause between descriptions to allow students time to locate the correct word in the word list.

4. Provide an answer card for students to check their work immediately.

Follow-up:

- Give descriptions of objects to be found in the home. You can divide these objects into categories such as *living room* or *kitchen.*
- Use the same listening activity in describing states in the United States.
- Have students write descriptions about animals for the other students to guess.

RECOGNIZING TYPES OF SENTENCES

Objectives:

Students will be able to

1. Recognize four types of sentences read by the teacher on tape

2. Identify types of sentences by marking abbreviations in the correct order on a game sheet prepared by the teacher

Description:

On a game sheet, students will write abbreviations in the correct order to identify four types of sentences read by the teacher on a tape.

Organization:

Small group, 20 minutes; individuals, 10 minutes

Procedure:

1. Prepare the game sheet shown below and make copies for children who use the tape.

Do You Know Me?

DEC.	DECLARATIVE	Makes a statement
INT.	INTERROGATIVE	Asks a question
EX.	EXCLAMATORY	Shows excitement
IMP.	IMPERATIVE	Gives a command

1. I am your teacher.	DEC.
2. Do you know me?	INT.
3. The house is on fire!	EX.
4. Go to your room!	IMP.

1. _____	4. _____	7. _____	10. _____
2. _____	5. _____	8. _____	11. _____
3. _____	6. _____	9. _____	12. _____

2. Prepare a cassette tape. Tell the children they are going to play a game called "Do You Know Me?" Explain the game sheet. Tell students there is a numbered line on the game sheet for each of the sentences you are going to read. They are to write an abbreviation on each line.

3. Explain that there are four kinds of sentences, and give examples and abbreviations for each kind:

> The declarative sentence (dec.) makes a statement: I am your teacher.
> The interrogative sentence (int.) asks a question: Do you know me?
> The exclamatory sentence (ex.) shows excitement: The house is on fire!
> The imperative sentence (imp.) gives a command: Go to your room!

4. Read sentences, allowing time for students to write abbreviations.

5. Provide an answer card so that students can check their answers immediately.

Follow-up:

• Record short stories using the four different types of sentences in each. Ask students to identify each sentence following the procedure described above.

• Tape students' spelling test using the four different kinds of sentences. Have students write each sentence as dictated on the tape.

• Dictate sentences based on science, math, or social studies.

SEQUENCING A STORY

Objectives:

Students will be able to

1. Put a story in sequential order
2. Create an ending for a story

Description:

Students will listen to a story, arrange cut-up comic strip pictures in the correct order to represent events in the story, and write an ending to the story.

Organization:

Small group, 20 minutes

Procedure:

1. Tell students that they are going to listen to a story while looking at a cut-up comic strip. As they listen to the tape, they should put the comic strip pictures in order.
2. Cut comic strips into squares and blot out the writing.
3. Have students paste the comic strips squares in the proper order on a sheet of paper and draw any squares necessary to complete the story.
4. Have students write in dialogue to complete the blotted-out sections.
5. Have students refer to the response card to check the proper sequence.

Follow-up:

• Have students bring comic strips, blot out the dialogue, and cut them into sections. Then, have them exchange comic strips with their classmates and create a story based on them.

• Have students make a class booklet of their own original comic strips.

CHALLENGE

Try these activities as you become acquainted with oral language experiences suitable for elementary school children.

1. Read a number of folktales. Prepare to tell one orally to a small group of classmates. Consider how you can introduce storytelling to young children.

2. Prepare a readers' theater lesson based on a familiar fairy tale. Use a duplicated copy to mark the script as needed. List the readers needed.

3. Prepare a cassette tape of directions for solving a puzzle (mental arithmetic) or drawing a picture on graph paper. Test your directions with another member of the class.

4. Select several books for reading aloud to children in primary grades. Select several for use with older students. Arrange to read one of these books to a group of children.

RECOMMENDED RESOURCES

Anastasiow, Nicholas. *Oral language: Expression of Thought.* Newark, Del.: International Reading Association, 1979.

Klein, Marvin L. *Talk in the Language Arts Classroom.* Urbana, Ill.: National Council of Teachers of English, 1977.

Tiedt, Sidney W., and Iris M. Tiedt. *Language Arts Activities for the Classroom.* Boston: Allyn & Bacon, 1978.

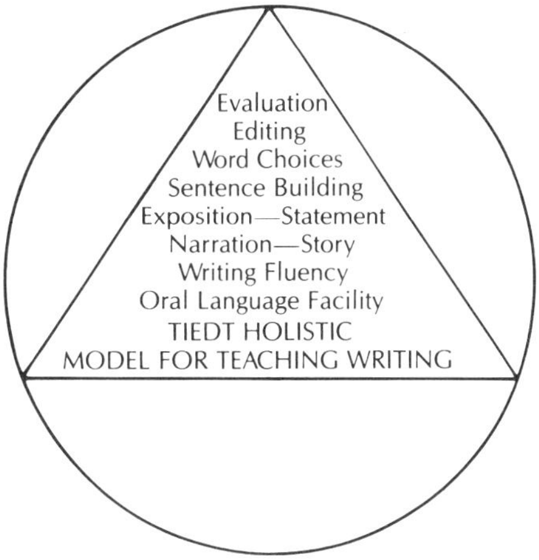

3

Developing Fluency

For many students the most difficult phase in writing is getting started. This problem, compounded by the fact that most students want their first draft to be perfect, makes progress extremely slow and tedious, and often produces writing that is disconnected and unimaginative. These interferences affect fluency, or the ability to put thoughts on paper easily, smoothly, with a ready flow of words.

Through fluency activities, students are encouraged to enjoy words and to draw upon their own store of words to find the right one. Since students' own words are more comfortable for them, they are able to use their own vocabulary with more power and vitality. Fluency exercises foster students' abilities to write freely and willingly, making it easy to transfer the thoughts in their heads to words on their papers.

The pleasant task for you, the teacher, is to bring children and words together joyfully. The more exciting you can make the study of words as communicators for your students, the more intrigued they will become with writing. Instill in your students a love of apt words and vivid images. Equally important, you will want to help create an atmosphere in which all students feel comfortable sharing their thoughts and feelings. Once you establish an environment that encourages and supports students' writing efforts, you will find that successful writing produces feelings of self-confidence, accomplishment, and satisfaction for both you and your students.

The lessons suggested in this chapter are designed to insure the success of your students' writing experiences and to eliminate any fear of failure on their part. The following model is helpful in creating the positive environment necessary for writing. This model forms the basic outline of procedures for each of the activities presented in this chapter.

Model for Successful Writing Experiences

1. State clearly what you expect students to do.
2. Provide a model or models of the activity.
3. Elicit oral responses from the students.
4. Write a group piece. (Omit this step when students no longer need it.)
5. Have students write the assignment independently.
6. Share the writing produced.

This chapter has been divided arbitrarily into three sections: Word Play; Parallel Poems, Stories, and Lists; and Poetic Forms. Whenever appropriate within each section, the activities are arranged so that the lessons described move from relatively easy exercises to more complex writing activities. These short fluency exercises are designed to be successful experiences for all of your students.

After reading this chapter you will be able to

1. Define fluency
2. Explain why fluency activities are important
3. Demonstrate specific activities that help to develop writing fluency

As you read and practice the activities in this chapter, you will recognize that you are capable of creating such activities yourself. Modify these exercises to meet the needs and achievements of particular groups or individuals in your own classes. In doing so, you make writing practice an exciting, rewarding adventure in learning.

WORD PLAY ACTIVITIES

From Mother Goose to T. S. Eliot, poets and storytellers have enjoyed the delights of playing with words as they write. Edward Lear, Lewis Carroll, Wallace Tripp, David McCord, and Shel Silverstein are just a few poets who have capitalized on the pleasure and playfulness of our language.

The word games that follow are intended to urge children to explore and experiment with the language. In experiencing pure play with words, children are able to creep deeper into their imaginations and feel more comfortable with their language. Encourage students to look for words that "have a taste on the lips, that have a perfume to the nostrils, rattling words one can throw into a box and shake, making a sharp, jingling sound." This is just the attitude toward words you will want to arouse in your students. The activities suggested here will encourage children of all ages to find some words to "throw into a box and shake," words that can challenge the "kickle snifters and other fearsome critters" they may meet in their wild imaginations.

WORD ASSOCIATION

Objectives:

Students will be able to

1. Demonstrate the ability to write words quickly on paper
2. Add additional words to their vocabularies

Description:

Associating one word with another and another is a method used to obtain ideas. It is also a process of quickly covering a paper with words. "Popcorn" is a game of word association in which students list as many words as they can, as fast as they can. The purpose is to write words and list ideas quickly. Quantity, not quality, is the prime consideration. This is an excellent stratagem to have at your fingertips when students say, "I don't know what to write."

Organization:

Large or small groups, 30–45 minutes

Procedure:

1. Tell your students that their imaginations are unusually fascinating because when they look at one word and think about it, their minds quickly jump to another word and another word and so on, much like popcorn popping in a sizzling hot pan. To motivate the students further you may want to read *Harold and the Purple Crayon* by Crockett Johnson (Harper & Row, Pub., 1958). This charming story of a small boy illustrates how one thought leads to another. Tell your students that no two people make the same associations. There is no one right answer.

2. Tell your students that they are going to play "Popcorn."

3. Demonstrate the game on the chalkboard. Suitable stimulus words to use might be *water, fire, snow, earth, weeds, bugs,* or *sky.*

4. Elicit associations from your students and write all responses on the chalkboard. The recording of the word associations can take a variety of forms. In the beginning it may be easier just to list the words in a column.

a. Column format

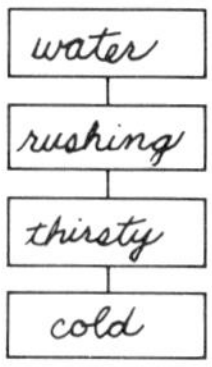

b. Clustering format

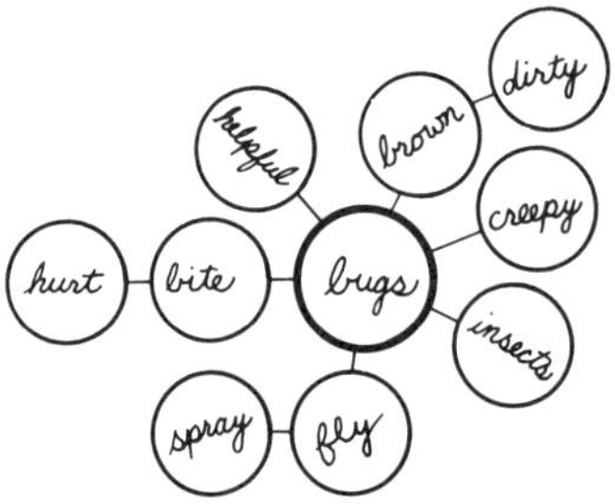

c. Explosion format

5. When your students understand the process, give them a new word and have them do their own word association. To achieve speed in setting pen to paper, allow only one or two minutes to list words.

6. Provide comfortable opportunities for students to share what they have written.

Follow-up:

- Have students group their associations into lines containing two- or three-word phrases taken sequentially from their list.
- Have students write a paragraph incorporating several or all of the words from their word association list.
- Have students play "Popcorn" with a friend, taking turns as they associate a new word with the previous word.
- Have students experiment with a new arrangement for writing the words on the page. Rather than writing in columns, students may choose to scatter the words, perhaps connecting them with arrows.
- Have students put the word *ME* at the top of their papers, followed by ten words that describe themselves. Then have each student pick a friend and ask that friend to eliminate three of the ten words and tell why.

WRITING ACROSTICS

Objectives:

The student will be able to

1. Use descriptive words in writing
2. Tell a story using this name format

Description:

These acrostics are based on names. The letters of the name (student's name, friend's name, nickname, name of an object, city, state) are written vertically. Then each letter is used as the first letter of the first word in that line (see examples[1]). The content of the writing should describe the word appearing vertically or tell a story about it.

M y friend
I s dainty,
C unning,
H elpful,
E legant,
L ittle,
L ovely,
E specially nice.
Susan Haselhofer

[1]The student examples in this chapter are from *Peanut Brittle,* the literary magazine published annually at El Roble Elementary School in Gilroy, California.

Haunted houses
Are frightening
Lonely scary rooms.
Lights are nowhere
On Halloween.
Wicked witches
Eerie noises in the night—
Everyone looks frightened.
Nights are scary on Halloween.

Lisa Garcia

On a scary night,
Cats screeching and meowing.
Trick-or-treating.
Ooooh!
Beware if you CARE!
Everywhere is a ghost.
Run if you DARE!

Andrea Barberi

Organization:

Large or small groups, 30–45 minutes

Procedure:

1. Tell the students that they are going to write acrostics. Explain acrostics.
2. Provide models. Use your own name to compose an acrostic. Students love it!
3. Have your students compose an acrostic as a class collaboration. Write their suggestions on the chalkboard using the appropriate form. You might suggest that students create acrostics on words such as the name of their school or town.
4. Have your students write their own names vertically on their papers and then describe themselves in words, phrases, or sentences, or tell a story about themselves. Encourage your students to ask themselves these questions: Can you choose words that will paint a portrait of yourself? What makes you who you are? How are you like your best friend? How are you unlike your friend?
5. Have students share their writing with others in pairs, small groups, or large groups. Keep in mind the sensitivity of the students in your class: "Tell all the *good things* you know about yourself."

Follow-up:

- Have your students draw self-portraits and display them on the bulletin board along with their acrostics.
- Have your students use their nicknames rather than their given names to form an acrostic.

• Have your students work with partners and write acrostics containing both partners' names.

• Have your students use the names of cities, states, or objects and describe them.

• Have students choose a word and use it to create a sentence: Each letter in the word becomes the first letter of a word in the sentence (for example, *POETRY* = People often exaggerate, telling ridiculous yarns).

NAME GAMES

Objectives:

The students will be able to

1. Compose a short poem about themselves
2. Identify rhyme
3. Play with the letters in their names

Description:

This activity requires students to write poems rhyming their names. To create the name poem described here, students should begin by listing all the words they can think of that rhyme with their names (first, last, or both). Then using the word list, students compose poems with their names as the focus. Length of the poems may vary, but three lines seems to be a popular length.

Jean, Jean
Often wished to be seen
On a movie theater screen.

Organization:

Large or small groups, 30–45 minutes

Procedure:

1. Read *Pierre* by Maurice Sendak (Harper & Row, Pub., 1962) to the class. (Any book that focuses on a child and the name of the child will do.) After listening to students' comments about the story, recite this little poem about Pierre:

Pierre, Pierre, Pierre
Was stubborn and unaware
Because he didn't care.

Ask students if that describes Pierre.

2. Tell students that they are going to write poems about themselves. Describe the name poem. Read the examples here and others you may write yourself.

3. Do a name poem about yourself on the chalkboard. Tell the students that it is helpful to begin by first listing all the words they can think of that rhyme with the name used in the poem. Ask the students to help you write your poem.

4. Ask students to share oral descriptions about themselves. Instruct students to write poems using their names. Suggest that they may make up funny, untrue descriptions or tell true stories about themselves.

5. Give students opportunities to share with each other.

My name is Sue
And I'm quite new.
You see I was born today at two!

My name is Lupe.
I'm having a great day.
We had a game and I got to play.

Follow-up:

• Make silhouettes of your students using the opaque projector. Display their name poems on their silhouettes.

• Have students keep this poem to use as part of a collection of writing they will do about themselves, called "The Magnificent House of Me Alone."

• Have students compose a name poem by writing their names vertically and using each letter as the first letter for that line of poetry.

• Have students write "two-word" poems about themselves. They may write as many lines as they wish, but each line may have only two words.

• Invite students to play with the letters in their names:

Elizabeth
Lizabeth
Izabeth
Zabeth
Abeth
Beth
Eth
Th
H

WRITING SHAPE POEMS

Objectives:

The students will be able to

1. Use descriptive words
2. Form a picture with words
3. Compose a shape poem

Description:

Children can shape poetry to be seen as well as to be read or heard. The subject of the poem dictates the shape, and descriptive words are arranged to form a picture. The message is conveyed through both words and image.

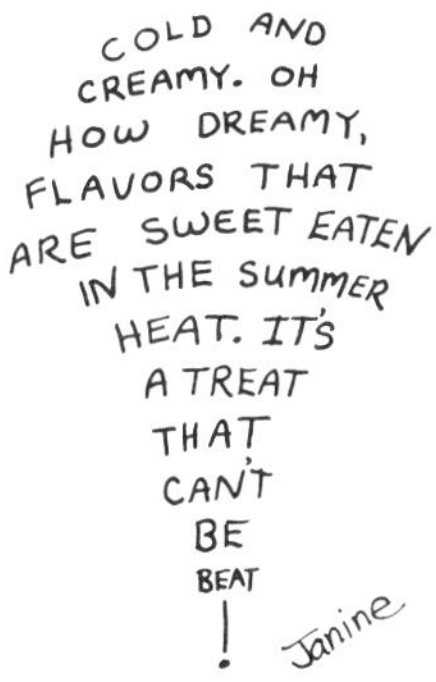

Organization:

Large or small groups, 30–45 minutes

Procedure:

1. Prepare overhead transparencies of several examples of shape poetry. *Street Poems* by Robert Froman (McCall, 1971) and *Poems to Hear and See* by Ian Hamilton Finlay (Macmillan, 1971) are two excellent sources of examples of shape poetry.

2. Tell the students they are going to paint pictures with words, like those you have just shown them.

3. Define shape poetry for the students.

4. Elicit examples from the class and put them on the chalkboard or overhead projector.

5. Tell students to experiment with shape poems on their own papers.

6. Provide opportunities to share. Using an opaque projector is a quick method of showing a student's poem to the entire class.

Follow-up:

• Have students enlarge their shape poems using the opaque projector. Tell students to mount their poems on large pieces of colorful paper and display them on a bulletin board.

• Have students recopy their poems on ditto masters, duplicate them, and assemble the poems into an individual booklet for each member of the class.

• Using only word, have students write the word in such a way that it suggests the meaning.

• Have students write noun and verb poems. A noun can be arranged to picture the meaning. Students may repeat the word to make the picture.

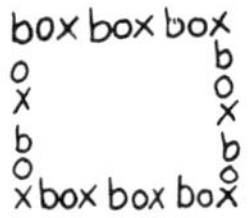

• Instruct students to experiment with poetry that includes a word picture within the poem.

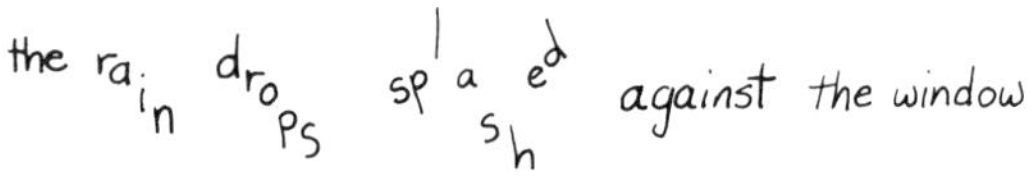

• Have students draw a simple outline picture of something they like (an animal, a friend, a food, a toy). Tell students to write their feelings about the object they have drawn on the inside of their picture.

• Have students lightly outline a picture of an object, then cover the outline with words that describe the object.

Objectives:

The student will be able to

1. Write personal opinions and feelings
2. Use abstract and concrete words
3. Use metaphors and similes

Description:

Writing definitions for words helps students move from abstract words (words for qualities, feelings, and ideas) to concrete words. After developing this ability, your students will be able to produce more exciting images and make their writing more appealing to the reader.

Misery is
having homework,
not having food on the table
when you come in from playing,
not knowing that someone cares about you,
having problems on your mind.

Brad Carlson

Winter is when
The red red robin looks for his food,
And the deer gallops at almost any noise,
And the fox is hunting for his food
Which he won't find,
And maple trees are leaking their sap
For our breakfast table,
And the snowball fights are just
Beginning over a crushed snowman.

George Redenbaugh

Organization:

Large or small groups, 30–45 minutes period

Procedure:

1. Read *A Hole Is to Dig* by Ruth Krauss (Scholastic, 1952) to your class.
2. After discussing the contents of the book, tell your students, "You are going to write definitions for words in terms of what those words mean to you." Provide models of words and definitions. *Words, Words, Words* by Mary O'Neill is an excellent source.
3. On the chalkboard, write an abstract word such as *wonder, surprise,* or *winter.*

Ask your students to share their ideas about the meaning of the word. Instruct your students to be very specific and to use concrete words, names of things they can see, feel, hear, touch, smell, or taste. Write their suggestions on the chalkboard under the word to be defined.

4. Provide another abstract word and instruct your students to copy it on their papers and list concrete words to define the given word.

5. Have students share their writing.

Follow-up:

- Compile a class booklet incorporating each student's list of images defining the given word.
- Have students illustrate some of the images used to define the given word.
- Have your students write a paragraph or short story developing one of the images in their definition.
- Write a list of words you think your students do not know. Have your students write definitions for the words without using a dictionary. Then have them compare their definitions with each other.

STREAM OF CONSCIOUSNESS

Objectives:

Students will be able to

1. Write continuously for a given length of time
2. Observe that their minds wander from one thought to another
3. Observe that their thoughts are the material for writing

Description:

Students will experience stream of consciousness writing by recording the free flow of thoughts running through their minds. Students sit quietly and let their thoughts move outward and onto their papers. This activity will help them to see that what they think and notice is the inspiration of writing. In this lesson students will write for three uninterrupted minutes.

Organization:

Large or small groups, 30–45 minutes

Procedures:

1. Explain stream of consciousness writing to your class.

2. Read models of this type of writing. Compose examples of your own or read the one that follows:

This will be hard writing because three minutes is a long time and I don't know what to write. Tom's pencil just broke. My stomach is growling. Janie wants to play at my house after school. I like her. She lets me ride her new bike. I wish it was recess. School's hard. Sometimes I hate school. David just sneezed. My birthday is soon. I wonder if we will have . . .

3. Call on students to share their thoughts at this moment. Do this orally to "warm-up" the class and stimulate ideas.

4. Demonstrate stream of consciousness writing by timing yourself for one minute and writing on the chalkboard all the thoughts passing through your mind.

5. Establish a quiet mood. Tell the students that for three minutes they are to write down everything that passes through their heads. They are not to lift the pencil from the paper. They do not need to write complete sentences. They are to write whatever pops into their heads. Suggest they write down everything they see, hear, or feel around them.

6. Have students choose partners and read to each other what they have written.

Follow-up:

- Have students turn over their papers and write for three more minutes. Then have them compare the two pieces of writing, making observations about the quantity and quality.
- Have students scatter about the room or outside the classroom to write for five uninterrupted minutes, recording everything they see, hear, and smell.
- Have the students write for two or three minutes from the viewpoint of another person or object.

JOURNAL WRITING

Objectives:

Students will be able to

1. Remember and record events in their lives
2. Practice different types of writing
3. Establish a habit of writing

Description:

Each student will keep a personal journal for a specified period of time. Keeping a journal encourages students to keep current accounts of how they are growing, what is happening to them, and how they respond to situations. It provides cumulative statements about who they are.

For the teacher, the journals provide a daily sample of students' writing, making it easy to observe how writing skills are progressing. The thoughts, feelings, and concerns that emerge from these journals help you to understand your students.

Organization:

Large or small groups, 30–45 minutes

Procedure:

1. Introduce the idea of a diary or journal by reading from published diaries. Reading from *The Diary of a Young Girl* by Anne Frank (Pocket, 1955) and the section about diaries in *Nobody is Perfick* by Bernard Waber (Scholastic, 1971) will provide examples for students. You may need to paraphrase the excerpts, depending upon the grade level you teach.

2. Distribute journals to your class. These can be several pages of writing paper stapled together or a composition notebook. Students may wish to bring a journal notebook from home.

3. Demonstrate on the chalkboard how to date an entry and then write what could be an entry in your own journal.

4. Explain to the students that since their journals are private writing primarily for themselves they will not be corrected for spelling, punctuation, or correct usage. Tell your students you will read them (with their permission) and perhaps write a comment or respond to something they have written.

Follow-up:

• If students have made several entries during a week, have them look over their week's writing and make some observations. Did their journal tend to be full of events or were there more reflective comments? Do they feel the same about the events now as they did on the day they wrote about them? How do they feel about keeping a journal? Does reading the journal help them to see things differently?

• Have students write short journals covering several hours, one day, or several days in the life of an inanimate object. These entries might carry such titles as "A Day in the Life of George Gobelsky's Football" or "The Diary of Lucy's Left Toeshoe."

• Have students work in pairs and write a journal in the form of a discussion. The journal entry will consist of a conversation between "me" and "you" (the other student) about a previously agreed upon topic. Use one journal.

• Have students keep historical journals. Have them choose a week in history and write about events of that week as if they were alive during that time. This project will require research.

Another activity that increases fluency is writing a poem or story that follows a definite language pattern or parallel construction. In patterned writing, consecutive lines may begin or end with the same words, or groups of lines may end in a repeated refrain. The structure suggests ideas and helps children to walk right in and feel comfortable, yet allows them the flexibility to write at their own level of skill and sophistication.

Encourage the children to borrow a theme or a pattern from a story or poem that they like. Imitation of good writing should be encouraged because student's writing improves when they imitate excellence. Borrowing does not discourage creativity. The demand for self-expression is extremely strong in young children, and their personalities emerge in the writing even though the form is borrowed or imitated.

WRITING COLOR POEMS

Objectives:

Students will be able to

1. Use metaphors
2. Use similes

Description:

Color is familiar to children and evokes vivid images, moods, sounds, and special associations. Writing about color is a comfortable way for children to begin to enhance fluency. In this activity students will use similies and metaphors to define colors.

Black

Black is . . .
　　midnight gold, strong and bold
　　being all alone
　　and a song with a moaning tone.
Black is . . .
　　a cat walking through the night
　　and a color that's not very bright.
Black is the dark pushing back the day.

Charmane Vaianisi

Organization:

Large or small groups, 30–45 minutes

Procedure:

1. Place a pyrex pie plate of water atop an overhead projector. Dribble a few drops of food coloring into the bowl. Magical forms begin to appear on the screen. Stir or blow the colored water for movement. Mix colors to create exciting visual experiences.

2. Discuss with the students how colors can make you feel, how they "sound," what images they bring to mind, how colors "taste" and "smell." Provide examples of color poems. *Hailstones and Halibut Bones* by Mary O'Neill (Doubleday, 1960) is an excellent source. You may want to read the following color poems written by children:

Yellow

Yellow is the taste of kernels
  popping in the pan.
Yellow is the sound of bees
  crying enormous tears.
Yellow is a feeling of
  pillows in the air.

Stacie Eaton

Yellow

Yellow is a flashlight
  That glows in the night.
Yellow means proud
  When you know you're right.
Yellow is a bright tasty
  Sugar cookie batch.
Yellow is a spark
  When you strike a match.
Yellow is moth balls
  That you think are icky!
Yellow is a lollipop
  That feels sticky!
Yellow is your teeth
  When you didn't brush 'um.
Yellow is snail guts
  When you crush 'um.

Michelle Freymann

3. Elicit oral examples from the students as they react to their color experience. (Blue is a whisper. Red is a shout.) From the student responses compose a group poem. Each line should begin with a color word.

4. When students are comfortable and freely contributing ideas, have them compose individual color poems.

5. Provide opportunities for students to share their writing. A student may wish to share one line or the entire piece of writing. Some may wish to share in front of the class, while others prefer to share in small groups. It will be up to you to be sensitive to the students' needs.

Follow-up:

- Combine students' individual color writings into a class color book.
- Have the students choose one line from their poem and develop the image.
- Display students' writings about color. This topic lends itself delightfully to exciting bulletin board presentations.
- Have your students write a one-color poem focusing on a specific color and shades of that color.
- Write a color poem in which each line contains a color word, not necessarily at the beginning of a line.
- Write a color cinquain.
- Write a story about a color.
- Have your students write acrostics using color words.

"I REMEMBER" STATEMENTS

Objectives:

Students will be able to

1. Improve their memory skills
2. Improve their ability to concentrate on details

Description:

Children are fascinated by the possibility of a ride backward or forward in a time machine, and remembering is a way of experiencing another time, in one direction at least. It is something we do naturally, and it is something we can do better with practice.

In this activity students write memory statements, beginning each line with "I remember" as in the following example:

> I remember a quiet evening when Dad came home
> with a great big grin on his face.
> I remember riding in a huge rickety yellow truck
> called Big Bertha.

Organization:

Large or small groups, 30–45 minutes

Procedure:

1. Tell the students, "We are going to take an imaginary ride backward in a time machine and write down events we remember from our past."

2. Provide examples, such as the student sample included here. Sharing memories of your own personal life can be highly motivating to your students. Begin each memory with the words "I remember."

> I remember when I used to jump on my mom's bed.
> My dad got mad!
> I remember when I had a new doll.
> Now it's thrown in the toy box.
> I remember when Mom took my picture with two teeth missing.
> I looked like a beaver.
> I remember when I did my best coloring.
> It took me a very long time
> And my little sister wrote all over it!
>
> Delica Morales

3. Elicit oral responses from the students. Have them share memories from their lives.

4. From these responses compose a group poem on the chalkboard to serve as a model for student work.

5. When your students are comfortable with the idea and are eagerly sharing memories of their past, invite them to jump into the time machine, recall times in their past, and write a poem on their own.

6. Group students into clusters of five or six each and ask them to read their memories to each other.

Follow-up:

- Time-machine statements can be used as an idea bank for future writing assignments. Have your students write a story about one memory mentioned in their poem.
- Have your students find another student in the class with a similar memory and have them compare the details of the event.
- Have your students contribute one line of their poems to a class collaboration poem
- Vary the beginning phrases or combine two phrases such as:

> I remember ___________.
> I wish ___________.
> or
> I used to be ___________,
> But now I ___________.

• Have your students write I remember statements around a theme such as

Times they remember really laughing
Times they were embarassed
Times when they forgot something
Times that were frightening

• Have your students make a timeline of selected events in their lives. (Later use this as a guide for writing their autobiographies.)

• Have your students interview their parents and write a story about the day they were born.

WRITING LISTS

Objectives:

The students will be able to

1. Follow a pattern
2. Demonstrate flexibility of thought by looking at ideas in a variety of ways
3. Write thoughts on paper quickly

Description:

Writing lists is an activity that quickly engages children's imaginations. The format is repetitious, a very natural and comfortable structure for children. They tend to be spontaneous and carefree with this assignment, particularly if you encourage some crazy or outrageous responses.

Organization:

Large or small groups, 30–45 minutes

Procedure:

1. Read "The Ten Best List" in *NOBODY IS PERFICK* by Bernard Waber.
2. Tell students they are going to write lists.
3. Elicit some list ideas from the class. Their responses will determine the assignment. The following topics have been successful in motivating students:

Ten Things I Could Never Tell
Ten Lies I Have Told
Ten Wishes I Have
Ten Things that Could Never Happen
Ten Things that Annoy Me
Ten Things I Do before I Come to School
Ten Ways to Ride a Bicycle

4. When a topic is picked, brainstorm the possibilities on the chalkboard.

5. Have students compose individual lists. If some children finish before others, have them go ahead and list more items. Then when time is called, have them choose the ten best from their list.

6. Give students the opportunity to share their writing. The following is an example of a student's list.

Ten Ways to Get into the Water

1. Dive in
2. Get pushed in
3. Hold your nose and jump
4. Grab a friend and go in together
5. Tiptoe down the steps into the water
6. Climb over the edge and go in slowly
7. Sit on the edge and slide in
8. Have your dad pick you up and throw you in
9. Run and jump
10. Go down the slide

Follow-up:

• Have students recopy their lists, illustrate them, and bind them into a book of lists.

• Discuss the idea of learning to see things in a variety of ways.

• Have students list activities telling how to build, cook, or draw something.

• Have students compose lists in pairs.

• Play a record and have students list what they hear while the music plays.

• Show a movie or slides to the class. Have the students list their reactions, or objects or events viewed.

WRITING DIALOGUES

Objective:

The student will be able to write a dialogue.

Description:

The use of dialogue can add sparkle and variety to narrative writing. The following activity invites your students to talk to someone or something they feel close to and with which they can identify. This may be a person, an animal, an object or themselves.

Organization:

Large or small groups, 30–45 minutes

Procedure:

1. Read *Do You Know What I'll Do?* by Charlotte Zolotow (Harper & Row, Pub., 1958) (or any book containing a great deal of dialogue or a monologue) to your class. Comment on the content of the book. If you are reading *Do You Know What I'll Do?* show the students that the entire book is a monologue, in which the little girl is talking to her brother.

2. Tell your students that they are going to write a conversation with another person, an animal, or an object. You may wish to limit their selection.

3. Role play a conversation with a student or a conversation with yourself. (What you role play will depend upon the selection you use to motivate the lesson.)

4. Have your students suggest situations for conversations. You may need to provide more examples.

Going to Bed with Wet Hair
(A Conversation with Myself)

Oh, my hair is wet!
I don't like going to bed with wet hair.
My pillow is wet in the morning.
I don't like going to bed,
My pillow gets my skin wet.
I don't feel good at night.
I get into bed and listen to the sounds.
Then I fall asleep with my hair wet!

Jessica Santana

The Football

I am a football, so nice and brown.
Everyday I am kicked around. I can't
stand it no longer! My air is running out
to absolute zero. I am getting flat, like a
flat straw hat! I'm suffering to death.
Please air me up! I can't stand it
no longer—being kicked around.

Vladimir Bello

5. Using an idea suggested by the students, write a conversation on the chalkboard.

6. Have the students write their own conversations.

7. Provide opportunities for your students to share their writing with a small group.

Follow-up:

- Have your students act out their conversations.

• Have students illustrate their conversations with cartoons using dialogue bubbles.

• Copy a published poem. Have your students write a conversation with the poet. The students copy a line from the poem and then write a line themselves. They continue alternating lines to the end of the poem, conversing with the poet to create a new poem.

• Read a story such as *The Biggest Bear* by Lynd Ward (Houghton Mifflin, 1952). Stop reading the story at a point where an emotional or particularly meaningful conversation occurs. Ask your students to write that conversation.

• Set up situations between objects and ask your students to write the conversation, for example, among the pots and pans in the kitchen after Christmas dinner.

• Have students pretend to be an object talking to itself, such as a discarded toy or a tattered book.

• Give your students photos of two people. Instruct them to write a conversation between the two people in the pictures.

REWRITING MOTHER GOOSE

Objectives:

The student will be able to

1. Identify rhyme
2. Parody nursery rhymes

Description:

Most children possess an outrageously healthy sense of humor. They mimic their teachers and classmates and tend to see the ridiculous, the funny side, of many situations. Mother Goose parodies provide an outlet for children's humor. This activity requires the students to rewrite nursery rhymes.

Organization:

Large or small groups, 30–45 minutes

Procedure:

1. Ask students who can remember Mother Goose rhymes to recite for the class.

2. Read more nursery rhymes to the class. *The Real Mother Goose* illustrated by Blanche Fisher Wright (Rand McNally, 1916) provides outstanding pictures to accompany the rhymes.

3. Read examples of parodies of rhymes found in *Granpa Grig Had a Pig* (Little, Brown, 1976) and *A Great Big Ugly Man Came up and Tied His Horse to Me* (Little,

Brown, 1973), both by Wallace Tripp. Explain the meaning of parody. Tell the students they are going to write parodies of the nursery rhymes.

4. Compose class collaborations of parodies of the nursery rhymes.
5. Have students write individual parodies, such as:

> There was an old woman
> Who lived in a shoe
> She had so many children
> She packed them into boxes
> And mailed them to the zoo.

> Dorinda D. Dorch
> Sat on the front porch
> Mixing some peach ice cream.
> Along came the gneeches
> And ate all the peaches
> And then ate Dorinda, too!

6. Have students share their rhymes with other classes.

Follow-up:

- Have students edit and recopy their rhymes, illustrate them, and bind the class compositions into a book, *The New Mother Goose.*
- Have students act out the rhymes in a game of charades. You may want to do this in small groups of two teams each or as a class activity.
- Have students write lost and found ads for the nursery rhymes. (Lost: black sheep. Last seen leaving the barnyard with Bo-Peep.) Mother Goose is full of lost or missing things.
- Have students create a Mother Goose Village in the classroom with scenes depicting famous rhymes.
- Have students pantomime the familiar Mother Goose rhymes.
- Have students create puppets, then act out and recite the longer rhymes.
- Have students rewrite the nursery rhymes and try to remove the violence, crime, and dishonesty.
- Give students a list of Mother Goose titles and have them rewrite them as newspaper headlines: Pupil Questioned about Tardiness ("A Diller, a Dollar, a Ten O'clock Scholar").

PATTERNED STORIES

Objectives:

Students will be able to

1. Identify the sequence of events in a story
2. Identify the storyline
3. Compose a story following a given story pattern

Description:

Patterned stories are stories written by students following the format or "pattern" of a given story or poem. This form of imitative writing is exceedingly useful and effective in teaching children to write, if you choose good models.

Organization:

Large or small groups, 30–45 minutes

Procedure:

1. Select a story or poem that will interest your children. It should contain a pattern that is predictable, identifiable, and repetitious. One example is *Alexander's Terrible, Horrible, No Good, Very Bad Day* by Judith Viorst (Atheneum, 1972).

2. Read the story or poem to the children in an enthusiastic manner. Your enthusiasm is essential to establish motivation.

3. Conduct a brief oral discussion about the selection. Identify the elements of the pattern that are to be imitated.

4. Invite student participation in composing a class story patterned after the selection. Record it on the blackboard so all can observe the story taking shape.

5. Refine this first draft. See if the story follows the pattern.

6. Invite students to compose individual stories patterned after the selection read.

7. Have students share their writing in small groups. The following is an example written by a third grade student.

It Was a Terrible, Horrible, No Good, Very Bad Day

Do you know what happened to me this morning? When I got up my little brother left his skateboard in front of my bed and I fell on it and I went flying into my brother's bath water and got my school clothes all wet! Then I said to myself, "It's going to be a terrible, horrible, no good, very bad day."

When I went to school, I was late because I got some candy. My teacher said I was late and I had to sit on the bench. And I said, "It's going to be a terrible, horrible, no good, very bad day."

When I went to lunch, I was the only one that had a jam sandwich. All the other kids had a meat sandwich. And I did not have a dessert in my lunch bag. They did! I said, "It's going to be a terrible, horrible, no good, very bad day."

Then when I was walking home, my little brother was at the corner of the block. When my brother and I were walking the rest of the block, we saw our mom leaving to go to the store and she locked the door on us! So now we have to wait an hour! And I said to my brother, "It's been a terrible, horrible, no good, very bad day."

Ginger Potter

Pattern Stories

Browne, Margaret Wise. *Where Have You Been?* New York: Hastings, 1963.

Charlip, Remy. *Fortunately*. New York: Parents Magazine Press, 1964.

Heide, Florence. *Some Things Are Scary*. New York: Scholastic, 1969.

Gwynne, Fred. *The King Who Rained*. New York: Windmill Books and Dutton, 1976.

Joslin, Sesyle. *What Do You Say, Dear?* Scholastic, 1958.

Krauss, Ruth. *A Hole Is to Dig*. New York: Scholastic, 1952.

Leodhas, Sorche-Nic. *Always Room for One More*. New York: Holt, Rinehart & Winston, 1965.

Mayer, Mercer. *If I Had. . . .* New York: Dial Press, 1968.

O'Neill, Mary. *Hailstones and Halibut Bones*. Garden City, N.Y.: Doubleday, 1960.

Simon, Mina, and Howard Simon. *If You Were an Eel, How Would You Feel?* Chicago: Follett, 1963.

Zemach, Margot. *It Could Always Be Worse*. New York: Farrar, Straus & Giroux, 1976.

See page 25 for additional ideas for working with pattern books.

Follow-up:

• Have the students illustrate their story (or choose a partner to illustrate their stories for them) and prepare picture storybooks to share with other classes or to put in the library.

• Have students write scripts for their borrowed tales and perform them for the class.

POETIC FORMS

Young children have a natural flair for poetry. They think and talk in comparisons. Elizabeth, an eight-year-old, for example, observed that "sledding is like a knife ripping through the snow." Children often use personification, metaphors, and similes in their dialogue, frequently describing an object or action by saying it looks "just like" something else. So children are using imagery orally before they know that it is a literary device. Your challenge as a teacher is to release these images and help students put them on paper.

Your students need to realize that poetry emerges from all of life. Poems can be written about ordinary things like washing your face, eating an apple, or getting out of bed, because sometimes ordinary things are the most important of all.

The poetic structures presented in this chapter teach a sense of poetic form based on the verse line, the syllable, and the use of words as pictures. The power of words is what makes the magic of poetry. Rhyming is *not* the necessary ingredient as so many children believe. Rather, poetry is an open, honest expression of the writer's feelings. For that reason students should be encouraged to begin writing poetry without rhyme and later experience writing poetry that rhymes.

WRITING CINQUAINS

Objectives:

Students will be able to

1. Identify syllables
2. Follow a pattern
3. Write a cinquain

Description:

Children will write the cinquain, a simple, concise, five-line poem containing twenty-two syllables. Words are carefully chosen in a two-four-six-eight-two syllable pattern to tell a story or describe something.

Organization:

Large or small groups, 30–45 minutes

Procedure:

1. Provide models of this form of poetry (see examples below). Read several cinquains to your students. Examples can be found in books for teachers on the teaching of poetry. One excellent resource is *Pass the Poetry, Please* by Lee Bennett Hopkins (Citation, 1972).

Snowman
Little snowman
Don't get cold when it snows
Or when that terrible, awful
Wind blows.

Steve Polleck

As I
See the flowers
Growing up the wall, I
Hope that no one hits them and makes
Them fall.

Kristi Prather

2. Describe the cinquain and present the outline for this form of poetry on the chalkboard. Elicit ideas for cinquains from your students. You may suggest some subjects such as nature, people, or objects. Remind your students that the words in a cinquain do not rhyme. Compose a few class collaborations so the students begin to feel at ease with this new structure.

3. Assign a topic and instruct your students to write a cinquain or let the students choose their own topics.

4. Share the students' writing. The students may prefer to share in pairs at first before sharing with the entire class.

Follow-up:

• Have students edit and recopy their cinquains for display on a bulletin board.

• Have the students collect the compositions and make a class book of cinquains.

• Copy the poems on leaf-shaped paper and hang the cinquains on a "poetree."

• Try a cinquain using the following pattern, which gives more direction to your students:

Line 1. Title—two syllables
Line 2. Description of title—four syllables
Line 3. Action—six syllables
Line 4. Feeling—eight syllables
Line 5. Another word for the title—two syllables

Children
Short, fat, tall, thin
Running, looking, shouting
Asking questions furiously
Learning

Lisa

• To practice parts of speech use this pattern:

Line 1. Noun
Line 2. Two adjectives describing the noun
Line 3. Three verbs showing what the noun does
Line 4. A short phrase about the noun
Line 5. Synonym for the noun in line one

Bird
Fascinating fisherman
Dives, dashes, darts
Feels good to fly
Freedom

Tommy Gambolie

• Have your students write a double cinquain. When the syllables in each line are doubled, the pattern becomes a five-line stanza with 44 syllables in a four-eight-twelve-sixteen-four pattern.

Objectives:

The students will be able to

1. Identify syllables
2. Follow a pattern correctly
3. Write a lantern poem

Description:

The lantern is a poem written in the shape of a Japanese lantern. It is a five-line poem containing eleven syllables in a one-two-three-four-one pattern.

Line		Syllables
1	—	1
2	— —	2
3	— — —	3
4	— — — —	4
1	—	1

Procedure:

1. Tell the students they are going to write lantern poems.
2. Provide models for this form of poetry. You may use the examples here, and you may also find it helpful to prepare more examples before you present the lesson. Explain the format to your students. If they do not understand syllables, you may have to refresh their memories.
3. Obtain ideas from the students. Use their suggestions to compose a group piece. You may wish to do several group collaborations to help your students gain confidence in writing this particular form of poetry.
4. Have the students write individual compositions. If some students seem hesitant, suggest that they work in pairs.
5. Provide opportunities for your students to share their writing.

My
anger
makes me hit
when I do not
wish.

John

Bait
wiggles
on the pole
waiting for fish.
Ugh!

Davie

Follow-up:

• Have your students recopy their poems on paper and mount them on lantern-shaped mobiles to hand around the room.

• After your students have tried writing several lanterns, have them string a series together in story form, for example:

Shells
g e n t l y
crunch under
my feet at the
beach.

Birds
of the
sea tip-toe
quietly by
me.

It's
fun to
play alone
walking on the
shore.

Denise

WRITING HAIKU POEMS

Objectives:

Students will be able to

1. Identify syllables
2. Follow a pattern
3. Observe details
4. Write haiku poetry

Description:

Children will write haiku, a form of Japanese poetry consisting of three non-rhyming lines, containing 17 syllables, five-seven-five respectively. The subjects of haiku are usually nature or the seasons of the year. When presenting this form of poetry to students, emphasize the importance of creating a single clear image or of capturing a moment in nature. Haiku is a delicate poetic form that can leave something implied but unsaid or provide a surprise image.

Organization:

Large or small groups, 30–45 minutes

Procedure:

1. Display something from the world of nature, such as a vase of flowers (either fresh or dying), an insect, or a rock.

2. Read examples that pinpoint the qualities of haiku. Many good books are available. *In a Spring Garden* edited by Richard Lewis (Dial, 1976) and *Don't Tell the Scarecrow* by Issa, Yayu, Kikaku and other Japanese poets (Four Winds, 1969) are two excellent sources.

3. Tell the children they are going to write haiku, and describe the form.

4. Refer to the nature display in the classroom and elicit ideas and thoughts about the display. The clustering idea described on page 14 will help facilitate ideas. Write the ideas on the chalkboard.

5. Carefully select some phrases and write a class haiku on the chalkboard. Demonstrate this form several times.

6. Ask the students to write their own poem using the display as the subject or something else related to the world of nature, as in these examples:

Clouds grow bigger fast,
Little drops of water fall,
A storm is so near.

Laura Mello

Ants are so small that
they can use a piece of grass
for a diving board.

Shauna Boomgaarden

Follow-up:

- Compile the finished products in a booklet and send copies home as a gift for parents to enjoy.
- Display the poetry on the bulletin board with the title "Moments to Remember" or "A Closer Look."
- Have students mount their haiku as a wall hanging. If several students have written about the same subject, it may be possible to combine their poems into a haiku series.
- Have students write a haiku for each season of the year.
- Have students write a haiku series on birth, life, death, the city, or country.
- Have students compose picture storybooks using haiku poetry.
- Have students write a haiku around a picture drawn by a student and representing the subject of the haiku.
- Share pictures or slides of the world of nature. Have students compose haiku to accompany the pictures.

Objectives:

Students will be able to

1. Identify opposites
2. Identify nouns, adjectives, and participles
3. Follow a pattern
4. Write a diamante (dee-ah-mahn′-tay)

Description:

Students will write the diamante, a seven-line, diamond-shaped poem created by Dr. Iris M. Tiedt. The diamante is a poem of contrast, beginning with a noun, gradually revealing differences, and moving to a noun that is the opposite of the original word. Students do not need to be concerned with rhyme or rhythm, but they must be familiar with the parts of speech. The pattern is as follows:

Line 1. One noun
Line 2. Two adjectives
Line 3. Three participles (-ing or -ed verb forms)
Line 4. Four nouns related to subject (Begin to make transition to opposite idea.)
Line 5. Three participles
Line 6. Two adjectives
Line 7. One noun (opposite of subject)

Organization:

Large or small groups, 30–45 minutes

Procedure:

1. Read several examples of the diamante to your students.

sun
bright orange
scorching, shining, burning
clouds, sky, stars, planets
dark, black, starry
night white
moon

Tina Vandenburg

slave
whipped tired
running hurrying crying
blacks whites Indians Chinese
sleeping loving fun
laughing playing
freeman

Pam McGee

2. Describe the diamante pattern and draw it on the chalkboard. (Duplicate this form for student use.)

—
— —
— — —
— — — —
— — —
— —
—

3. Ask students to think of nouns that are opposites, for example, summer-winter or man-woman.

4. Compose a class diamante on the chalkboard using a pair of opposites suggested by the class. Tell the students that it is easier to write a diamante if they begin with lines one and seven and then proceed to fill in the remaining lines. Do several with the class. If necessary, review the parts of speech used in the diamante.

5. Have the students write individual diamantes. If some students have difficulty composing, suggest that they work in pairs.

Follow-up:

- Have students edit and recopy their poems. Using colored crayons, have them trace diamond shapes around the poem until there is no space left on the paper. Display the poems on the bulletin board.
- Have students compare their poems to see if they contrasted similar subjects.
- Have students illustrate the change described in their diamantes, drawing several pictures to show the story.
- Have students write diamantes in pairs or groups, creating collages to accompany the poems.
- Have students work in groups of six. Give each student a piece of paper. Each student writes the first and last lines of a diamante, a pair of opposites. Then have students pass their paper to the next student for the second line and so on until the student receives his or her original piece of paper.

WRITING LIMERICK POETRY

Objectives:

Students will be able to

1. Compose poetry using rhythm
2. Compose poetry using rhyme
3. Follow a poetic pattern
4. Write a limerick

Description:

Students will write the limerick, a poem written in rhyme with a definite rhythm. Limericks were made popular by Edward Lear. This light verse form bears the same name as the city in Ireland where it originated.

The limerick has five lines. Lines one, two and five rhyme, and lines three and four rhyme (*a a b b a*).

________________ a
________________ a
____________ b
____________ b
________________ a

Lines three and four are shorter than the other lines, and line five usually ends with a funny or surprising twist. Limericks can be about anything. Popular limericks use people, places, or animals as subjects.

Organization:

Large or small groups, 30–45 minutes

Procedure:

1. Tell students they are going to learn to write limericks. Provide many examples of this verse form. *Book of Nonsense* by Edward Lear, *Out On A Limerick* by Bennett Cerf and *Book Of Ogden Nash* by Ogden Nash are excellent sources.

   Describe the pattern. Demonstrate that limericks, like music, have a certain beat. Suggest that the students clap out the rhythm.

2. Elicit limerick ideas from the students. You may need to give them a first line. Compose several group limericks on the chalkboard.

3. Have students write their own limericks.

4. Provide the time for students to share orally what they have created, for example:

There once was a man named Ned
Who fell as he jumped out of bed.
He stepped on a crow
And it bit his toe,
And he screamed and then fell on his head.

Kristi Prather

There once was a boy named Mike.
He liked to ride his bike.
One day in a wreck
He fell and broke his neck.
So now the boy rides a trike.

Donald Yamaoka

Once in the Kingdom of Hose
There was a young girl named Rose.
She stood on a chair
Ten feet in the air
And balanced a flower on her nose.

Mike Selletti

Follow-up:

- Have the students illustrate their limericks.
- Have students edit, recopy, and illustrate their limericks and bind them into a class book.
- Have students pantomime their limericks. Do this in small groups to gain maximum participation.
- Have each student write a series of limericks about a given topic such as an animal, a friend, or a character from literature.
- Set up a learning station and have students compose limericks as verses for greeting cards. Provide various kinds of colored paper in assorted sizes and a variety of writing or coloring tools. The learning station might be identified by the table tent shown below.

CHALLENGE

Imagine yourself as the teacher in an elementary classroom.

1. Develop a lesson for teaching a poetic form not included in this chapter, either a traditional verse form or one you create yourself.

2. Design a learning center around the theme "Let's Have Fun with Words," asking your students to explore the many ways words reach out and touch us. You may include activities involving all the language arts.

3. Collect or prepare examples of the fluency exercises presented in this chapter. You will then have additional models to use in teaching the lessons. Anthologies by children such as *Miracles* (Simon & Schuster, 1966) edited by Richard Lewis, and books by Lee Bennett Hopkins and Kenneth Koch will provide more examples of the activities described in this chapter.

Brown, Rosellen, and others. *The Whole Word Catalogue.* Virgil Books; Teachers and Writers Collaborative, 1972.

Cheyney, Arnold. *The Writing Corner.* Pacific Palisades, Calif.: Goodyear, 1979.

Dodd, Anne Wescott. *Write Now.* New York: Learning Trends, 1973.

Hopkins, Lee Bennett. *Pass the Poetry, Please.* New York: Citation Press, 1972.

Welech, David, and Susan E. Elliott. *A Year of Writing Activities.* New York: Scholastic, 1979.

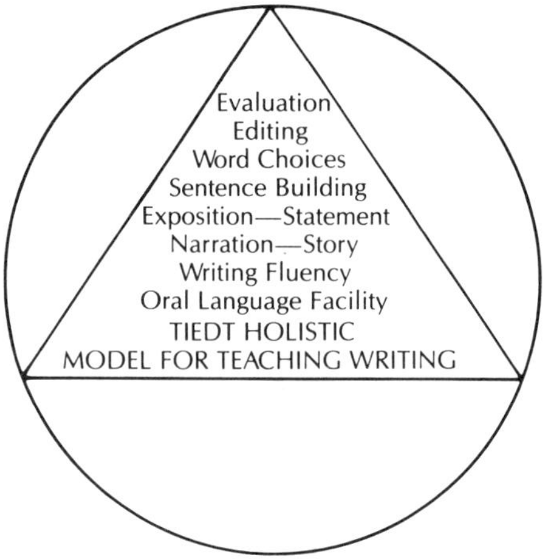

4

Narrative Writing

The desire to tell a story is a natural impulse, as common as crying or laughing, eating or drinking. If something happens your students want to tell you about it. When they've heard a joke or experienced something new or recalled a vivid memory, they want to share it with someone. The step from writing fluency to narration is, therefore, an easy and enjoyable progression for most young writers.

Narration results from telling or giving an account of experiences or events, whether true or fictitious. It can appear in such forms as a joke, a fable, a fairy tale, a folktale, or a short story.

Good narrative rarely relates action alone. It describes the action intermingled with scene, characters, and places. This chapter, which focuses on the craft of narrative writing, presents activities in which these elements of story writing are considered altogether as well as one at a time.

To promote success in these writing adventures, be aware that a positive attitude on your part as well as on the part of your students will increase self-confidence, cooperation, and willingness to experiment with the risky task of exposing thoughts on paper. Careful preparation and structuring of lessons is an important key to competent writing instruction. Aspects of a good lesson include planning prewriting experiences, selecting topics of interest to students, giving clear directions, and providing comfortable opportunities to share writing. Each lesson presented in this chapter incorporates these necessary ingredients to help you create a supportive environment.

After reading this chapter you will be able to

1. Define narrative writing
2. Teach students the elements of a story
3. Demonstrate specific activities to teach students the various types of story forms
4. Teach students to write a narrative paragraph

SIMPLE NARRATIVE FORMS

The imaginative power of children is awesome if we but open the door for them and then step aside. They seem to have an intuitive sense of the dramatic steps of narrative, especially if they have had a background rich in literary experiences of all forms.

If you require your students to create stories, give them the opportunities to listen to some of the best by such colorful authors as Hans Christian Andersen, the Grimm Brothers, Beatrix Potter, Rudyard Kipling, Jane Yolen, and Lawrence Yep. Provide recordings of stories read by famous artists. If possible, learn to tell some of these tales from memory, and encourage your students also to practice the art of storytelling. Capitalize upon each student's enjoyment, wonder, and excitement in listening to the magic tales of mystery, adventure, and friendship.

The lessons that follow provide writing activities that allow students to explore several narrative forms.

WRITING JOKES

Objectives:

Students will be able to

1. Identify the beginning, middle, and end of a story
2. Write a joke or anecdote

Description:

Students will write stories they have heard. Those who are not easily encouraged to write anything else will attempt to write a joke or an anecdote that they know. The simplest kinds of narrative contain the traditional ingredients of a story: a character, a problem, a climax, and a solution. The joke has an easily identifiable beginning, middle, and ending, as in this example:

Susie was sitting on the steps of a house when a lady approached and asked, "Little girl, is your mother at home?"

"Sure," said Susie.

"Good," said the lady, "then I'll just knock on the door." So she knocked and knocked but there was no answer. She knocked louder and louder but still no one came. She looked at Susie and asked, "Didn't you say your mother was at home?"

"Oh, yes," Susie said, "my mother is at home."

"Then why doesn't she answer the door?"

"Because," said Susie, "she's not here. This isn't my house!"

Organization:

Large or small groups, 30–45 minutes

Procedure:

1. Read a number of jokes to the class. Good sources are *Bennett Cerf's Book of Laughs* (Beginner Books, 1959) and *Witcracks: Jokes and Jests from American Folklore* by Alvin Schwartz (Lippincott, 1973). You might also share a humorous moment in your life with your students.

2. Explain that a joke or an anecdote works best when it includes:

   a. A situation
   b. A complication
   c. A climax
   d. Something funny

3. Elicit examples from the class. Encourage students to share amusing experiences with the class or with each other.

4. Compose a joke as a class collaboration. Write it on the chalkboard. Do two or three so that students get the idea.

5. Identify the beginning, middle, and end of the jokes.

6. When you feel students are "catching on," invite them to write their own jokes or stories.

The Ghost

Once there was a man who was very tired and he couldn't find a hotel room. At last he found one. It was a haunted room, too! When he was asleep, he heard something say, "I'm the ghost with the bloody finger." Then a moment later he heard again, "I'm the ghost with the bloody finger."

Quickly the man yelled back, "Look in my luggage and you'll find a Band-Aid."

Delia M.

The Three Prisoners

Once there were three men. They were all in front of a firing squad to be shot. Then the squad leader said, "Ready, aim . . ."

At that moment one of the prisoners said, "Flood." All of the squad went to get ready for a flood. There really wasn't a flood and the prisoner escaped.

Then the firing squad leader said, "Ready, aim . . ."

The second prisoner called out, "Tornado." When everybody on the firing squad went to prepare for the tornado, he escaped.

There was only one prisoner left. The firing squad leader shouted out, "Ready, aim . . ."

And the prisoner yelled out, "Fire!"

Allen P.

Follow-up:

- Some jokes may be appropriate for acting out in one-minute plays.
- Collect the stories and compile a "Funny Book."
- Illustrate some of the jokes and present them in comic-strip format.
- Have students simply retell a joke or funny story they have heard.
- Collect single cartoons and cartoon strips from the newspaper. Cut out the dialogue and have students create new dialogue to fit the picture.
- Have students collect funny stories from members of their families, write them down, and bind them into a "Family Fun Book."

WRITING FABLES

Objectives:

Students will be able to

1. Recognize the fable as a narrative form
2. Write a fable

Description:

In this activity students will write a fable after reading or listening to several examples of fables. The best known fables are those collected in Greece by Aesop some 2,500 years ago. James Thurber is a modern day fabulist.

Organization:

Large or small groups, 30–45 minutes

Procedure:

1. Ask students to tell you what they know about fables. Brainstorm or cluster the ideas.

2. Read several examples of fables by Aesop. Tell students that the fable is one of the oldest and shortest prose forms. The characters are usually animals given human voices to make a statement about how humans think and act. A moral is always attached to the end of a fable.

3. Read a fable and ask students to identify the moral. Suggest other proverbs or morals. Elicit ideas from the students.

- He who plots to harm another often comes to harm himself.
- If you do not share your good fortune with others, don't expect them to share in your misfortunes.
- Before you take advice, be sure it is given for your sake.
- Slow and sure is better than fast and careless.
- Prepare today for the needs of tomorrow.
- He who is too greedy may end up with nothing.
- Don't count your chickens before they are hatched.

4. Choose one proverb and compose a fable as a class composition. Write it on the chalkboard as students suggest sentences.

5. Ask students to choose a saying and to compose fables individually, as shown here:

The Turkey and the Farmer

One fall day a turkey was eating his grain. The farmer wanted him to get very fat for Thanksgiving. That day each hour the farmer fed his turkey more and more grain. He wanted him to get very fat for Thanksgiving. It so happened that the farmer's daughter told the turkey about what her father was going to do, but the unwise turkey didn't listen.

"I don't care," said the turkey. "I'll hide so the farmer won't get me."

So the farmer's daughter walked away and said, "Okay, if you want to die, don't listen to me."

So that night the farmer got his gun ready and went into the barn and shot the turkey.

MORAL: Listen to what your friends have to say before you disagree.

Stacey

The Ant and the Mouse

There once was a mouse that never worked. He always went to parties. One day he saw an ant working like a horse. He said, "Look at him working."

The ant said, "When winter comes, you won't have any food." The ant was right. When winter came, the mouse didn't have any food. He only got a piece of bread. "Next time you come for food, I won't give you any. I worked hard for this food," the ant said.

The mouse barely survived that winter, but the next winter the mouse worked hard for his food.

MORAL: Prepare today for the needs of tomorrow.

Antonio

Follow-up:

- Publish a collection of fables written by students.
- Have students make filmstrips of their fables. The technique is simple:

1. Measure and cut strips of paper to fit the filmstrip machine.
2. Mark the paper so that it contains boxes measured to fit the opening.
3. Have students draw pictures with a fine-line felt pen.
4. Then lightly rub baby oil over the paper strip.
5. Let it dry. The strips become transparent and will project onto the screen when put into the filmstrip machine.
6. Have the students show and narrate their fables.

- Encourage students to work with partners to compose fables.
- After reading fables, have students pantomime selected fables and ask the rest of the class to guess the moral.

REWRITING FAIRY TALES

Objectives:

Students will be able to

1. Identify elements of a fairy tale
2. Identify point of view
3. Rewrite a fairy tale

Description:

In this activity the students are asked to rewrite a known fairy tale from another character's point of view. *Cinderella* might be written from the stepsister's point of view and called "That Terrible Cinderella." *Hansel and Gretel* might be written from the witch's point of view, or *The Three Pigs* might be written from the wolf's point of view.

Organization:

Large or small groups, one or two 30–45 minute periods

Procedure:

1. Read several fairy tales to your students. *Little Red Riding Hood, Cinderella, Hansel and Gretel,* and *The Three Little Pigs* are excellent examples. Discuss the fairy tales with your students. Explain that they are based on universal themes such as love, greed, jealousy, and bravery, and contain clearly defined characters. The characters are frequently kings, queens, princes, and princesses with a problem to solve. Good wins out over evil with a hero or heroine accomplishing seemingly impossible tasks. Discuss the story elements, particularly the problem. Identify who is telling each story.

2. Compose a class version of Cinderella as told through the eyes of the stepsisters, a different point of view. Help students identify the motivation of the characters to aid them in telling the story.

3. Tell students to select a fairy tale to retell from a different point of view. Some students may wish to work in pairs to rewrite a fairy tale, while others may feel comfortable writing the tale by themselves. Here the wolf retells the story of *The Three Little Pigs:*

The Mean Little Pigs

You all know the three little pigs' side of the story, but no one ever asked for the real story. Listen to what I have to say.

Once upon a time on a cold and windy day I went to this cozy yellow straw house and knocked on the door. Inside was a little pig. I asked him if I could come in and warm my hands. All of a sudden he slammed the door right in my face! He slammed it so hard, the house caved in!

I went to the second house. It was made out of hard brown boards. I asked if I could come in and warm my hands. All of a sudden this little pig slammed the door right in my face! He slammed it so hard the house fell in!

I went to the third house. It was made out of strong red bricks. The pig inside said, "What's going on here?"

I said, "Can I come inside and warm my hands?"

The frightened little pig said, "But you're a wolf and very dangerous. You can't come into my house."

Now I was getting pretty cold outside, so this time I said, "If you don't let me in, I'll huff and puff and blow your house down."

The smart little pig said, "Go ahead." He knew I couldn't blow down his house. Instead I climbed upon the roof and slid slowly down the chimney and landed in a pot of boiling water. I leaped up into the air screaming and ran through the door and down the street. I only wanted to warm my hands. I wouldn't hurt those three little pigs!

Dionne P.

Follow-up:

- Edit and illustrate the tales and bind them in a book for the library.
- Read the fairy tales to other primary classes.
- Compare the rewritten fairy tales with the original stories.

- Rewrite the fairy tale in play form and perform the play.
- Script the story as a readers' theater performance.
- Encourage students to rewrite a familiar fairy tale by updating the situations, locations, and vocabulary to create a modern tale.
- Change only the ending of the original fairy tale.

HOW AND WHY STORIES

Objectives:

Students will be able to

1. Recognize this story form
2. Write a how-why story

Description:

The how-why tales (which Kipling called "Just-So Stories") challenge students to test their powers of invention. In this lesson students will compose their own how-why or just-so story.

Organization:

Large or small group, 45 minutes

Procedure:

1. Show pictures of animals and ask questions relating to the physical characteristics of the animals such as, "Why does the pig have a curly tail?" Read several stories from the *New Illustrated Just-So Stories* by Rudyard Kipling (Doubleday, 1952). These are relatively simple stories that attempt to explain such oddities as why the zebra has stripes or how the elephant got its trunk.

2. Call attention to the way the author begins each story. Rudyard Kipling's *Just-So Stories* contain a style and language that is so appealing to students that it soon spills over into their stories.

3. Ask additional "why" questions and elicit responses from the class. From these responses develop a class story that answers one of the questions previously asked.

4. Encourage students to write a how or why story. Some may choose to work with a partner.

How the Turtle Got His Shell

Once upon a time, long, long ago, the turtle had no shell. He lived in trees, mossy lakes and in the ground. One day the turtle was hunting for insects and along came a knight in shining armor. He tried to kill the turtle by stabbing him. Suddenly a tremendous crash was heard throughout the valley! The knight had lost his balance and fallen off his horse. A giant piece of steel fell from the knight and wrapped itself around the turtle. After about a week, the steel rusted and made a hard, brown substance that covered the back of the turtle. That's how the turtle got his shell.

Jill F.

Follow-up:

- Compile a class book of "just-so stories."
- Have students work in groups and act out some of the stories.
- Have students "tell" their stories to other classes.
- Script just-so stories for play presentations.
- Rewrite the stories as news flashes.

WRITING A TALL TALE

Objectives:

Students will be able to

1. Identify hyperbole (exaggeration)
2. Write a tall tale

Description:

Students will write tall tales following examples such as Paul Bunyan, Pecos Bill, Davy Crockett, and John Henry. Students will find it easy to reach into their own interests and experiences to find a suitable topic for the outrageous treatment of the tall tale. In this activity students will use exaggerations to make a point.

Organization:

Large or small group, 45 minutes

Procedure:

1. Begin the class period by telling an outrageous lie. Ask students if they remember any time in their lives in which they exaggerated to make a point. Ask if they have ever said something similar to these statements: "When my friend moved away, I cried for weeks." "Her smile warms up the whole school!" "That basketball player must be ten feet tall!"

2. Tell students they will be writing stories using hyperbole, the literary device of using exaggeration to make a point.

3. Read several examples of tall tales. You might include the following student example.

Paul Bunyan

In Greathole, Alaska, you might meet Paul Bunyan. He's the most talked about person in the world. Here are some facts not usually known about him.

On May 11, 12, and 13, 1851, Paul Bunyan was born. By the time he was 11 he was fifty feet tall! Going to school was a problem so he spent his days leaping from mountaintop to mountaintop. He never did learn to read. That was no problem because there weren't any books big enough for him to hold!

Paul was a friendly boy and made friends quickly. His best pals were the giant redwoods. They stood together in the forests for hours and sometimes even days discussing what Paul would be when he grew up.

Mike L.

4. Explore ideas for tall tales with your class.
5. Compose a tall tale as a class composition.
6. Invite students to work in pairs to compose tall tales.

Follow-up:

- Have students prepare filmstrip presentations of their tall tales.
- Present these tall tales to other classes.
- Group students into small response groups and have them read their stories to each other.
- Write a poem consisting of a gigantic lie in each line.
- Have a "Can You Top This?" contest in which each student writes a stupendous lie.

ELEMENTS OF A STORY

When is a story a story? Frequently a piece of prose that is meant to be a story is not a story because the main character solves no problem. Solving a problem is vital to storytelling. A story is a story when someone wants something, and he or she gets it only by overcoming one or more obstacles. This comprises the plot or plan. The plot plus characters and setting make up the basic elements of a story.

As you read stories to your students, discuss the basic elements of the story. In identifying the *who, what, why, where* and *when* in a story, students will determine the characters, plot, and setting. If you talk about these ingredients for stories as you read to your students, they will become familiar with these concepts and will approach story writing with more confidence.

This section presents procedures to help students acquire skill in developing characters, setting, and plot. Also included are dialogue and point of view exercises, activities that embellish the telling of a story.

CHARACTER DEVELOPMENT

Objectives:

Students will be able to

1. Demonstrate the ability to describe a character
2. Demonstrate the ability to use specific words and details
3. Identify ways to describe a character

Description:

Students will learn to develop characters. Stories take on life when writers describe their characters so well that they become alive to the reader. In writing clear descriptions writers frequently exaggerate one distinctive characteristic. This activity provides suggestions that help students to write vivid characterizations.

Organization:

Large or small group, 45 minutes

Procedure:

1. Read a vivid character description to the students.

2. Ask students to name traits found in characters. Elicit responses such as greed, shyness, cruelty, strength, kindness. List these traits on the board.

3. Model the activity. Begin by making a statement about yourself, such as "I am quite clumsy." Develop this characteristic in terms of:

a. *How you do things.* "Jogging down the road can be dangerous for me if I'm not watching where I'm going. My feet seem to find every loose pebble in the path."
b. *Synonyms, similes, metaphors.* "I frequently move in an awkward manner. I walk like a tired elephant."
c. *What people say about you.* "When I'm out jogging, my neighbors worry and often tell me to be careful."
d. *Something you've done.* "One day while walking down the sun-baked brick

road, my high-heeled shoe became stuck in the soft tar, and I walked right out of my shoe!"
e. *What you are not.* "I am certainly not a candidate for ballet school. I would find it very difficult to move gracefully continually."

4. As a class, develop one of the character traits using the form shown here.
5. Have students identify one of their character traits and develop it as modeled.
6. Review ways to describe a character. Emphasize that a description including something of the life and personality of the character will tell us a great deal more than just a description of physical traits.

> I am extremely shy. Whenever I walk into a room filled with strangers or even people I know, I keep my head down and my eyes down until someone talks to me. I guess I am truly a bashful person just like Snow White's little dwarf. "Don't be so unsocial," the kids say. Out on the playground I stand alone by the first grade building. I'm not unfriendly, but I'm not comfortable around a lot of people.
>
> Sarah T.

Follow-up:

- Illustrate the character according to the description.
- Act out the characterization.
- Write a story around this character trait.
- Have students think of people in their neighborhood, observe them, and write about their character traits.
- Describe a character, using enough specific detail to enable another student to paint the character's picture.

DESCRIBING SETTING

Objectives:

Students will be able to

1. Use specific details to describe a place, a time, or a mood
2. Identify setting in stories
3. Write a setting

Description:

Students will write settings.
Vivid descriptions of settings help the reader visualize and prepare for what is

to happen in the story. This activity will allow students to create an atmosphere for a story.

Organization:

Large or small group, 45 minutes

Procedure:

1. Have students describe how it looks outside on Halloween night or how it feels Christmas morning. Explain that setting is an extremely important element in a story. The time, place, and mood of the story are established through the story's setting. A sad, gloomy story, for example, might begin with a description of a gray, dreary day. A comedy might begin by describing the day in lighter, brighter terms.

2. Read several examples of settings from books appropriate to your grade level. Anne Frank's diary (Pocket, 1955), *Tom Sawyer* (Airmont Books, 1962) and the *Wizard of Oz* (Grosset & Dunlap, 1980) contain examples of effective setting descriptions. Identify the time, place, and mood of setting that you read.

3. Show students a picture that definitely indicates a time (of year or day), place, or mood. As a class, brainstorm words to describe the time, place, and mood of the picture. Compose a paragraph to describe the setting for the picture.

4. Pass out pictures from magazines. Have the students identify the specific details of the setting and write it as a paragraph, thus:

> The stream ran freely through the melting snow. The small block of snow moved slowly down the cool waters. The trees were as thin as toothpicks. The snow on the lightly covered ground felt like powdered silk. The surroundings were peaceful. The air was cool and crisp. The tall full-needled pine tree stood boldly. The animals in the woods were tucked away in their burrows and nests. The sky was clear and beautiful. Everything was wonderful that day at the stream.
>
> Dawn P.

Follow-up:

- Place all the pictures on the ledge of the chalkboard. Have students take turns reading their setting descriptions while classmates match them with the appropriate pictures.
- Mixup and redistribute the paragraphs and have students illustrate the setting described.
- Describe a character and write the character into the setting.
- Construct a diorama as described in the paragraph.
- Describe the setting in a picture as it might be described in a mystery. (Students should choose more cautious, haunting, mysterious words where possible.)

- Describe the same setting in terms of anticipating an exciting adventure.
- Describe the setting in terms of a fairy tale.

WRITING PLOT

Objectives:

Students will be able to

1. Define plot
2. Identify plot in a story
3. Outline episodes in a plot

Description:

In this activity the students will identify events in the plot development of several stories. Students will also be asked to outline episodes in a plot.

Organization:

Large or small group, 45 minutes

Procedure:

1. Quickly read or review a known fairy tale with the class.

2. Explain that the plot is an essential ingredient in an effective story. It is the plan, the story line, the sequence of events leading to a change. The main character seeks a goal, but he or she is prevented or hindered from reaching this goal by one or more obstacles. There is usually a conflict producing a certain amount of tension for the reader.

3. Read the *Three Billy Goats Gruff, The Gingerbread Boy,* or any short folktale. Elicit the plot outline from the class.

4. Provide students with copies of *Little Red Riding Hood, The Three Little Pigs,* or any short folktale. Instruct each student to outline the plot of the story. Encourage them to discuss the story and reach agreement about the sequence of events in the plot.

5. Assign each student the task of creating an outline for a plot, as in this example:

Plot Outline

1. My grades at school had dropped this semester.
2. We had no plans for Easter.
3. I wanted to go to Disneyland for Easter.
4. My parents said we could go if my grades improved.

5. There were only a few weeks left until Easter.
6. I'm not too good in math.
7. I'm on the little league baseball team.
8. I had a friend do lots of my homework.
9. Then we took the math test.
10. I waited nervously for the teacher to tell me my score.
11. I did not get good grades.
12. We did not go to Disneyland for Easter.

Dan B.

6. Remind students that something must change. They will need to give the reader certain information. Include what exists now, the goal or important change, and the steps toward that goal as well as what happened afterward. Remind students that they may find it easier to write from their own experience.

Follow-up:

- Write the outline as a story with setting and further character development.
- Make a picture story book from the outline.
- Write another episode in the life of this character.
- Identify the plot in a feature article in the newspaper.

WRITING DIALOGUE

Objectives:

Students will be able to

1. Transcribe conversations heard
2. Identify purposes for using dialogue
3. Use quotation marks

Description:

Dialogue is conversation. In stories it is extremely useful in developing character, in keeping the reader interested, in providing humor, and in adding realism. Simple dialogue can reveal a remarkable amount of information. In this activity your students will be asked to recall a real conversation and write it down. What the characters say should appear in quotation marks. Remind students that each time the speaker changes, a new paragraph begins.

Organization:

Large or small group, 45 minutes

Procedure:

1. Read dialogue from any story appropriate to your students' interest level.

2. Discuss dialogue or conversation and point out what the writer revealed about the character, setting, or plot through the dialogue.

3. Have students role play familiar situations such as being called for breakfast, arriving home from school, discussing what to do in the evening.

4. Demonstrate on the chalkboard a conversation you have heard.

> Mrs. C: "Do you know your lines?"
> Sara: "I think so. I practiced all day, but my knees are shaking."
> Mrs. C: "Oh, you'll do fine, Sara. I'm really looking forward to seeing the play. Break a leg!"

Teach students how to use quotation marks, if they do not know.

5. List the information this simple dialogue reveals.

> a. It's late in the day.
> b. Sara is in a play. She has practiced a lot.
> c. Sara is insecure and nervous.
> d. Sara knows her lines.
> e. Mrs. C. is familiar with the theater.

6. Now have students recall a conversation they have heard or they have had. Have them write the conversation, as in this example:

> "John, get up. Time to get up. Turn off your blanket."
> "Okay, Mom, okay. Aaaahhhh."
> "Breakfast is ready, hurry up."
> "What are we eating?"
> "Eggs and cinnamon toast. Your favorite breakfast. HAPPY BIRTHDAY!"
>
> John W.

Follow-up:

- Role play several of the conversations.
- Have students read their conversations in read-around groups and list information they learn through the dialogue.
- Have students choose a relative and write a conversation they have had with that person.
- Create a humorous scene with dialogue.
- Describe specific situations and let students choose to write a dialogue for one of the situations.
- Distribute pictures of people or objects and ask students to write a dialogue as it might take place in the picture.

Objectives:

Students will be able to

1. Identify point of view
2. Define point of view
3. Write from two points of view

Description:

Point of view is defined by Brooks and Warren as "the mind through which the material of the story is presented."[1] Your students have probably noticed, when observing an event with someone else, that they each may have a different way of looking at it. Writing can be improved if your students understand that people feel and observe differently. Consistency in point of view provides organization and unity to a story. In this exercise students will practice writing from two points of view.

Organization:

Large or small group, 45 minutes

Procedure:

1. Show an action-packed beginning of a film or filmstrip. Run it for a few seconds. Then stop the film. A good film is *Hunter in the Forest* (*Encyclopaedia Britannica*.)

2. Ask several students to tell what they saw. Notice the difference in detail and interpretation.

3. Tell students that each observer has expressed one point of view.

4. Review with students the definition of point of view and factors that can influence point of view such as age, sex, and experience.

5. Review the plot of *Little Red Riding Hood.* Have students role play the story from the point of view of the wolf telling the story to his buddies, Grandma talking to the Senior Citizens, or Little Red Riding Hood sharing at school. Discuss any differences that would occur, such as detail and language changes.

6. Have students describe their school desks from the point of view of the desk and from their own point of view, as in these examples:

[1]Cleanth Brooks and Robert P. Warren, *Scope of Fiction* (Englewood Cliffs, N.J.: Prentice-Hall, 1960), p. 607.

Desk's Point of View

Being a school desk is not easy. People are always sitting on me and playing on me. People come in from recess and breathe all over me. People sweat on me, too. I wish they would leave me alone.

Student's Point of View

It's good to have my own desk. With my own desk I have a place to keep my pencils and books. I can bring something special from home and if it is small enough it will fit in my desk and be safe. My desk is my own place in the classroom.

Shari R.

Follow-up:

- Illustrate the description in the paragraphs students write from the point of view of the desk.
- Put the paragraphs and the illustrations into a book.
- Discuss the paragraphs in terms of looking at something in a different way.
- Have students select a picture, study it, and write a comment on the situation in the picture from the point of view of one character (person, animal, or object) in the picture.
- Have students act out a brief scene in which two children fight and the teacher helps them settle the scuffle. Have one-third of the class write a description of what happened from the point of view of one child; have one third write from the other child's point of view; and have the remaining third write from the teacher's point of view. Compare points of view.
- Have students draw a picture of a tree and then describe it as if they were sitting on the top branch. In another paragraph they should describe the tree as if they were sitting under it.

PARAGRAPH DEVELOPMENT

The paragraph is one of the critical building blocks necessary for most longer pieces of writing. In narrative writing, paragraphing is not as highly structured as it is in expository writing. Nevertheless, learning to write a strong paragraph is an essential skill in developing effective prose.

The definition of a paragraph can vary, but generally the following interpretation is appropriate. A paragraph is a series of sentences that tell about one subject or topic. Usually the paragraph contains a topic sentence, several supporting sentences, and a concluding sentence.

Essential to a good paragraph is focus. Food is too general a topic to discuss in a short paragraph, but if the subject is limited to oatmeal cookies or sliced brown bread, then it is easier to describe succinctly in a paragraph. The paragraph reproduces a picture in words, and like a photograph, a paragraph can be sharp or out of focus. Encourage your students to write about something very specific.

Students need to be aware of when to indent for a paragraph. In narrative writing indentation is used whenever a new character speaks and when there is a change in time, place, or action. You need to explain to students that indenting does not always indicate that a paragraph follows. They can observe indentation in a reading textbook or any story that includes dialogue.

Allow students to write about a subject of interest to them. They write more clearly, more vividly, and with more vitality when they write about something familiar and interesting. Therefore, offer several choices rather than single topics as paragraph writing assignments.

MAPPING

Objectives:

Students will be able to

1. Organize information
2. Generate ideas for writing
3. Demonstrate the technique of mapping

Description:

Mapping is a process of organizing information. It is a method of outlining thoughts in a visual illustration. Students write the topic in a circle in the center of the page, then add spokes out from the circle, and write key concepts on the spokes. Details are filled in on additional prongs.

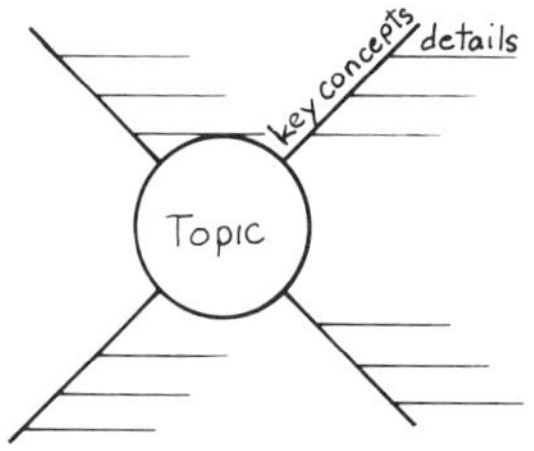

Organization:

Large or small group, 45 minutes

Procedure:

1. Talk about maps. What are they? Why are they useful? How are they used? When do you use them? (They show us how to get someplace.)

2. Tell students today they are going to learn how to map some of their ideas. They will make a picture outline of something they are thinking about.

3. Propose a topic for writing, such as "I feel angry (or good) when . . ."

4. Demonstrate the process on the chalkboard.

5. Suggest another topic. Have the class respond and complete an outline as a group.

6. List the following on the chalkboard.

> I feel proud when . . .
> It is a good day when . . .
> I admire __________ because . . .

7. Elicit other topics from the students.

8. Ask students to choose a topic and complete a map individually.

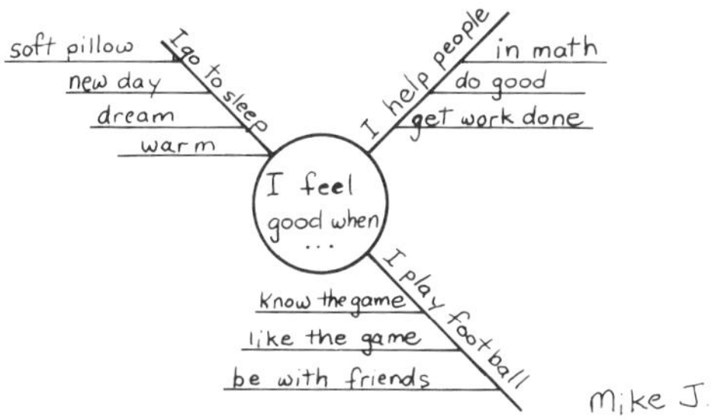

Follow-up:

- Have students develop a paragraph using the ideas from one of the spokes.
- Have students write a paragraph using each spoke of ideas.
- Have students map a story in their reader or one you have read aloud as a way of demonstrating comprehension.
- Have students map science or social studies lessons to help them visualize and understand concepts.

PARAGRAPH PATTERN

Objectives:

Students will be able to

1. Recite the pattern for a paragraph
2. Write a paragraph using this pattern

Description:

The purpose of this lesson is to provide a pattern for paragraph development as follows:

1. Choose a topic that is specific, not general. ("Pets," for example, is too broad; "dogs" is better, and "poodles" is better yet, but "my poodle" is specific.)
2. State a point of view, idea, or opinion about the topic. ("My poodle is an extremely active dog.")
3. Support your statement with a minimum of three reasons. (The poodle chases cars, barks at airplanes, and jumps on visitors.)
4. Restate the main idea in a different way. ("I wish my poodle were not quite so nervous.")

In this activity students will write a paragraph using these guidelines.

Organization:

Large or small group, 45 minutes

Procedure:

1. Tell students the purpose of the lesson. Illustrate the paragraph pattern on a chart available to students for daily reference.
2. Work with the entire class to compose a model paragraph on the chalkboard following the formula.
3. Give students a general topic such as friends, colors, food, toys. Instruct students to write a paragraph following the guidelines.

Muffin

My dog Muffin tries to act like a human. When we go on long trips and then stop for gas, she sits in the driver's seat and puts her paws on the steering wheel like she's driving. When we get to our destination, she is always the first one out of the car and the first into the house. At dinner time she sits at the table waiting for her food. It's almost like having a sister.

Eric M.

Follow-up:

- Have students edit and illustrate the paragraphs and bind them into a class book.
- Continue a discussion of the topic by stating another opinion and developing it in an additional paragraph. (Use mapping.)
- Write a daily paragraph about any object you or a student brings to class.

• Have a student perform an action. Invite students to write a paragraph about what they saw the student do.

• Have students write a paragraph with the topic sentence in the middle or at the end.

OBSERVATION

Objectives:

Students will be able to

1. Recall details
2. Observe specific details
3. Write specific details

Description:

The power to evoke mental images comes from sharp observations. The skill of observing, as with most skills, improves through practice. In this activity students will describe an object in great detail. You will want to repeat this exercise frequently.

Organization:

Large or small group, 45 minutes

Procedure:

1. Ask the students a series of questions:

   a. Do you put your right sock on first or your left?
   b. What color are your best friend's eyes?
   c. Without looking, describe what the teacher is wearing.

2. Comment on the accuracy of the student's observations.

3. Tell the students that good writers are good observers, and they are going to practice observing specific details.

4. Read examples of detailed observations selected from library books.

5. Describe any large object in the classroom or choose a small area in the classroom and begin to identify specific details. If you have decided to write about the classroom door, the details might be as follows: "Above the doorknob there is a long narrow scratch about six inches long curling upward on the left end. Several kick marks appear at the base of the door." The emphasis should be on looking closely at the object being described. Like a zoom lens on a camera, the students are to move in and notice smaller and more specific details.

6. Now ask students to describe an object such as their pencil or desk top.

> My pencil looks like it was pulled through the tenderizing machine at the meat counter. I chew it so much that not much is left of my stubby yellow pencil. It's only two or three inches long now and has no eraser left on the end. There is almost no writing left on the side of my pencil.
>
> Terry M.

Follow-up:

- Have students gather in small groups and place the objects described on a table. Instruct each student to read his or her description and then ask the group to name the object described.
- Collect the descriptions, mix up the papers, and redistribute them to students. Ask each student to illustrate the object described in the paragraph.
- After viewing a film in slow motion or discussing examples of people, animals, and plants in motion, ask each student to describe every motion necessary to carry out a rather routine action. Students might describe all of the movements in getting off a bike, combing their hair, or yawning.
- Have students go outside the classroom with notebooks and pencils. After everyone finds a place to sit, give each student a piece of string with which to outline a circle about one foot in diameter. Ask each student to observe the area and record in detail all that is seen inside it.
- Use pictures to teach close observation of a subject. Cut out pictures of faces. Have students write descriptions including adequate detail to enable someone else to visualize the face described. Collect the descriptions, pass them out to students, and have them illustrate the descriptions. (Make certain students do not receive their own descriptions.)
- Have each student choose a partner and tell each pair to sit back-to-back with paper and pencil. Ask students to describe their partners in detail without looking.

DESCRIPTION USING THE SENSES

Objectives:

Students will be able to

1. Write a description appealing to the reader's five senses
2. Use metaphors
3. Use similes

Description:

Teaching students that they can improve their writing by including details of sight, sound, smell, taste, and touch produces writing that is interesting and exciting. Emphasizing sensory awareness helps students to be more specific in their writing. In the following activity, students will describe an object in terms of what they see, touch, hear, taste, and smell.

Organization:

Large or small group, 45 minutes

Procedure:

1. Introduce this lesson by reading any book that illustrates the use of the five senses in description. *Hailstones and Halibut Bones* (Doubleday, 1960) by Mary O'Neill is filled with good examples. Discuss how the author brings vivid pictures to the mind of the reader.

2. Tell students they are to write a description of an object in terms of taste, touch, sight, smell, and sound. Demonstrate on the chalkboard. Pick an object such as a leaf, pine cone, shell, book, or chalk.

3. Have students describe it in terms of the five senses. ("The pine cone smells like a forest and scratches like daddy's beard.") Encourage students to use similes or metaphors in these examples. Point out the use of these figures of speech and define them if necessary.

4. Have the students give similar descriptions orally using other objects in the classroom. Begin with ordinary objects and elicit accurate observations about them.

5. Give each student a different object and have each one write a description. Instruct them to observe closely with their five senses and to write only what they see, smell, taste, hear, and touch.

> On the floor lies a large gray-blue, slick and silvery piece of pipe. It hurts when it comes banging down again and again like the slamming of a door. I can almost taste the hot sparks as metal hits metal in a smoky collision.
>
> Jonathan T.

Follow-up:

- Have students illustrate their descriptions.
- Edit descriptions by critiquing them for accuracy.
- Identify details that students wrote that proved to be helpful and those that proved to be misleading.
- Younger students may begin by listing sense words to describe objects or make statements such as:

The chalk tastes like ____________.
The chalk feels like ____________.
The chalk sounds like ____________.

The chalk looks like ___________.
The chalk smells like ___________.

• Consider one sense at a time. Put an object in a bag. Have a student reach in without looking and use the sense of touch to describe what he or she feels. The class should guess what is in the bag.

• Present a series of numbered vials containing various substances. Students are to smell them and describe each one. Students will be surprised to discover how limited their vocabulary is for describing odors.

• Provide a learning center where students can practice using the sense of touch. At the center place a group of ten objects similar in size and shape—lemon, walnut, golf ball, and so on. Instruct students to close their eyes and take an object from the group. Tell them to get to know the object so well that when it is put back with the others, they can pick it out by feel alone. Have them write a short paragraph about their object.

CHALLENGE

To prepare yourself for teaching narrative writing, try several of the following activities:

1. From books for children collect at least five examples of good character descriptions and five examples of good setting descriptions that you can use in the classroom.

2. Read two fairy tales and, in chart form, identify the characters, setting, and plot for each tale.

3. Consider your role as a teacher of composition. Write a dialogue between you and a student in which you discuss the value of writing.

4. Read several fables. Select a moral (proverb) and write a modern fable of your own that you can share with students.

5. Develop a chart or poster listing the elements in a story and provide examples of each element.

6. Using all of your senses, describe a holiday such as the Fourth of July, Cinco de Mayo, Christmas, or Hanukkah.

7. Think of all the animals you encounter. Choose one of these animals and observe the animal for a short time. Describe in specific detail all the smaller movements that work together to form the action you are observing, for example, a dog scratching a flea bite.

RECOMMENDED RESOURCES

Carlson, Ruth Kearney. *Sparkling Words.* Geneva, Ill.: Paladin House, 1979.

Dodd, Anne Wescott. *Write Now.* New York: Learning Trends, 1978.

Potter, Robert. *Writing Sense.* New York: Globe, 1975.

Wermuth, Linda. *Imagination and Language.* Englewood Cliffs, N.J.: Prentice-Hall, 1976.

Zavatsky, Bill, and Rod Padgett. *Whole Word Catalogue 2.* New York: McGraw-Hill, 1977.

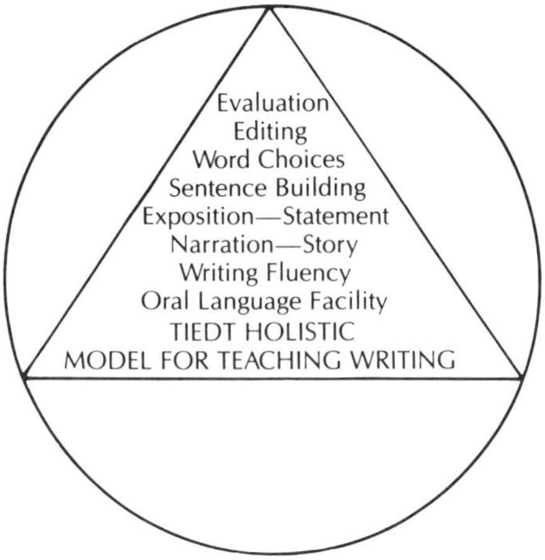

5

Expository Writing

Exposition is the act of explaining. Expository writing includes the technical paper based on research as well as the essay written from personal experience and observations. This type of writing is required almost daily—the information sent to parents or a report written for a committee. In the world of work, exposition is used for log entries, office memos, or quarterly reports to stock holders. In school, expository writing is required in all subjects. It is often done under pressure of class or test conditions, which means the skill must be automatic so that effort is directed to content.

Expository writing is like the writing of a computer program. The focus of the statement must be clear and followed by facts that support the concept. If the reader cannot progress to a logical conclusion, the information has not been given correctly.

The teaching of exposition requires the development of models that, like a computer program, can be applied to different kinds of material. As students learn about letter writing, for example, they need to learn that this form can be used in writing a letter to a friend or, with minor changes, in writing a request for a college application. The paragraphs written for an English composition class are developed in the same manner as those written for science.

The teacher's role then is one of educating the student to recognize expository forms and providing enough practice so that mastery of these forms results. This learning takes time and is difficult because the content used in the writing must first be learned by the student through direct personal experience, reading, or observation.

Just as elementary school students sometimes draw over and over again a subject they feel they draw well, student writers may repeatedly write about only one subject. It is the responsibility of the teacher, then, to help students expand the topic by introducing a variation of the theme; for example, the fourth grader who writes only about horses could be asked to write from the point of view of the veterinarian or to describe the workings of the stables.

Writing requires concentration, and for most elementary school students this means a quiet workshop atmosphere. The classroom environment for expository writing should be free of unnecessary distractions. Students can read, take notes, design folders, or write essays, but excessive movement or talking is likely to distract the writer.

The teacher's guidance is of prime importance from the topic selection to the final draft. Because of the importance of instruction, all work should be done in the classroom. Books or notes from books can be brought to the class from home, but materials should stay in the room in order to be available during the directed lesson.

The recent emphasis on proficiency standards brings renewed interest to the art of expository writing and, like computer-based education, it is confusing without a step-by-step plan for teaching. The four stages described in this chapter are appropriate for elementary students:

1. *Categorizing.* Students need to develop vocabulary and organizational skills necessary for composition and to learn the formula for paragraph writing.
2. *Description/observation.* Exposition requires details and an organized method of presenting them.
3. *Report writing.* One report a year is sufficient because of the time needed to teach and complete the assignment. The final report provides a model for the student's future use.
4. *Letter writing.* The student will learn to write a basic letter.

Currently teachers are finding many uses for expository writing beyond the simple paragraph. Students can, for example, write statements in a process journal recording what they have learned each day. Letters written by students facilitate home and school communication and enable the teacher to evaluate the thoroughness of student learning. The models taught as part of the expository writing experiments become a permanent part of the students' knowledge as they take an active part in community life.

After completing this chapter you will be able to

1. Guide students to organize information

2. Demonstrate the formula paragraph to students
3. Help students use expository writing in various ways
4. Devise stimulating activities to encourage students to practice letter writing

CATEGORIZING

Students as young as five years of age can list words associated with general topics. By first grade, they can identify subgroups and see relationships for grouping. In second grade, the concept is used during math in teaching about number families and in spelling through teaching about the combining of words to make compound words.

Because of the importance of categorizing, the classroom teacher should provide frequent lessons that require the students to list words for a specific category and guide them in the identification of groups within that general topic. This chapter begins with a complete lesson in developing this skill.

The second lesson presents the formula for writing a basic paragraph: a topic sentence, three substantiating sentences, and one concluding sentence—a form that can be applied to all expository writing. The activities described in this section are recommended as teaching strategies for students in grades one through eight.

CATEGORIZING

Objectives:

Students will be able to

1. List words for a specific topic
2. Group them under specific categories

Description:

Students dictate words that are associated with a topic, and the teacher writes them on the board or a large sheet of paper. Pupils then state categories and identify words that belong to each group.

Organization:

Whole class, 30 minutes

Procedures:

1. Write a word on the board that has some meaning to students (such as *dog*). Ask, "What comes to your mind when I say *dog*?" List the words supplied by the students on the board or chart paper.

collie	protection	guide dog	German shepherd
big	pet	helper	dog food
mean	cat	friend	tricks
teeth	fight	puppy	obedience
bark	large	animal	black

2. Ask, "Which words seem to go together?" When specific categories emerge from class discussion, write the categories on the board and number them. Ask the class which category each word belongs to, and then write the number of the appropriate category beside the word, for example: (1) reasons to have a dog, (2) things dogs do, and (3) how dogs look.

collie	1—protection	1—guide dog	German shepherd
3—big	1—pet	2—helper	dog food
3—mean	cat	1—friend	2—tricks
teeth	2—fight	puppy	2—obedience
2—1—bark	3—large	animal	3—black

Note: This step must be repeated several times before individual writing assignments are introduced.

Follow-up:

• Have students dictate sentences using the words in one category. Write the sentences on the board in paragraph form, for example: *Dogs can do many things.* They *bark* when someone rings the doorbell. They can get into *fights* with other dogs. Some dogs *protect* buildings and houses. Ask students to suggest a concluding sentence.

• Have each student write a similar paragraph following the five sentence pattern using words from a different category.

• Students work in small groups developing and categorizing lists.

• Students work in small groups using words from each category. When groups of sentences have been completed, have students put all of the sentences in order for a sample report.

PARAGRAPH WRITING

Objective:

Students will be able to

1. State the formula for writing a basic paragraph
2. Write one paragraph

Description:

Students will learn the parts of a basic paragraph; they will then write a paragraph.

Organization:

Whole class; two periods, 30 minutes each

Procedures:

1. Say, "A paragraph is a series of sentences related to one subject or topic." Ask students how many subjects or topics are contained in a paragraph.
2. Say, "A sentence that tells the main idea of the paragraph is called the *topic sentence.* Some of the other sentences help us understand the topic sentence." Ask students to explain the topic sentence.
3. Read simple paragraphs and have the students identify the topic sentences.
4. Say, "To write a paragraph, you must first choose a topic and write the topic sentence."
5. Say, "The second step is to write other sentences to help the reader understand the topic sentence."
6. Write a paragraph together. Select a topic from the following list:

J. had just been made captain of the football team.
It had started to snow.
Suddenly Henry heard a noise.
It was my birthday.
If Pat could get an *A* in reading, s/he could earn a dollar.
It looked like summer.
Sandy could see the town.
I am afraid of cats.
Lunch was ready.
I wish ___________.
I would like to be ___________.
My best friend is ___________.
My favorite food is ___________.

7. Tell the class they will each choose a topic sentence from this list and write a paragraph.

Follow-up:

• Have students suggest other topics or topic sentences for writing. Include topics related to science, math, or social studies.

• Introduce transition words: first, second, third. Add others such as: at first, then, finally. Older students can use furthermore, moreover, in addition, etc.

• Combine this lesson with categorizing. To extend the lesson have students write a series of paragraphs about the same topic.

OBSERVATION

Exposition is writing for the purpose of sharing information. Students often write about something they have seen or heard rather than actually experienced. They need to develop the skills of identifying what they have seen, organizing information about it, and relating the facts in a sequence.

A wealth of material for classroom use is available from electronic media as well as printed sources. In the sample lessons that follow, science, reading, and television provide subjects for students' expository writing.

OBSERVATION

Objective:

Students will be able to

1. Explain an idea shown in pictures or on charts
2. Use writing as part of a science lesson

Description:

Students will examine a chart, discuss it, and write a paragraph explaining the material shown by the chart.

Organization:

Whole class; 30 minutes

Procedures:

1. Have the students complete a science lesson on color from, for example, the McGraw-Hill Elementary Science Study (ESS) Kit entitled "Colored Solutions." Put this chart on the board:

Color Chart

Primary Color	+	Primary Color	=	Secondary Color
Red	+	Yellow	=	Orange
Yellow	+	Blue	=	Green
Blue	+	Red	=	Purple

2. Point to the chart. Have students describe what is shown and dictate summa-

ry statements about the information in the chart. If they cannot do this, provide sample summary statements:

> New colors can be obtained by putting two colors together.
> When primary colors are combined, they form secondary colors.
> Mixing colors can give surprising results.

3. Using one of these beginning sentences, or one of their own, students write a paragraph describing the information given on the chart.

> Mixing food colors can have surprising results. When red is added to yellow, orange is formed. Yellow and blue make green. Purple is made by putting blue and red together.
>
> David Norris

Follow-up:

- Exchange papers for editing. This activity is ideal as a beginning step in revising and correcting copy. The passages are short and the words used are shown on the chart so that spelling corrections can be made easily.
- Summarize charts in other subject areas. Make charts for cultural groups, ratios, hobbies, pets, and current events.

OBSERVING SETTING

Objective:

Students will be able to

1. Describe a setting
2. Make inferences about a setting from written material
3. Make a map or a sketch indicating spatial relationships

Description:

Students produce a map or sketch on which they label important landmarks, physical features, and details of a setting.

Organization:

Whole class or small group; approximately 60 minutes

Procedures:

1. Select a story from a reading text in which setting is an important component, for example

At the foot of these fairy mountains, the voyager may have descried the light smoke curling up from a village, whose shingle roofs gleam among the trees just where the blue tints of the upland melt away into the fresh green of the nearer landscape.

Washington Irving, "Rip Van Winkle"

2. Say, "Think of the setting as what you would see in the background if this story were a movie or television show." Have students list words, or groups of words, that identify aspects of the setting.

light smoke
village
shingle roofs
foot of mountains

3. When specific information is not given, then clues must be used. Tell students they must "read between the lines." Example: "Sidney and Sam watched their kites sail high over the wires." The reader infers that the day was windy and there was danger from the wires.

By using the information from the selection within the text, have the students draw a map or picture showing important details. Have students label parts that are especially difficult to illustrate.

Follow-up:

- Display sketches and maps with the selection from the text or story.
- Reverse the procedure; have the students look at a map or picture and write sentences. To extend the lesson have students write inference statements suggested by pictures and maps.

WRITING FROM OBSERVATIONS

Objective:

The students will be able to

1. Observe an action
2. Relate the action to time and place
3. Write a short report about the action

Description:

Students will write a newscast based on action observed.

Organization:

Entire class; 60 minutes

Procedure:

1. Have the class watch a nationally televised newscast. If possible, video tape the newscast for future reference. Students should complete a data sheet (page 109) while viewing the program.

2. Select one news item that is of interest to students. Ask the following questions regarding the news item and write the answers on the board:

a. Who was involved?
b. What happened?
c. Where did it happen?
d. How did it happen?
e. Why did it happen?

3. Students dictate the answers to the above questions based on the one news item selected. They then rewrite the news item or select data from another event in the news and write a different item. Example: Students view a news segment and select a story about a fire in California.

a. Who is involved?	Fire fighters
b. What is happening?	Fighting 1,500 acres of fire in Patterson, California
c. When and where does it happen?	Patterson, California, July 30, 19_____
d. How did it happen?	Arson by persons not yet identified
e. Why did it happen?	Unknown

Today firefighters fought a 1,500 acre brush fire in Patterson, California. The fire fighters were limited in the work they could do because of the steep and rugged ground. The fire was started by an arsonist and police are looking for clues.

Colleen Heaps

Follow-up:

• Replay the broadcast and identify introductory and closing phrases. Students then rewrite their story so that it sounds like a news broadcast.

• This activity is ideal as a homework assignment that all can complete. Have students write a news item using the format for this lesson as a model.

• Use this format for individual stories centered on school or community news.

• Read any of these newscasts written by students in groups so that all can hear. Use a television studio layout to simulate a TV newscast, or use a radio arrangement with a central microphone.

• Begin with newspaper stories and follow the same lesson. Extend the lesson to a television or radio format for classroom activity.

News Worksheet

Student____
Channel________________________Time____________Date____________

Topic	Place

For one topic listed above, write the answers to these questions:

1. Who is involved?____
2. What is happening?______________________________________
3. When and where does it happen?____________________________
____
4. How did it happen?_______________________________________
5. Why did it happen?_______________________________________

REPORT WRITING

Students write many reports in school—book reports, science experiments, descriptions of people and places, animals and resources, outer space and inner self. Students can learn how to make their reports more effective.

Collect material at various reading levels as resources for the students. Reports require students to use information beyond or supplemental to their own range of experience, and generally this knowledge is obtained through reading. To prevent verbatim copying from books, teach students how to take notes. Also encourage them to use other sources of information, such as interviews. They must learn to organize material and to follow this organization as they write the report.

Because the process is unfamiliar, children will need plenty of time. Allow at least ten hours of classroom time for students to read the material, take notes, organize information, and write their reports. One research report per year is sufficient for students in grades two through six; two reports may be assigned in grades seven and eight.

LOCATING INFORMATION

Objective:

Students will be able to use the tables of contents and indexes in books

Description:

Students will locate information for each other from books and identify the location of the topic within the book.

Organization:

Whole class, 30 minutes. (After one sample has been demonstrated, the remainder of the assignment may be completed during unstructured class time.)

Procedures:

1. Select a topic that will be used for the teaching of report writing. Go to the school library to make certain that a number of books are available at various reading levels on the subject you have chosen. Collect books on that general topic. Subjects usually found in a variety of books are:

sports	transportation	foods	animals
biographies	recreation	health	human body

2. Make a large chart and place it on the wall in the classroom. Write each student's name on the chart. Next to each name have the student write the subject selected for the written report.

General Topic: *Animals*

Name of Student	Animal Selected
1. Sandy	Vampire Bats
2. Kit	Arabian Horses
3. Brad	Hamsters
4. Kara	Snakes of Texas
5. [etc.]	

3. Distribute several strips of paper, about six inches long, to all students.

4. Distribute books and pamphlets at random to students.

5. Review the location, purpose, and use of the table of contents and indexes within books.

6. Direct the students to locate subjects within the books, identify which student is studying that subject, write the name of that pupil on a slip of paper, and place it in the book.

Sandy's subject: Vampire Bats

7. Keep all materials in a central location while teaching report writing. The students' names may be written on labels and pasted on the shelves of a bookcase to designate a space for each student's research materials. Each book is then placed above the name of the student who will use it. If more than one student could use the book, place it above the name of the student who has the fewest resources. (In grades two through four, one book per student is sufficient.)

In addition to reference books, composition books for note taking and all other materials involved in this assignment should be kept on these shelves. While learning to write a report, students should keep all books and materials in the classroom. They may bring material from home or from libraries, but all writing should be supervised by the classroom teacher.

Follow-up:

- Students who have many books above their names may need to limit their topic. If no information can be found for a selected topic, the student needs to choose another topic.
- Exchange charts with another class that is also learning to write reports. Students can identify books for students in the other room.
- Extend the lesson by including other printed material such as pamphlets and magazines available to students.

Objectives:

Students will be able to

1. Locate paragraphs containing useful information
2. Write the main idea from each paragraph in a notebook
3. Organize notes under general categories
4. Construct a simple outline

Description:

Students will practice taking notes and organizing them under various subject headings. They will make a sentence outline.

Organization:

Whole class, 45–60 minutes (Consider also using the reading period and other subject periods to allow adequate time for students to work on their reports.)

Procedure:

1. Distribute a composition notebook to each student.

2. Students read about their topics from the books previously selected. They identify paragraphs that tell about their subjects. In the notebook, the student writes sentences or phrases that summarize the main idea of each paragraph, forming a simple outline. If the general topic is "Transportation," for example, and Kim's topic is "Bush Pilots," Kim might make the following notes:

> Bush pilots help in the Arctic.
>
> Bush pilots help find lost people.
>
> Crisscross flying

In taking notes, students write on only one side of the page and skip lines so that the statements can be cut apart later.

3. When all resources have been read and notes completed, students divide a large sheet of paper (18″ × 24″) into sixths. General categories that the student selects are written at the top of each section of the unfolded paper. Kim's paper might look like this:

Training	Job Description
Hazards	Benefits
Future	Feats Accomplished By Bush Pilots

4. Each subject heading suggests the topic sentence for one paragraph of the student's report. Students may wish to determine in a conference with you or a peer the best order in which the topics can be presented in the report.

5. To develop the outline for their reports, students cut their statements from the notebook and paste them under the appropriate subheading. (Some words and phrases may be discarded at this stage.)

6. Students at this time also will be designing folders in which the reports can be organized and made available for reading by other students in the class.

7. The report is then edited and rewritten. The completed report can be used as a model in other subject areas.

Follow-up:

- Display reports in the local or school library for enjoyment by others.
- In a departmentalized school, work with other subject area staff so that a report for a science or social studies class can be developed in your class.
- Have students work in teams of two or three to prepare a report.

MAPPING TO ORGANIZE A FIVE-PARAGRAPH REPORT

Objectives:

Students will be able to

1. Outline information presented in a story
2. Write a five-paragraph report on the story

Description:

Students will read a selected story, use mapping to outline the information presented in the story, and write a five-paragraph report following the formula given.

Organization:

Large group presentation, 45 minutes (reported)

Individual reading of books, varies

Writing of individual reports, 45 minutes

Editing and rewriting, 45 minutes

Procedures:

1. Select a short book or story to read aloud to the class, for example, a familiar folktale such as "Red Riding Hood" or "Sleeping Beauty."

2. After reading the story aloud to the class, ask them to help you map the story. Place the story title in the center of the chalkboard, then ask students to list the characters. Next, have them list the places identified in the story. Finally, list the events that occurred. Write their suggestions on the board to complete a map that looks something like this one.

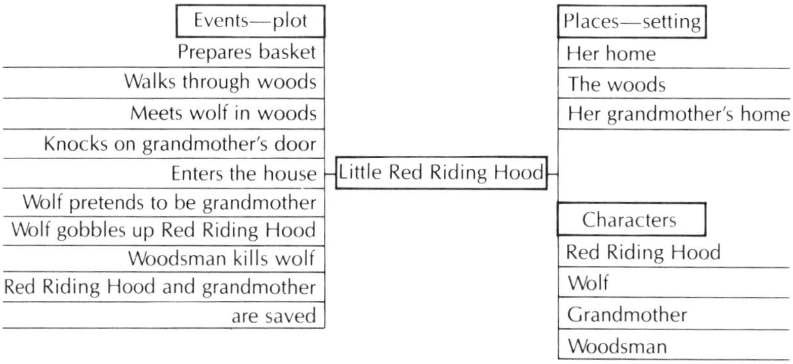

3. Show students how to write a five-paragraph theme or report based on the information they have organized. Write the report collectively on the board with students supplying the necessary information as you call for it. Point out that the paragraphs will follow the same pattern they have already begun using (Topic sentence, 3 supporting sentences, 1 concluding sentence). The resulting report will be something like this:

Little Red Riding Hood

"Little Red Riding Hood" is a story that most of us know. The characters include a heroine, a hero, and a villain. The setting is in three different places. The events move rapidly along to a satisfactory conclusion. This story is a favorite folktale.

The characters include a heroine, a hero, and a villain. Red Riding Hood, of course, is the heroine, a sweet little girl. The woodsman who rescues Red Riding Hood and her grandmother is the hero. The villain is the wicked old wolf who gets his just desserts. These characters are clearly described.

The setting of the story moves us to three different places. The story begins in Red Riding Hood's home, where she is preparing a basket for her grandmother. Then, she begins walking through the woods, where she first meets the wolf. Finally, the story concludes inside her grandmother's house. The three settings are quite different.

The plot moves along rapidly. Red Riding Hood prepares her basket and sets off to visit her sick grandmother. When she meets the wolf, we know that he represents danger. The story concludes satisfactorily when the woodsman saves Red Riding Hood and her grandmother from the wily wolf. The events are logical and well-organized and follow a clear time sequence.

"Little Red Riding Hood" is a favorite with young children. They like the story because it contains some scary elements. The wolf is pictured as wicked with big, sharp teeth. When he is killed in the end, everybody is happy. This story will continue to delight children.[1]

4. Help students outline the structure of this five-paragraph essay or report so they can apply it to other compositions. Show them, too, the relationship between the expository paragraphs they wrote and this longer work.

One Expository Paragraph	The Five-Paragraph Essay
Topic sentence	Introductory paragraph
Support sentence 1	Paragraph about support sentence 1
Support sentence 2	Paragraph about support sentence 2
Support sentence 3	Paragraph about support sentence 3
Concluding sentence	Concluding paragraph
5 sentences	25 sentences

5. Have students individually map another story that you read aloud to them, then compare their results. Ask them to compose the introductory paragraph and discuss it before students continue. Let them complete the five-paragraph essay independently.

6. After the papers are completed independently, have students work in pairs to see if each one has followed the formula by counting the sentences in each paragraph (5), identifying the topic sentence in each paragraph, reading each sentence aloud to see if it "sounds right," and checking to see that supporting sentences relate to the topic.

[1]Iris Tiedt, *The Language Arts Handbook* (Englewood Cliffs, N.J.: Prentice-Hall, 1983).

7. Students who complete this assignment can apply the method to a book they read independently. As they begin writing the reports, confer with them at three checkpoints: mapping, completion of the introductory paragraph, and completion of the five-paragraph report.

Follow-up:

- Have students prepare a report for science or social studies, adapting the structure used in mapping fiction to fit the topic. They may need such categories as characteristics (of an animal), products (of a country), contributions (of a statesman).
- Have students map a feeling. Discuss the categories they might use.

THE I-SEARCH PAPER

Objectives:

Students will be able to

1. Determine how to find information they need
2. Use various sources of information
3. Organize the information they collect
4. Prepare a formal report

Description:

Students will choose topics that interest them and list ways of finding the information they need. They will collect data and organize it into a formal report. This activity is recommended for older or advanced students.

Organization:

Large group planning, 45 minutes
Individual collection of data, one week
Individual writing of first draft of report, one week
Small group editing, three 45-minute periods

Procedures:

1. Ask students to list five things they would like to know, for example:

> I would like to know how to repair my bicycle.
> I would like to know how words get into the dictionary.

Give them time to think about this list. After they have made the list, have students select one of the items to investigate.

2. Discuss ways of finding information. Make three columns on the board to organize resources, thus:

In the Library	Talking to People	Writing for Information
The Reader's Guide	Interviews	City officials
Atlases	Telephoning	State agencies
Almanacs	Visit a business	U.S. government agencies
Encyclopedias		
Books about subject		

3. Have students begin keeping a process journal in which they record their progress and make notes. Each entry should be dated. Schedule time for students to work in the library; suggest other ways of finding the information they need.

4. After a week's time for collecting information, guide students in organizing their reports. You may schedule one period for each of the following parts:

a. Statement of the problem: What did you investigate?
b. Procedures: Describe how you went about your search.
c. Findings: What did you find out? Outline the information or prepare graphs. Write paragraphs to summarize information.
d. Conclusion: What will you do now? How will you use the information you discovered?

5. After students have completed the first draft of their I-Search paper, have them work in pairs to edit their papers. Prepare a checklist on the board of things they should watch for—clarity of meaning, good vocabulary, punctuation.

Follow-up:

- Have students prepare a cover for their reports and illustrate them as appropriate. Place the reports on a table where they are available for reading.
- Discuss what students learned about the process of locating information. What will they do next time? Have students observe that they did not just copy from an encyclopedia. Why not?
- Have students outline the process of preparing a report on another topic. They can think through the process without writing another complete research report.
- Use these procedures in science or social studies classes.

Letter writing must always have a purpose. It is the responsibility of the classroom teacher to find various ways to motivate this form of expression. The following are suggested purposes for letter writing by students:

1. Write to a sports hero.
2. Write to television stars or singers.
3. Send a holiday greeting to a hospital patient.
4. Send a holiday note to senior citizens in a residential home or hospital.
5. Ask relatives about life when they were younger.
6. Write to parents explaining the need for homework binders, plans for next week's open house, and so on.
7. Write an excuse for absence *to be signed by parent.*
8. Write for free information.
9. Write to political figures.
10. Write letters to school staff to express appreciation or offer suggestions.
11. Write thank you notes after a holiday expressing appreciation for gifts.
12. Make suggestions to the cafeteria director.
13. Send to parents a daily statement that describes one new item learned each day.

Letter writing can be the vehicle to teach manners and proper penmanship as well as effective communication.

THE THREE-PART LETTER

Objective:

Students will learn to write a three-part letter.

Description:

Students will write a three-part letter. To maintain letter writing as a high-interest activity, introduce it only when an actual need exists for writing a letter.

Organization:

Whole class; 30 minutes

Procedure:

1. Have a large model of the three-part letter displayed. Say, "This is the form of

a three-part letter. This part is the greeting. It tells you who will receive the letter."Ask students to explain what the greeting is and to identify it by name.

Greeting, Body of the letter. Signature	Dear Alan Alda, Thank you for providing the television program M.A.S.H. My friends and I enjoy watching it together. Tracy Smith

2. Say, "This part is the body of the letter; it tells the message." Ask students to explain and identify the body of the letter.

3. Say (as you point to the signature), "The last part is the signature; it is the writer's name." Ask students to explain and identify the signature.

4. Have students write a letter. You may wish to consider having monthly themes for letter writing so that in September students write to a sports or entertainment star, in October to distant relatives, and so on.

Follow-up:

- Mail the letters through the school. Review the procedure used by post offices for handling mail. Many post offices permit study excursions. When the post office is located near a school, the cost is minimal.
- Provide mail boxes within the classroom for mail between students.
- As a class write letters that can be copied for individual use.

WRITING A FIVE-PART LETTER

Objective:

Students will write a five-part letter.

Description:

Students will write a longer, five-part letter. Present this lesson as many times as necessary for mastery.

Procedure:

1. Display a large chart of the five-part letter and a sample letter.

Sample Chart

HEADING
Street
City, State ZIP
Date

Greeting:
Body of the letter

Closing,

Signature

Sample Letter

123 First Street
Chico, CA 95877
November 1, 19_____

Dear Terry:
We are so happy that you can spend Thanksgiving with us. We have your room ready for you. Plan to stay as long as you wish.

Yours truly,

Kim

2. Say, as you point, "This is the heading of a five-part letter. The heading gives the address of the person who is sending the letter and it gives the date the letter was written. The heading is placed near the top of the right side of the page." Have students explain the content of the heading and identify it by name.

3. Say, while showing, "This is the greeting. It usually starts with the word *dear*. The greeting is placed at the left margin, and a colon is placed after the greeting."

Have students give oral responses individually and as a group, naming this section, purpose, location, and the punctuation mark needed.

4. Say, again as you point, "The third part of the letter is the body, which contains the message of the letter. The first word of each paragraph is indented."

Students give responses identifying the body of the letter and its function.

5. Say, as you indicate on the chart, "The fourth part of the letter is the closing. Notice the comma after the closing."

Students identify the closing and review the punctuation mark necessary.

6. Say "The fifth part of the letter is the signature. It is the writer's name."

Students will identify the signature by name and purpose.

7. Review with the students the following checklist for writing a five-part letter (which may be written on a chart for proofreading):

Did You

a. Capitalize each word in the heading?
b. Separate city and state with a comma?
c. Use the correct state abbreviation?

d. Separate the day and the year with a comma?
e. Have five parts to your letter?
- heading?
- greeting?
- message—the body?
- closing?
- your name?

Follow-up:

- Mail the five-part letters and share responses.
- Learn more about the five-part letter through examining actual letters.
- More mature students can use the formal business letter form including the inside address. Have students use this form to write for free materials or information. Have students bring in sample business letters their parents have received to serve as models. Students will enjoy making creative letterheads.

CHALLENGE

1. Make charts for use as models with the three-part and five-part letter writing units.
2. Compile a bibliography that lists free material students can request during letter-writing units.
3. Write samples for activities described so that you will have them to use as teaching aids.

RECOMMENDED RESOURCES

Bergman, Floyd L. *The English Teacher's Activity Handbook.* Boston: Allyn & Bacon, 1976.

Michel, Lois A. *Another Way Out.* New York: Holt, Rinehart & Winston, 1974.

Reeves, Ruth, ed. *Ideas for Teaching English: Successful Practices in the Junior High.* Urbana, Ill.: National Council of Teachers of English, 1966.

Tovey, Duane R. *Writing Centers in the Elementary School.* Bloomington, Ind.: Phi Delta Kappa Educational Foundation, 1979.

NCTE Committee. *All About Letters.* Urbana, Ill.: National Council of Teachers of English and the United States Postal Service, 1979.

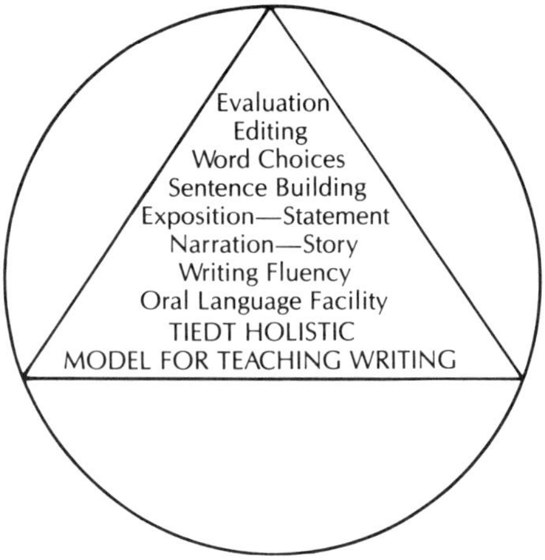

6

Writing Effective Sentences

Have you read a Western Union message lately? While walking down the street, do you hear short, choppy telegram-like talk? Probably not. Few people communicate that way.

Without formal grammar instruction, a child bridges the gap from two-word combinations to telegraphic speech, and then graduates to sentences. Since a child learns to speak in sentence form without formal instruction, the concept of the sentence need not be taught when the child begins to write. The child begins writing sentences intuitively. After students are writing in quantity, we can help them learn to write more effective sentences.

If you accept the fact that a child intuitively knows the form of sentences, then you can build on that skill by looking at more sophisticated skills such as sentence combining. The focus of this chapter is on examining the structure of sentences (grammar) and explaining ways to help students polish their sentences and develop style. Grammatical terminology, such as parts of speech and punctuation, will be used throughout the chapter. Since students are expected to be familiar with these prerequisite skills, it would be helpful to review these terms as you model the lessons. As they practice writing better sentences, students will need a "working knowledge" of grammatical terms.

The lessons in this chapter are designed to help students write more mature sentences. After reading this chapter, you will be able to

1. Involve students in a discovery method by having them build sentences based on oral language experiences
2. Perform sentence imitation and patterning by sharing literary forms and directing students to write sentences that imitate these models
3. Use dictation methods so that the students will develop an "ear" for powerful sentence forms
4. Teach punctuation within the context of oral and written language experiences

This chapter shows how to make students aware of the intuitive connection between spoken and written language. The student is first exposed to more complicated structures. The ultimate purpose of this chapter is total involvement with sentence building, and its goal is to share techniques that lead to more mature sentence development as described in the main subdivisions:

1. Transcribing and Expanding
2. Sentence Building
3. Sentence Modeling
4. Using Punctuation

TRANSCRIBING AND EXPANDING

A child acquires sentence structure as early as one-and-a-half years of age through hearing language. The intuitive connection that the child made at that early age can be reinforced through later grammar instruction as children become aware of how English grammar works. The activities of this section provide stimulating springboards to language study.

This section focuses on transforming short, choppy phrases into sentences. Students intuitively manipulate choppy phrases so that they speak in sentence form. The activities of this section give practice in writing sentences.

BABY TALK

Objectives:

Students will be able to

1. Transcribe short phrases into sentences
2. Listen to conversation critically

Description:

Students will record examples of "baby talk." The class will be divided into pairs. One member of the pair will utter the "baby talk" and the other member will expand it into sentences.

Organization:

Pairs, 30 minutes; large group, 15 minutes

Procedure:

1. Instruct the class to listen to the talk of 1½- to 3-year-old children and to write what they hear. Assign this as investigative homework.
2. After a few days, have the class brainstorm examples of baby talk, such as:

Daddy go	food highchair
doggy eat	go bank
nana	outside please
nite-nite time	water on

3. Instruct the class to expand these phrases into the intended message of the child and to compare their sentences to see if they all have the same message, as shown here:

Phrase	Suggested Sentences
Daddy go	Where did Daddy go?
	Daddy, let's go.
doggy eat	The dog wants to eat.
	The dog is eating.
nana	I want a banana.
nite-nite time	I want to go to bed.
go bank	Let's go to the bank.

4. Arrange the class into pairs and have one member utter the baby talk while the other member writes the sentence.

5. Use the reverse procedure. Have students examine complete sentences and jot down the key words that the baby would utter. This is good practice in identifying the topic or main idea.

Follow-up:

• After the class has brainstormed and discussed baby talk, identify the kinds of words that are missing (function words, verb endings, pronouns). Discuss whether the child communicated even though the utterances were not in sentence form. Tell the class about the acquisition of language, a process they experienced as small children.

• Set up the class for team competition by challenging opposite teams to transcribe an utterance into a sentence. Give the teams points based on the number of seconds it takes to transcribe (for example, five seconds = five points). The team with the lowest score wins.

PHONE CONVERSATION

Objectives:

Students will be able to

1. Listen to the ending of a conversation and "guess" the other segment of the conversation
2. Write a dialogue in sentence form

Description:

Students will role play a mock phone conversation. Then, a student will role play one side of the conversation. Students will write the other end of the conversation.

Organization:

Pairs, 15 minutes; large group, 30 minutes

Procedure:

1. Break the class into pairs and have each pair write a phone conversation. Tell them that they'll role play this conversation so they should write a script, for example:

Aunt: Hi, Ryan, what are you doing?
Ryan: Watching cartoons.
Aunt: Oh, yeah, which ones?
Ryan: Popeye, Batman.
Aunt: Do you like them?
Ryan: Ya.
Aunt: Which cartoon are you going to watch next?
Ryan: Cartoons are over, I'm going outside.

2. After the students have written the scripts, have them role play the conversation. Have them role play half of it; then have one speaker remain silent, so that only one side of the conversation is heard.
3. On the board or overhead transparency, write what was heard and have the

class copy that. Then, have them write in what they think would be the other end of the conversation, for example:

Ryan: Popeye, Batman.
Aunt: ___________
Ryan: Ya.
Aunt: ___________
Ryan: Cartoons are over. I'm going outside.

4. When the role playing is finished, have classmates read their scripts and then compare theirs to the original.

5. After two or three conversations have been role played and the students have practiced the model, divide the class into small groups so that all pairs have a chance to role play their conversation. Have students follow the same procedure when they work in small groups.

6. Circulate among the groups and answer any of their questions. If there is not enough time to role play all the conversations, collect the student scripts and prepare them for the next day by blotting out one end of the conversation. Make copies for the class, thus:

Conversation of Two Friends

Sue: Mom said I could go.
Jill: ___________
Sue: I know.
Jill: ___________
Sue: It's the best movie.
Jill: ___________
Sue: At 2 P.M.

7. Pass the "blotted-out" scripts to the class and have them write in the missing part of the conversation. Remind them that the missing part of the conversation should be written in sentence form.

Follow-up:

- Have the class discuss the activity and write a summary of conversations. Discuss when we talk in sentences or in phrases. Discuss how we develop an "ear" for language.
- Have students write a phone conversation between two super heroes, such as Batman, Superman, Wonder Woman or The Incredible Hulk.

NEWSPAPER HEADLINES

Objectives:

Students will be able to

1. Use newspaper headlines to write a sentence
2. Select key words and rearrange them into a new sentence

Description:

After looking at a newspaper headline, students will use the words in the headline to write a sentence.

Organization:

Large group, 45 minutes

Procedure:

1. Have students clip newspaper headlines and bring them to class.
2. Hang a string across the front of the room. Gather the headlines from the students and hang them on the string by using paper clips.

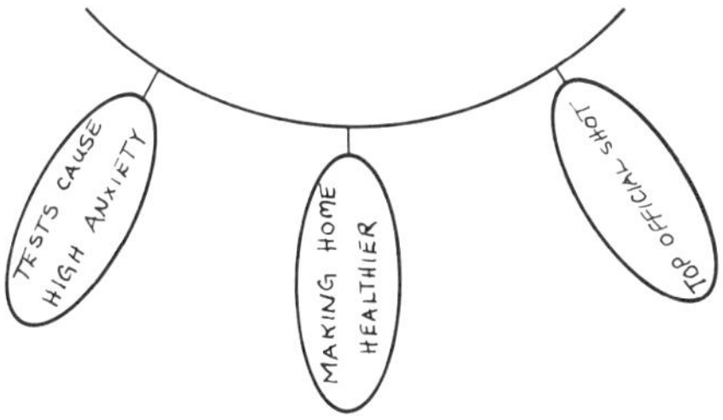

3. Brainstorm other headlines and list these on the board so that the students will have plenty of choices. Instruct students to select ten of these headlines and write them in sentence form. After students have finished writing sentences, have them read their sentences to the class.
4. Help students develop an "ear" for the sentence by accepting or rejecting sentences they hear. For additional practice, point to headlines on the line and ask students to volunteer other sentences that sound right.

Headlines	Sentences
High Anxiety	Tests can cause high anxiety.
Making Home Healthier	What will make the home healthier?
Top Official Shot	The President was shot.

5. Bring in headlines that have double meanings and discuss ambiguity. Here are two examples.

1. Ship Sails to France
   a. Ship = transport

Transport white sails to France.

b. Ship = a boat
   A boat sails to France.

2. Race Riots
   a. Race = nationality
      Race riots shake the city.
   b. Race = a contest
      Riots occurred at the race track.

Follow-up:

- Have students arrange themselves into small groups and compare their headline sentences.
- Select a panel of six students who will read headlines to the class. A volunteer from the class will then say a sentence using each headline. Arrange the class into teams. Time the answers and give points according to the number of minutes it takes to give a sentence.

TELEGRAM

Objective:

Students will be able to isolate key words and write complete sentences.

Description:

Students will write telegram messages and will then transcribe these messages into sentence form.

Organization:

Large group, 25 minutes; small groups, 20 minutes

Procedure:

1. Write an example of a telegram on the board, such as:

   HAPPY BIRTHDAY STOP WILL MISS PARTY STOP
   SEE YOU AT 6 P.M. LOVE DAD

Tell students that the STOP represents a period.

2. Have students rewrite the telegram into sentence form, for example:

   Have a happy birthday. I won't be able
   to come to the party. I'll see you at
   6 P.M. instead. Love, Dad

3. Divide the class into small groups of three or four and have the group write telegrams. Duplicate sample telegram forms. On the back of each form, have students write a corresponding message in sentences.

Telegram Message

TO: ____________________
STREET ADDRESS: ____________________ TELEPHONE ________
CITY & STATE: ____________________ ZIP CODE ________

MESSAGE ____________________

FROM: ____________________
ADDRESS: ____________________

4. Read the telegrams orally and challenge class members to repeat the messages in sentences.

Follow-up:

- Shuffle the telegrams and invite friends from outside the class to transcribe the message.
- Arrange a scavenger hunt. Hide objects around the room. Have students write clues in telegram form. Insert each telegram into an envelope. Invite another class to come to your room and, using the telegrams, find the objects. Have students write the message in sentence form.
- If the school has a public address system, get permission to have the students give the morning announcements in telegram form. Have the class transcribe the announcements into sentences. Discuss whether the telegram communicated adequately.

• Have students listen to a TV commercial and then transcribe that commercial into telegram form.

SENTENCE BUILDING

When students are aware of the difference between a sentence and a sentence fragment, they are ready to take a closer look at sentences and consider various aspects of sentence building. This section provides a variety of activities designed to add "spice" to the sentence. Students will learn how to enrich sentences by adding colorful adjectives and dynamic verbs—verbs that *show,* not tell. By experimenting with word order, they will see that there is more than one way to write a simple sentence. And finally, students will learn how to combine sentences with the use of conjunctions. Writing more complicated sentences is the main goal of this section.

ADDING ADJECTIVES

Objectives:

Students will be able to use adjectives within the context of a sentence to add variety.

Description:

Students will brainstorm a list of adjectives and add these to given sentences.

Organization:

Large group, 45 minutes

Procedure:

1. Give students trite adjectives such as *cute, great, big, super,* and *beautiful* and have them list as many synonyms as possible. List these adjectives on the board.
2. Instruct the class to write two- or three-word sentences, such as:

The boat raced.
The dog barked.
A watch ticked.
The baby cried.
Beans simmered.
John screamed.

Challenge students to the "longest sentence battle" by seeing who can write the longest sentence by adding adjectives only.

3. Show them a sentence pattern that consists of a series of adjectives separated by commas: A, A, A, A, A N V.

The soft, chubby, cuddly, red-faced baby cried.
The crimson, oval, over-baked beans simmered.
The round, gold-plated, tarnished watch ticked.

Follow-up:

- Provide a dictionary and a thesaurus for each student, if possible. Have students list adjectives and their synonyms on paper and use these adjectives to write sentences. Tell them that using the reference books will help them expand the number of adjectives that they can use.
- Show students how to use adjectives with compound subjects.
- Write adjectives on one-word flashcards. On another set of one-word cards write the words of a sentence. Give each student one card. Have the sentence group go to the front of the room and unscramble themselves into a sentence. Then, have the adjective group go to the front of the room and blend in.

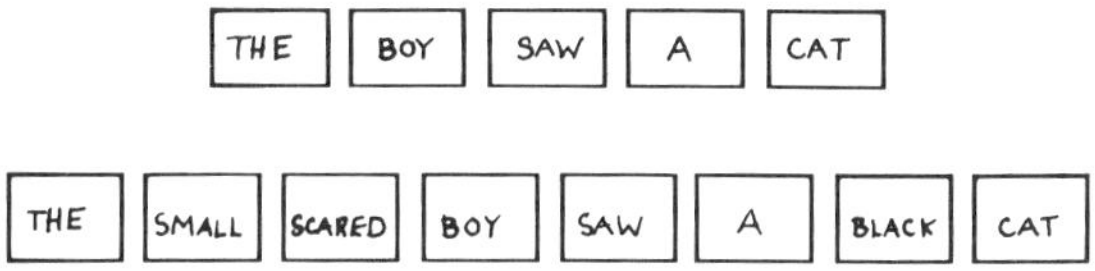

Vary this activity rearranging these cards on the flannelboard.

REARRANGING WORD ORDER

Objective:

Students will be able to

1. Put words into sentence form
2. Move parts of the sentence around without losing sentence meaning

Description:

Students will look at sentence parts and combine them into a sentence. Then they'll move the sentence parts around to form a new order.

Organization:

Large group, 15 minutes; pairs, 30 minutes

Procedure:

1. Explain to the class that the two parts of the sentence are subject and predicate. The subject usually answers the question, "Who? What?" Begin with the

action verb as a predicate that answers the question, "Can I do it?" Questioning is modeled like this: Can I *run*? Yes. *Run* is a verb. Can I *he*? No. *He* is not a verb. Make a chart on the chalkboard with three columns.

Subject	Verb	Phrase
Who? What?	Can I do it?	with a________
		on a________
		by a________

2. Have the class brainstorm a list of words for each column.

boy	run	on a bus
girl	skip	in a house
Mrs. Garcia	play	down the street
rat	hit	down the block
mouse	throw	with a dog
house	ride	with a bat

3. Group the class into pairs. Have each pair write ten sentences, and then read their sentences aloud to see if they "sound" right.

The boy run down the street.

Does that sound right? No.

The boy runs down the street.

When each pair has ten sentences that "sound" right, have them exchange sentences with another pair and proofread the sentences.

4. Now, have the students rearrange their sentences by changing the order. Have them look at the way the chart can be rearranged, such as:

1. subject	verb	phrase
2. verb	subject	phrase
3. phrase	subject	verb
4. subject	phrase	verb
5. phrase	verb	subject

5. Provide a model sentence and rearrange it on the board in a variety of ways. Have students write as many "scrambles" as possible for their sentences, as shown here:

1. The boy runs down the street.
2. Down the street the boy runs.
3. The boy, down the street, runs.
4. Down the street runs the boy.

Follow-up:

- Introduce other columns, such as adjectives, adverbs, and verb phrases, and have the students write even longer sentences with greater variety.
- Make this a team competition. Give the entire class the same key words. Have each class member work with a sentence. Have the team select its five best sentences. Write these on the board and then have the entire class vote to select the sentence with the most variety. The team which wrote that sentence wins.

SHOWING, NOT TELLING

Objectives:

Students will be able to

1. Choose action verbs instead of "being" verbs
2. See that action verbs "move the sentence along"
3. Write sentences that "show" rather than "tell"

Description:

Students will write sentences that use only action verbs.

Organization:

Large group, 45 minutes

Procedure:

1. Tell students that the verb is the most important part of the sentence. Show them the difference between a verb that shows action and one that tells something. List telling statements on the board.

> John is angry.
> Sue seems sad.
> Joanne is becoming a nurse.
> Mom was happy.

2. Have students replace these "being" verbs with action verbs.

> John is angry.
> John kicks the fence violently.

Point out that now they know how John feels (angry) because of his action (kicking the fence).

3. Now that an action verb is the first selection when writing a sentence, have students choose more vivid verbs by asking, "How?" Write this example on the board:

José ran across the street.

4. Have the students brainstorm the many verbs that tell how someone ran. List these possibilities on the board:

<u>Ran</u>

raced	streaked
trotted	galloped
skipped	jogged

Have students visualize Jose performing each of these actions. Discuss how these verbs show the exact action.

5. Challenge the students to write at least ten sentences that contain action verbs (using synonyms for the verb *ran*).

6. Using this model, have the students transform "being" sentences into "action" sentences, such as:

Being: Mom was happy.
Action: (What was she doing?) My mom smiled.
Exact: (How did she smile?) My mom grinned from cheek to cheek.

Follow-up:

- Employ the "Instant A" technique by requiring students to use action verbs. As soon as an action verb is used, give that person an A. Give no grade if a "being" verb is used. When a student rewrites a sentence using an action verb, give a make-up grade of B.
- Dramatize the action verbs by acting out verb choices. Do not hesitate to have students jog, skip, or gallop across the room. Tell them to ask themselves if they can dramatize a verb they choose. If they can't dramatize the verb, then select one they can act out. Have students use the thesaurus to select more specific verbs.

COMPOUND SENTENCES

Objectives:

Students will be able to

1. Write a one-sentence response to a picture
2. Write a compound sentence

Description:

Students will bring a picture to class and write a one-sentence response to the visual stimulus. Using the conjunctions *and, but, or,* students will work in pairs to write compound sentences.

Organization:

Large group, 45 minutes; pairs, 45 minutes

Procedure:

1. Instruct the class to bring from home either a magazine picture or a baby photo; have them mount the photo on construction paper. Line the photos on the chalkboard.

2. Have the students select one photo, take it to their desks, and write one-sentence captions for the picture. Have the students share their captions with the class.

I had a bad day!

3. Divide the class into pairs and have each pair share the same photo. Tell each pair to write two short sentences for their photograph. Then have them work together to combine these two sentences with a conjunction (*and, but, or*) to form a compound sentence to caption the photograph.

> My tooth ached, and I had a bad day!
> I had a bad day, but my brother didn't.

Follow-up:

• Write the captions on the board and have the class write compound sentences by drawing a line between any two sentences that could be joined by "and." Do the same with the conjunctions *but, or.*

SENTENCE COMBINING

Objectives:

Students will be able to use conjunctions to join sentences together.

Description:

Students will use words from columns to form complex sentences.

Organization:

Large group, 45 minutes

Procedure:

1. Write three columns on the board. Put short sentences in columns A and B and conjunctions in column C.

Column A	Column B	Column C
It was early.	He screamed.	whenever
He jogged.	The alarm rang.	because
They laughed for days.	Two trucks crashed.	when
Mother hit the ball.	I was angry.	although
The snow stopped.	Everyone cheered.	before

Tell students to mix columns A, B, and C together to make sentences.

2. Have students take turns reading their sentences orally.

Whenever he jogged, he screamed.
When it was early, the alarm rang.
Everyone cheered because Mother hit the ball.
The snow stopped before the two trucks crashed.

Follow-up:

- Have students make two columns of short sentences to combine with column C. Then, follow the procedure outlined above.
- Have students play a round robin game in which each student adds one word to the sentence. Every time they need to use a conjunction, they should say *hiccup.*

Hiccup I fall down, I cry.
I run hiccup I see the ice cream man.

SENTENCE COMBINING

Objectives:

Students will be able to

1. Rewrite short, choppy sentences into longer, meaningful ones
2. Combine sentence parts
3. Use conjunctions

Description:

Students will employ sentence-combining techniques to eliminate choppy sentences.

Organization:

Large group, 45 minutes

Procedure:

1. Have students write three sentences that are closely related, such as:

I watched a TV show.
It was short.
It was exciting.

Have them pass these sentences to a classmate to rewrite into one sentence, such as:

I watched a short, exciting TV show.

2. Now, write these pronouns on the board:

+ who
+ that
+ which

Tell the class that these words can be used to connect sentences. Have students look at this pattern.

He bought a bike.
+ The bike had ten speeds.
+ that
He bought a bike that had ten speeds.

3. Arrange the class into pairs and have them list sentence combinations using + who, + that, + which. Have students write their patterns on the board and challenge classmates to combine them, thus:

The girl found a doll.
The doll had a broken arm.
+ that
The girl found a doll that had a broken arm.

Follow-up:

- Have students clip examples of these combinations from a magazine or newspaper and bring them to class.

• Put the pronouns + who, + that, + which on flashcards and give each student a set. Challenge each class member to find examples of shorter sentences that could be combined by using the pronouns. Supply magazines and have students copy sentences.

• Set up learning centers in the classroom. The purpose of the centers is to give students practice writing sentences. Use these themes at the centers: sentence starters (subjects only); sentence endings (predicates only); "what if" statements; "I used to think" statements.

SENTENCE MODELING

Selecting passages from literature as dictation material serves multiple purposes. In attempting to write like the skilled author, the children use more mature sentences. They are also motivated to read the book from which a passage is selected.

Single sentences also can be chosen to present more advanced syntactical (grammatical) forms to young writers. Children write sentences following the same structural framework. Thus, children experiment with more mature varieties of sentences guided by structures used in literature they can read.

DICTATING

Objectives:

Students will be able to

1. Listen to dictated sentences and write these sentences correctly
2. Write similar literary forms in their own sentences

Description:

Students will listen to a story, then write a passage dictated by the reader.

Organization:

Large group, 45 minutes

Procedure:

1. Select a passage containing examples of various sentence types. Give each student a pencil and lined paper and direct them to write exactly what you say to them.

2. Dictate a passage to them sentence by sentence. Spell difficult words and read the punctuation marks, but otherwise let them try spelling correctly. When finished with the dictation, show them the original passage on an overhead

transparency or a printed page. Have students compare their dictated message to the original. Direct them to make any necessary corrections.

3. Repeat the dictation on a daily basis with other selections so that students are continuously exposed to good literary forms and composition skills in context. Use an excerpt like this one from *Peter Rabbit* that contains excellent examples of sentence structures.

> But Peter, who was naughty, ran straight to Mr. McGregor's garden and squeezed under the gate. First he ate some lettuce, then some French beans, and then some radishes. Feeling rather sick, he went on a little farther to look for the parsley patch.

Follow-up:

• Vary this activity by using the same passage two days in a row, but omit assistance with the punctuation on the second day. Then evaluate punctuation.

• Dictate student-written samples.

• Dictate fables or nursery rhymes and have students write a different ending.

SENTENCE MODELING

Objectives:

Students will be able to

1. Model a sentence after a famous quotation
2. Underline segments of a sentence that could be replaced with original work

Description:

Students will select favorite quotes, remove parts of the sentence, and replace these segments with their own writing.

Organization:

Large group, 45 minutes

Procedure:

1. Have students select quotations, such as, "Most folks are as happy as they make up their minds to be." Write the quotable sentence on the board and have the class help underline segments of the sentence that could be removed, for example:

> Most folks are as happy as ___________.

Have each student write in his or her own concluding segment. When finished, read all sentences orally so that student responses can be compared, for example:

> Most folks are as happy as uncaged birds.
> Most folks are as happy as parents who are holding their newborn child for the first time.

2. Take quotable quips from any cartoon and follow the same procedure.

Follow-up:

- Incorporate sentence modeling with the context of a paragraph by giving students a well-developed paragraph to imitate.
- Use the same method with good samples of conversation and rhyme. Have students bring in favorite written passages.
- Show students that they can imitate a favorite song. Suggest to the younger children that they use the theme songs for their super heroes, such as this imitation of "Superman."

> Supermom
> It's a bird,
> It's a plane.
> No, it's Supermom.
> Able to cook pancakes every morning,
> Able to leap carpools in a single bound,
> Able to fix any scraped knee,
> It's Supermom.

USING PUNCTUATION

As yet another way of training the child's "ear for language," show students how punctuation marks are related to intonation. A brief pause may indicate the need for a comma whereas a full stop signals the need for some kind of ending mark. The specific mark also is signaled by intonation, the rising or falling of the voice or an unusual sense of excitement.

Punctuation is taught within the context of the student's writing rather than as unrelated drill. Students learn to use quotation marks as they write dialogue. Models from literature are used through direct observation of a piece of writing or through the dictation methods described in the preceding section.

EDITING PUNCTUATION

Objectives:

Students will be able to

1. Mark the ends of sentences with end punctuation marks
2. Mark internal pauses in the sentence with commas

Description:

Students will role play sentences and make appropriate gestures for the punctuation marks.

Organization:

Small group, 25 minutes; large group, 20 minutes

Procedure:

1. Divide the class into teams of three or four. Have the team members compose their own original sentences and write the words on separate cards.
2. Have three students use black felt pens to make punctuation flash cards.

3. Now have a team come to the front of the room and hold up the words to their sentence. Select a class member to unscramble the words so that they form a sentence.
4. Have students choose the end mark and hold up that flashcard.

Follow-up:

- Involve the entire class by having students write these sentences correctly on separate sheets of paper. Challenge them to rewrite longer sentences following a different order.
- Have each student make punctuation flashcards. Write a sentence on the board and have the students flash the end mark. Give the sentence orally and have the students flash the correct mark.
- Have two students pantomime a fake conversation. Have the students look at the body language involved and then flash an end mark.
- Label titles and pauses the same way by using commas and quotation marks on flashcards. Play the games mentioned above, but include these marks as well.

• Duplicate a passage taken directly from a classroom book. Give this passage to the students and have them discuss the punctuation marks. Dictate a passage directly from a book and then have them check their punctuation against that in the book.

CHALLENGE

1. Find literary models that specifically pattern each of these sentence types: simple sentence, compound sentence, complex sentence, compound-complex sentence. Choose literature that is appropriate to the middle grades, for example E. B. White's *Charlotte's Web* (Harper, 1953), and the upper grades, for example Laurence Yep's *Dragonwings* (Harper, 1976). Copy the original sentence and then prepare a sentence frame by omitting the content and retaining only the structure of the sentence. Students can then create new sentences following the author's model.

2. Prepare a piece of writing that contains many short sentences. Use it as part of a lesson that asks students to rewrite the selection, combining sentences to make the writing flow.

RECOMMENDED RESOURCES

Nilsen, Don, and Alleen. *Language Play: An Introduction to Linguistics.* Rowley, Mass.: Newbury House, 1978.

Tiedt, Iris M. *The Language Arts Handbook.* Englewood Cliffs, N.J.: Prentice-Hall, 1983.

Weaver, Constance. *Grammar for Teachers: Perspectives and Definitions.* Urbana, Ill.: National Council of Teachers of English, 1979.

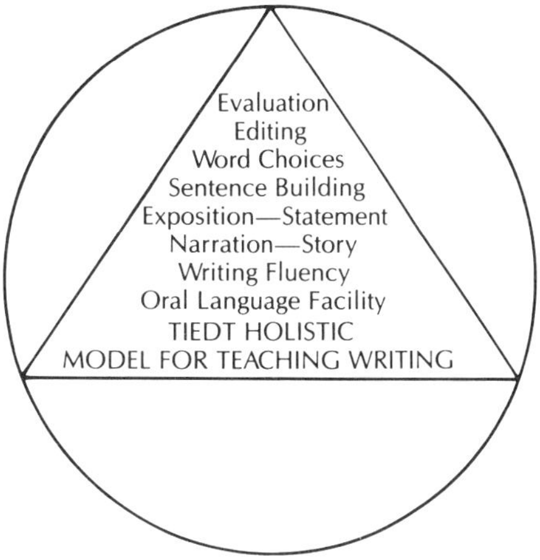

7

Making Effective Word Choices

Words are among the oldest things around us. They have been handed down through generations and across countries. Words are the tools of good thinking and the necessary equipment needed by all for communication. Through words, students can transmit experiences, beliefs, and knowledge. The more words students have at their command, the clearer and more accurate their thinking will be. Students who are proficient with words can express their own thoughts and feelings effectively and understand those of others.

Children learn early that words are useful tools in their environment by asking for people they need, such as *ma ma, da da,* or things they want, such as *cookie, water.* They soon find words to label objects they see, such as *dog, horse,* or *toy.* As a child grows, so does the child's vocabulary, with the help of parents, playmates, and then teachers. In school children learn rhymes and riddles and later on the conventions for using words in our language.

Teachers are the role models who show students how to use words to fit any situation. A good teacher shows students the magic of words and the advantages of developing good writing skills. Through developing interest in using and playing with words, you can help children learn to concentrate, to see relationships and analogies, to form intelligent guesses, to follow directions, spell, define, use a dictionary, to use figures of speech and oral and written imagery.

You and your students will find playing with words a great joy. Children love telling a joke or repeating a riddle. They find delight in forming a new word by changing a letter, writing words backwards, or making a word puzzle for others to solve. They need to know that words can be as explosive as firecrackers, or as gentle as raindrops. Words are the oldest heirlooms we have, the greatest treasures we own. You can help your students understand what words mean and how they influence people's thoughts and feelings, their behavior, and their personalities. Children need to realize that words make a difference in how people live, think, and behave.

As a teacher you can vary your program to include skills ranging from word structure to figurative language. After reading this chapter you should be able to

1. Describe a number of strategies for developing word choices with your students
2. Teach your students skills involving syllables, prefixes, vocabulary development, homonyms, synonyms, idioms, proverbs, and similes

This chapter is divided into four main subdivisions: Word Structure, Word Meanings, Word Play, and Figurative Language. A wide variety of activities that can be adjusted to your teaching style allows you flexibility in meeting the learning needs of your pupils. The materials needed for the lessons are readily available in the classroom or are easy to obtain. Step-by-step procedures and follow-up suggestions show you exactly how to present the lessons. When applicable, suggestions for adapting a lesson to another discipline are included. Your participation with the students in these activities should create a climate in which the power of words can spread like butter on hot gingerbread!

WORD STRUCTURE

SYLLABLES

Objectives:

Students will be able to

1. Divide words into syllables correctly
2. Write sentences leaving a blank for a word and specifying the correct number of syllables

Description:

After reviewing syllables with the teacher, students will divide words into syllables and write puzzle sentences in which other students can fill in a word of a specified number of syllables.

Organization:

Whole class, 15 minutes; individuals, 35 minutes

Procedure:

1. Tell students that they will be working with one-, two-, three-, and four-syllable words. Place the following words on the board and call on students to divide them into syllables.

bear
distant
understand
enjoyable

2. Write the following on the board.

finally
girl
temper
fertilizer

a. My dad has a bad ___________. (2)
b. I need some ___________ for my plants (4)
c. The boys were glad to know that they ___________ made the team. (3)
d. The little ___________ was absent from school today. (1)

Tell students that they are to read the sentences and look for the number clue that tells them how many syllables should be in the word. When they have found the answers, they are to write each sentence with the correct word in the blank by syllables. Example:

I need some fer-ti-liz-er for my plants.

Go over the sentences with the students.

3. Have students brainstorm lists of one-, two-, three-, and four-syllable words on the board. Example:

one	two	three	four
good	ba-by	to-ma-to	for-get-ta-ble

4. Explain a word game called "String Me Along." Have students brainstorm at least ten words under each of the above lists. Tell students they are to write sentences for 15 of these words, leaving the String Me Along word out of each sentence. Students should give a number clue at the end of each sentence, and write their answers on another paper for reference.

5. When they have finished writing their sentences, students may exchange papers and fill in the blanks.

Follow-up:

- Have students write sentences combining one-, two-, three-, and four-syllable words.
- Have students write slogans for bumper stickers by syllables. Example: flow-er pow-er.

PREFIXES

Objectives:

Students will be able to

1. Use words with prefixes in sentences
2. Write creative sentences matching animals with prefixes

Description:

After reviewing prefixes with the teacher, students will match animals to prefixes to write creative sentences.

Organization:

Whole class, 45 minutes

Procedure:

1. Explain to the students that a prefix is a syllable added at the beginning of a word to change its meaning or to make it into another word. Place these prefixes on the board:

> un- not, the opposite of
> re- again, back
> pre- before
> dis- not

2. Tell students that you are going to read four sentences with a word omitted from each sentence. They are to guess the correct word for the sentence. You will give them a clue by pointing to the prefix they should use. Give examples thus:

Point to *un.*
a. My dog is very __________ when he doesn't have a bone. (unhappy)

Point to *re.*
b. I had to __________ the meat because it was not done. (recook)

Point to *pre.*
c. Mother had to __________ the food just before the guest arrived. (preheat)

Point to *dis.*
d. If you are a magician, you can make anything __________. (disappear)

3. Have students brainstorm words beginning with these prefixes. Here are a few examples:

prefix	preschool	recharge	discharge
rebuild	unfed	discomfort	return
preview	refill	unafraid	unpleasant

4. Place the words *elephant* and *refill* on the board. Ask students to give you a sentence using both the animal and the prefix word. Example: The elephant came back to the waterhole to *refill* its trunk. Have students brainstorm names of animals on the board. Tell students that they are to match ten animals with ten prefixes in creative sentences of their own. Have students give you prefixes to fit into these sentences. Read sentences.

The robin was worried because her young were __________. (unfed)
Mr. Whale wanted to __________ the films about ocean life. (preview)

Follow-up:

- Have students form groups and put their prefix sentences together to write funny stories.
- Have students make lists describing themselves and using their prefixes. Example:

I dislike
I'm unhappy when
I'm unafraid of
I feel it is unnecessary to

WORD MEANINGS

There is a strong need for vocabulary development throughout the child's curriculum because vocabulary correlates with success in all academic areas. The key to vocabulary growth is the teacher's own interest. If you are a teacher who is curious about words, you can share that curiosity with the children.

In this section you will find activities on the origin of words, homonyms, synonyms, and vocabulary building.

WORD ORIGIN

Objectives:

Students will be able to

1. Locate the origins of several words
2. Write imaginative meanings for their names

Descriptions:

After going over the origins of several words, students will write creative meanings for their own names.

Organization:

Partners, 45 minutes

Procedure:

1. Tell students that words come from many origins such as:

    Greek or Roman gods
    Inventors
    Historical persons
    Sounds they make
    Literary characters
    Other languages

    Tell students that they are going to look up several words to see which of these categories they represent. Place these words on the board:

    splash
    sandwich
    echo
    pasteurize
    scrooge

    Provide several reference books, such as encyclopedias and dictionaries, and borrow books on word origins from your school or city library. Let students work with partners to find answers.

    a. Louis Pasteur, inventor
    b. Named after the Earl of Sandwich, historical person
    c. Greek nymph, Greek or Roman gods

d. Derived from the sound
e. From Charles Dickens' *A Christmas Carol,* literary character

2. After students have discussed these words, have them pretend that their names came from one of these categories. Tell students that they are going to write imaginary meanings for their names. Example:

> *Sheilah* comes from the Greek word meaning *lovely*. Any child given this name will always be delightful and charming.

3. Have students create large name cards describing the origins of their names. Tell students to decorate their name cards with fancy borders and drawings.

Follow-up:

- Have students locate the origins of vegetable and animal names.
- Have students find words borrowed from other languages and mark their origins on a world map to show that many words in our language come from abroad.

VOCABULARY

Objectives:

Students will be able to

1. Use dictionaries and encyclopedias to locate meanings of words
2. Build vocabulary by writing creative questions using their new words

Description:

After reviewing meanings of words with the teacher, students will be able to write creative questions using their new words.

Organization:

Pairs, 45 minutes

Procedure:

1. Write the following on the board: Would a *sandleaf* be found on the beach? Ask students to answer yes or no and tell why. Pick a student to look the word up in the dictionary or an encyclopedia.

> *Sandleaf* is one of the lowest, poor leaves on a tobacco plant, small and often sandy.

Tell students they can't always tell what a word means by the way it sounds.

2. Write the next two sentences on the board. Have students repeat pronunciations after you for the underlined words in the sentences. Choose three students to look up the definitions of the underlined words. Ask the rest of the class to guess the correct response.

> Could your family sit at a stammtisch? (yes)
> Can you die from a phi? (no)
> Is a petty officer in charge of animals? (no)

3. Tell students that they are to find a partner, locate five words that they think no one else will know, and write a creative question for each. Tell students to write the meanings on another paper so they can refer to them. Here are some words to get them started:

> gizzard
> horehound
> calash
> swag
> urn
> terrella
> stickleback

Have students exchange papers and answer their partner's questions.

Follow-up:

- Have students make a class dictionary of their new words, showing pronunciation, meanings, and a drawing for each new word. Have them add other interesting words.
- Have students take a turn each week in announcing a new word on a bulletin board, by using a drawing, the definition, and the pronunciation.

HOMONYMS

Objectives:

Students will be able to

1. Distinguish between different sets of homonyms
2. Make creative book titles about their homonyms

Description:

After reviewing homonyms with the teacher, students will use homonyms to create titles for imaginary books, and write a brief description for each book.

Organization:

Large group, 15 minutes; pairs, 30 minutes

Procedure:

1. Tell students that they will be working with words that sound alike but have different meanings and spellings. Write these sets of homonyms on the board:

> flour, flower
> blue, blew
> ate, eight
> board, bored

Ask students to give the meaning of each word.

2. Draw a picture of *ate* and *eight* on the board and write the following title: He ate all eight!

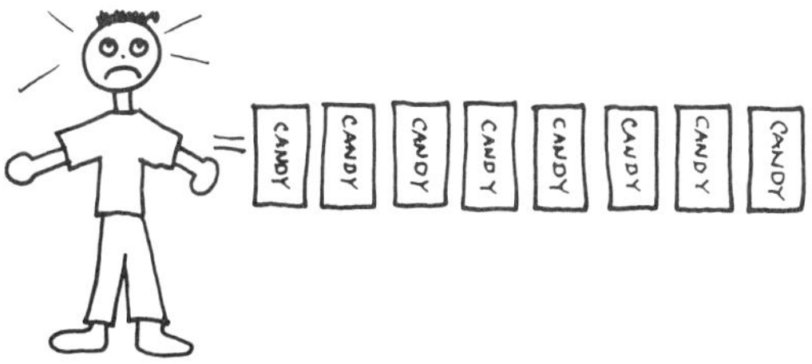

Tell students that this is a made-up title for a book. Next have the students complete the description of the imaginary book. Example:

> This is a story about a little boy named Tommy who ate eight candy bars at the school picnic and became very sick.

3. Write several titles on the board and have students give you possible descriptions of each.

> Be a dear, and let out the deer.
> We are sealing the ceiling before dad arrives.
> Our uncle is an hour late!
> I have been in the bin for hours!
> Hey! Get out of the hay!

4. Have students brainstorm more homonyms on the board. Here are some examples:

banned, band
bridal, bridle
maid, made
inn, in
steal, steel
Greece, grease (Discuss dialect differences in pronunciation.)

5. Tell students they are to choose two sets of homonyms to use in creative titles for their book jackets. They are to design their book jackets and give a description of the title on the inside of each book jacket.

Follow-up:

- Have students write sentences leaving a blank in each sentence for another student in the class to fill in the homonym. Example:

  It is wrong to ___________ from anyone. steel or steal

- Have students brainstorm higher-level homonyms.
- Have students write a short play using some of their homonyms.

VOCABULARY

Objectives:

Students will be able to

1. Make alphabetical lists for several categories
2. Build their vocabularies by using categories

Description:

With the aid of dictionaries, students will write alphabetical lists for several categories within a time limit.

Organization:

Groups of four, 45 minutes

Procedure:

1. Write the letters of the alphabet on the board. Tell students that they are going to play a game called "Are You Listed?" To start it off, they are to name an animal for each letter of the alphabet. Example:

A, aardvark
B, baboon
C, cougar
D, dalmatian

2. Place students in groups of four and pass out dictionaries and paper. Students will need to use several sets of encyclopedias. Tell each group to make their own list from a category you will give them. Give students helpful hints on how to work in the group. You may wish to have the following hints on the board ahead of time:

a. Decide quickly who is going to do what letters.
b. Find out what your hardest letters are and do them first.
c. If you choose a word no one has heard of, be sure you can prove it is a real word.
d. Help each other in the group, but do not let the other groups hear you!
e. If words for the letters *x*, *y*, and *z* are very hard to find, you may omit those letters.

3. Give students three minutes to list the letters *A* to *Z* vertically on their papers. When everyone in their group is finished, they are to choose one person from their group to call out "Are you listed?" Have students brainstorm several categories on the board. Suggested categories are:

girls' names
boys' names
nouns
things found in the home
words that describe people (adjectives)

Follow-up:

• Have students write a list of things they like to do. This time instead of one-word answers, they may use phrases or sentences. Example:

A, always look at television
B, bicycling in the country

• Have your students do this activity for social studies and science. Examples:

Make an *ABC* list of cities of the United States.
Do you know your birds? flowers? famous women?

SYNONYMS

Objectives:

Students will be able to

1. List synonyms of words
2. Write descriptive sentences using synonyms

Description:

Students will write descriptive sentences using more precise synonyms.

Organization:

Large group, 10 minutes; small groups, 35 minutes

Procedure:

1. Write the word *frightened* on the board. Tell students that frightened means to be afraid. Ask students to give you other synonyms for the word frightened. Examples:

terrified	startled
alarmed	unnerved
panic-stricken	horrified

2. Explain to students that when writing their stories and sentences they need to use precise words. Go over these examples with students.

Billy was *terrified* as he looked at the spooky picture on TV.
Billy was *alarmed* to learn that his younger sister was not home yet.
Billy was *panic-stricken* when he could not find the key to his house.
Billy was *startled* by his sister, who was hiding in the hallway.
Billy was *horrified* when he looked at the injured man's face.

3. Divide the class into groups and have each group make lists of words with their synonyms. They are to follow the example above and write precise sentences for each synonym. You may wish to place lists on the board. Students should use dictionaries to compile lists, for example:

Happy—gay, joyous, merry, pleased, delighted, elated

Follow-up:

- Make 3 × 5 cards and write one synonym on each. Have students act out each word.
- Have students use their synonyms for more precise writing in history.

WORD PLAY

In this section students will work with idioms, proverbs, malapropisms, and advertising skills. Because the activities are fun, children think of them as games. The real motive for using these activities, however, is to give students practice in interpreting the given language. Some activities encourage art work, which children enjoy.

Objectives:

Students will be able to

1. Discuss the meanings of idioms listed
2. Use and interpret idioms

Description:

After reviewing a list of idioms with the teacher, students will write advertising posters using the idioms.

Organization:

Large group, 10 minutes; pairs, 35 minutes

Procedure:

1. Write the following idioms on the board:

> My cousin Tommy was *born with a silver spoon in his mouth.*
> The dancer had *cold feet* before going on the stage.
> It was hard for me to keep a *straight face* when I saw him fall into the pool.

Explain what idoms are. Discuss the meanings of the idioms in these sentences.

2. Tell students that they are going to write advertising posters using idioms.

> Don't settle for a *raw deal.* Come to Jake's car lot for the truth!

Have students suggest ways to make their posters appealing, for example, by using large letters, pictures, bright colors. Group students in pairs. Explain that each person is to do a poster, but partners can help by sharing ideas and working on both posters together.

3. Pass out construction paper and crayons. Have students brainstorm a list of idioms on the board. Discuss the meanings. Here are examples:

> Kick the bucket—to die
> A chip off the old block—a person who is like his father
> My cup of tea—the sort of thing that appeals to me
> When in Rome do as the Romans do.—Adapt yourself to the customs and manners of the people around you.
> A dog's life—a wretched, unpleasant existence
> Pass the buck—shift responsibility
> Let the cat out of the bag—divulge a secret

4. Tell students that advertising is a form of persuasion. They will need to make their posters both convincing and attractive. Write the following on the board:

> Don't live a dog's life, ___________.

Have students brainstorm ideas to fill in the blank on a poster. They could name a place to vacation, or property to buy, such as a home or a car. Write several idioms on the board with blanks for students to fill in. Next, have students list subjects of posters, such as travel or business.

Follow-up:

- Have students write fairy tales using idioms.
- Have students work in groups to write cumulative stories using idioms.
- For an art lesson students can make drawings that illustrate idioms and compile them in a class booklet.

PROVERBS

Objectives:

Students will be able to

1. Translate meanings for proverbs listed
2. Write short stories to explain their proverbs

Description:

After reviewing proverbs and their meanings with the teacher, students will create stories explaining their proverbs.

Organization:

Partners, 45 minutes

Procedure:

1. Write the following proverbs on the board:

A watched pot never boils.
When the cat's away, the mice will play.
People who live in glass houses shouldn't throw stones.

Explain proverbs. See if students can interpret the three proverbs on the board.

2. After reviewing several proverbs with the students, write the following on the board:

Once upon a time, there was a boy named Tommy who had a younger sister, Sue. Before their mother left for work, she asked them to clean the house. Tommy and Sue . . .

Ask students to tell you which proverb might match the incomplete story. (When the cat's away the mice will play.)

3. Have students suggest possible endings for the story. Write the ending and then write the proverb at the bottom.

4. Have students brainstorm more proverbs on the board and discuss the meanings with you. Here are a few examples:

Never look a gift horse in the mouth.
Rome wasn't built in a day.
Experience is the best teacher.
Birds of a feather flock together.
Make hay while the sun shines.
Those who pay the piper call the tune.
All that glitters is not gold.

5. Tell students to find a partner for the next part of the lesson. They are to write a short story for one of the three proverbs listed on the board. After students have finished writing their stories they can illustrate them on construction paper with the proverb at the bottom of the page. Display in the classroom.

Once upon a time, there was a boy named Tommy who had a younger sister, Sue. Before their mother left for work, she asked them to clean the house. While she was gone, Tommy and Sue played all day. Next thing they knew mother was home again. Tommy and Sue were in trouble!

When the cat's away, the mice will play!

Follow-up:

- Have students select their favorite proverb, the one that has the most meaning for them. The students can write it on a 5 × 7 card, cover it in transparent contact paper, and keep it on their desks.
- Have students role play the stories they have written about the proverbs.

TOM SWIFTIES

Objectives:

Students will be able to

1. Write character names paired with adverbs
2. Write sentences using their characters and adverbs together

Description:

After reviewing Tom Swifties with the teacher, students will be able to create characters for their own Tom Swifty sentences.

Organization:

Whole class, 10 minutes; partners, 35 minutes

Procedure:

1. Write these sentences on the board:

   "I'll hurry," said Tom swiftly.
   "I'm freezing," said Tom coldly.

   Tell students that they are going to write funny sentences called Tom Swifties. You will give them the adverbs and they are to create characters and sentences to match with their adverbs.

2. Write the following adverbs on the board:

   pointedly
   sheepishly

   Name a character that matches each adverb. Examples:

   Mr. R. U. Sharp (said pointedly)
   Mrs. C. D. Wool (asked sheepishly)

3. Place the following sentences on the board.

> "__________," Mr. R. U. Sharp said pointedly.
> "__________," Mrs. C. D. Wool asked sheepishly.

Ask students to tell you what the characters might say, and fill in the blanks. Examples:

> "Give me that knife."
> "Is that your lamb?"

4. Have students work in pairs to write their Tom Swifty sentences. Help them generate their own adverbs.

Follow-up:

- Have students display Tom Swifty characters on a bulletin board with stories.
- Have students use their Tom Swifties in puzzles for other students to solve by finding the correct match.

MALAPROPISMS

Objectives:

Students will be able to

1. Recognize malapropisms used in sentences
2. Make sentences of their own using malapropisms

Description:

After learning the meaning of the word *malapropism,* students will be able to create malapropisms in sentences.

Organization:

Large group, 45 minutes

Procedure:

1. Write the following sentences on the board:

> The mother sang an *alibi* as she rocked the baby to sleep.
> The weary scout leader *strangled* into camp.
> My brother has a *repetition* for getting into trouble.

Tell students that each of the sentences contains a malapropism. A malapropism is misuse of a word that sounds like the correct word. (Mrs. Malaprop is a character in *The Rivals,* a play by Richard Sheridan.)

2. Have students locate the malapropisms in the sentences on the board and identify the correct word. Tell students they are to write sentences that include malapropisms.

3. Let students brainstorm words that can be used as malapropisms in sentences. Examples:

subscription, prescription
conversation, conservation
advocate, allocate

4. Let students create their own funny sentences using original malapropisms. Call on several students to share their sentences with the group.

Follow-up:

- Have students write commercials using malapropisms.
- Have students write conversations with a character from history using malapropisms they have created.

ADVERTISING

Objective:

Students will be able to

1. Write creative names for places of business
2. Make posters using their creative business names

Description:

From a list of examples students will create names for two business establishments and do an advertising poster about the one they've chosen.

Organization:

Whole class, 15 minutes; individuals, 30 minutes

Procedure:

1. Write the following example on the board:

jewelry store
florist shop
car lot

Tell students that they are to give you names for the businesses listed. Examples:

beauty salon
fish market
pet store
shoe store
bakery
health food store
motel
motorcycle shop
dress shop
music shop

2. Have students brainstorm a list of establishments on the board, for example:

florist shop, The Daisy Shop
car lot, Wheelin' and Dealin' Sam's
jewelry store, The Crowning Glory

Tell students they are to write creative names for two businesses from the list and then make an advertising poster for one. Pass out construction paper and crayons.

Follow-up:

• Have students write creative names for different people, such as a clown, a dentist, and a doctor, and make business cards for the characters they have created.

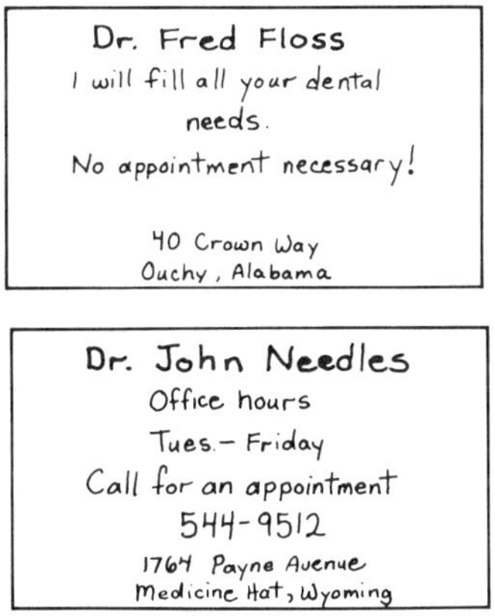

• Have students write a skit using their creative names for people and businesses.

Through the introduction of figurative language in the classroom, students learn to use forms of expressions that they didn't know existed. In this section you will find activities to help your students use similes and personification. The activities are designed to be fun and easy to present.

SIMILES

Objectives:

Students will be able to

1. Make comparisons (similes)
2. Write descriptive words

Description:

Students will write and illustrate similes.

Organization:

Large group, 15 minutes; individual, 20 minutes

Procedure:

1. Write the following on the board:

a clock
father's voice

Tell students that they are to use their imaginations by giving comparisons for these phrases; what besides a clock makes a ticking sound? (Example: a person's heart.) Father's voice could be very musical. What could it be compared to? (Example: a violin.) Explain that these comparisons are called *similes.* A simile usually starts with the word *as* or *like* ("ticks like a heartbeat"). Give other phrases and encourage students to think of fresh comparisons. Examples:

His nose is as long as (an elephant's trunk).
My father is as tall as (a redwood tree).
Her perfume smells as sweet as (warm rose petals).
My leg is as stiff as (a fence post).

2. Pass out construction paper and crayons. Students should divide each sheet of construction paper into six equal parts. Write the following words on the board.

clouds
ocean
rainbow
waterfall
thunder
snow
beets
butterfly
night
snail
mouse

Tell students that they are to choose six of these words, write a comparison for each word, and draw a picture about it in one of the squares.

3. Call on students to share their comparisons when they have finished.

Follow-up:

- Have students pick their favorite similes to be placed in a class booklet.
- Have students write comparisons describing their parents for cards on holidays or birthdays. Example:

MOM, you are
- as gentle as a morning breeze
- as sweet as a cinnamon roll
- as beautiful as an evening star.

Happy Birthday!

ANIMAL SIMILES

Objectives:

Students will be able to

1. Make comparisons using animal similes
2. Use descriptive words creatively in sentences and stories

Description:

After reviewing similes on the board, students will be able to make comparisons using animal similes in short stories.

Organization:

Large group, 45 minutes

Procedure:

1. Place the following similes on the board:

The little girl was as graceful as a deer.
The queen's dress was as beautiful as a peacock's feathers.
Mrs. Jones sings like a canary.

Give the meaning of the word simile. Ask students to explain the meanings of these sentences. Place the following list of animals on the board and ask students to give a one-word description of each. After they give the common comparison we all know, ask them to suggest fresh comparisons. Example:

giraffe, tall
lion, strong
elephant, big
bee, busy
fox, sly
turtle, slow
butterfly, pretty
wet cat, mean
owl, wise

2. Discuss how we often compare people to animals. Have students form pairs. Tell each pair to choose two animals and write a short story comparing its main characters to these animals. Examples:

> Once there was a little girl named Sally, who was as graceful as a deer. Sally met a queen who wore a dress as beautiful as a peacock's feathers.
>
> Once upon a time there was a lady named Mrs. Jones whose singing was as lovely as a canary's. While she sang she worked very hard around the house. Everyone said she was as busy as a bee.

3. Children can draw pictures illustrating their stories.

Follow-up:

- Have students rewrite their stories using fresh comparisons instead of the trite expressions illustrated.
- Have students make a rebus using their animal similes. They will rewrite the story replacing words with pictures wherever possible.
- Have students create poems using their animal similes.

PERSONIFICATION

Objectives:

Students will be able to

1. Write stories using personification
2. Use their senses in developing creative stories with the use of stickers

Description:

With the use of stickers, students will be able to use their senses of sight, smell, hearing, feeling, and tasting in developing stories using personification.

Organization:

Large group, 45 minutes

Procedure:

1. Write the word *bird* and list the senses on the board, thus:

bird: hear
feel
see
touch
taste

Ask the students to pretend that they are birds and describe some of the senses a bird experiences, for example:

Hear: the wind howling through the trees
a dog barking below
Feel: the wetness of a fresh spring day
cool raindrops sliding down my back
the softness of my babies' feathers
See: all my friends flying around
the beautiful colors of the trees
the breathtaking rainbow above me
Taste: luscious squirmy worms
branches between my beak as I build my nest

2. Have students give themselves names suitable for birds. Examples:

Clever Clarise
Bustin' Bruce
Chirpin' Charlie

3. Tell students that you want them to write a short story and include the senses they have been discovering. Each student should pretend to be a bird, as in this example:

> Hello, my name is Clever Clarise. I am a beautiful yellow bird, and I live high up in the air in a very strong oak tree. I am having a wonderful time flying around with all my friends and enjoying the wetness of this fresh spring day. I must hurry now, for I hear my babies chirping for those luscious worms I have been storing. See you later!

4. To make the lesson more interesting, buy stickers for your students. Children love being able to choose what birds, animals, or perhaps cars they would like to be. Have students place a sticker on their paper and draw scenery around it.

Follow-up:

- Have students write poems using their senses and stickers.
- Have students make up math word problems using animal stickers.

CHALLENGE

These activities prepare you to teach lessons on word usage.

1. Develop a chart focusing on specific groups of words that would help children develop their vocabularies, for example:

   Color words: red, ruby, crimson, lavender, purple
   Synonyms for say: murmur, scold, howl, snicker, counsel

2. Visit your local library to examine the kinds of books about language that are available for children. Look in the nonfiction section under 400. Browse through the books, noting possible content to be presented in lessons.
3. Find a book on word origins, for example, *Word Origins and Their Romantic Stories* by Wilfred Funk (Grosset, 1950). Make a poster focusing on an aspect of word origins, for instance:

   Words Borrowed from French
   Words Based on People's Names
   New Words in Science

4. Prepare a chart for students: Words to Avoid in Writing. Include such words as: a lot, get, just.

RECOMMENDED RESOURCES

Laird, Charlton. *The Miracle of Language.* New York: World, 1953.

Nilsen, Don and Alleen. *Language Play: An Introduction to Linguistics.* Rowley, Mass.: Newbury House, 1978.

Pooley, Robert C. *The Teaching of English Usage.* Urbana, Ill.: National Council of Teachers of English, 1974.

Tiedt, Iris M. *The Language Arts Handbook.* Englewood Cliffs, N.J.: Prentice-Hall, 1983.

Tiedt, Sidney W. and Iris M. Tiedt. *Language Arts Activities for the Classroom.* Boston: Allyn and Bacon, 1978.

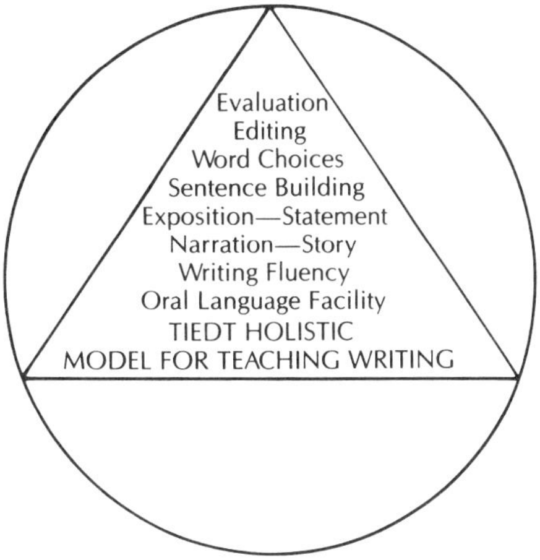

8

Editing

revising, rewriting, and proofreading

Few students carefully edit their writing as a matter of course. If we want to reverse the TIDE, we must teach students how to EDIT. As they edit their own work and that of others, they learn much about the qualities of effective composition.

Students should become aware early in their schooling of the importance of editing as part of the total process of writing, and they should learn to perform this task consistently. Consistency is the key word, for without consistent practice there is little progress. Because students do not revise, rewrite, and proofread automatically on their own, they must be trained not only to see the importance of these high-level skills, but also just how to carry out these processes. Activities must be designed to make the process a personal commitment.

The complex process of editing includes revising, rewriting, and then proofreading. Revision and rewriting involve checking for organizational and stylistic elements. Students should be encouraged to omit, add, reorganize, and to change completely. Knowing the criteria by which their final version will be assessed provides a concrete guideline to aid the students' revision efforts. Bear in mind that focusing on one or two specific matters for each selection is about all an inexperienced writer can handle. Appropriate standards must be maintained for each level of ability. It is well to remember, furthermore, that revision is best accomplished over a period of time. After putting a piece of writing aside, the writer can approach revision with renewed energy and insight.

Proofreading the revised composition is the final step. Discuss proofreading techniques that you and your students find effective. Successful strategies include reading the composition aloud or reading for one aspect of writing at a time, for example, spelling or punctuation. A checklist can be helpful in reminding students of what to look for.

Schedule time for self-editing, a vital element of the revision process. If you treat this private time as important, the students will naturally follow your lead. This quiet period with the teacher monitoring progress will train students to work through this important step.

After revising carefully, students should be directed to rewrite the selection in their best handwriting or printing. Students should be made aware of handwriting as part of the communication process. Because handwriting must be legible, students should work on specific skills if difficulties exist. What better way to enhance interest and enthusiasm for good penmanship than in writing their own original creations? When handwriting is taught in the context of composition, students learn to recognize it as a tool of expression that serves their needs. Handwriting is no longer merely an end in itself. Require good handwriting in all subjects to achieve consistently good work. Add interest to the teaching of handwriting by discussing the history of the alphabet and modern manuscript writing. For older students, calligraphy can provide a link between the process and the product.

Even at the point of rewriting, students should be encouraged to make changes. When the rewriting is completed, students should proofread the final copy.

Will every paper have to be revised and rewritten? No. Not every paper will be "published" nor developed to the fullest extent. There will be writing assignments given to encourage fluency, creativity, and thought. There will also be open-ended compositions left for later development.

After reading this chapter, you will be able to

1. Develop a strong editing program
2. Provide activities involving peer, group, and self-editing
3. Encourage student editing as their writings are made public

Providing students with a variety of peer, group, and self-editing activities, consistently scheduling time for editing, providing techniques for student editing, and ensuring a real and varied audience are positive ways of involving students in editing. Through such procedures students will make editing a personal habit with all of their writing.

EDITING AIDS AND EXERCISES

With the organized use of editing aids such as correction symbols, a record of past writings, and personal dictionaries, the editing process becomes an integral part of the writing experience. Presented as a vital step in the total process, editing is less an added requirement and more a natural occurrence to be handled accordingly.

The following exercises may not directly teach students how to write; however, they help teach students how to edit as part of the writing process. Through such relevant activities, students learn how to focus on one aspect of their writing. They can then apply their knowledge and skill in other writing and editing experiences.

Included in this section are exercises that force the students to "take a second look" at the written form. These exercises also reinforce lessons on specific concepts taught in class. Poetry, for example, is a creative writing experience. Yet, it too provides a medium for practicing editing skills.

KEEPING A WRITING NOTEBOOK

Objective:

Students will be able to keep a collection of all of their writings.

Description:

The students write the final copy of their compositions on loose-leaf paper in a notebook reserved for this purpose. The students will be required to write a rough draft and then revise it. The notebook helps the students to organize their work and enables them to refer to their previous writings.

Organization:

Entire class, 45 minutes; individuals, ongoing

Procedure:

1. Have the students purchase a loose-leaf notebook in which they can insert various sheets such as progress charts, individual dictionaries, assignment descriptions, and guidelines, as well as further development of their writings.

2. Explain the use of the binder and the form to be followed.

a. Write on one side of the page, allowing for additions, corrections, or comments on the back.
b. Follow the margin on the left side and leave a one-inch margin on the right.
c. Write on every other line to allow space for corrections.
d. Describe the heading students should use for each assignment. Example:

Assignment (Narrative) Name (Mary Jones)
Date (September 8, 19—)
Title (The Recurring Dream)

e. At the end of the paper, the student should write the trait(s) being evaluated. You can write your comments there also.

Follow-up:

• An optional requirement could be a responding comment from the student writer that commits the student to a goal for the next composition. Example:

Description: Your descriptions are very general. I would like to know about *your* feelings and reactions. For example, how did you feel when the wind blew against your face?

Student Response: I will make my descriptions more specific and include details about how I feel. Example: As the wind tossed my hair and refreshed me, I could sense beads of perspiration tingling on my skin.

• Have the students refer to their previous evaluation(s) and response(s) before writing a new assignment. This review will refresh their memory and enable them to focus on those elements in a constant effort to improve.

• Younger students will be able to handle a writing folder more easily than a notebook.

PERSONALIZED SPELLING DICTIONARY

Objectives:

Students will be able to

1. Keep a record of words that they repeatedly misspell
2. Refer to this dictionary when editing

Description:

To become more aware of the need for correct spelling and of their individual spelling difficulties, students will keep a record of troublesome words in their ringed notebook or a small separate notebook that is securely bound and can be used through several grades.

Organization:

Individuals, ongoing

Procedure:

1. Have the students purchase a small, securely bound notebook. Avoid the spiral ones. Notch the pages as in a dictionary.
2. Inform the students that they are to keep their dictionary notebook with them whenever they edit their works.
3. As the students write, however, they should not let their concern for correct spelling hinder the writing process.
4. When the students edit, have them use a dictionary to locate the correct spelling of words about which they are unsure. They must record those words in their notebooks.
5. When peer-edited compositions are returned to the students, they should be required to add to their personal dictionaries the proper spelling of any words they have misspelled. They should put a check beside any word they misspell again in subsequent writings.
6. The students should make a special effort to memorize those spelling demons.

Follow-up:

- This procedure must be followed consistently to raise the awareness level of the students and to reinforce the importance of correct spelling.
- Use the words from the personalized spelling dictionaries to form personal spelling lists.
- At the end of the year, have the students save their dictionaries and instruct them to use the dictionaries again the following year, or collect them and pass them on to the next teacher.
- Make a chart similar to this example and duplicate copies for the students to place in their ringed composition notebooks.

Name______________________________

Personalized Spelling Dictionary

____

A

____

B

____

C

Objectives:

The students will be able to

1. Use the correction symbols in proofreading
2. Make the necessary revisions indicated by the correction symbols

Description:

The students are introduced to the chart of correction symbols, to be used as a reference aid. Each symbol is discussed and demonstrated in a short paragraph. Students use these symbols in successive lessons and apply them in the editing process.

Organization:

Large group, one class period

Procedure:

1. Duplicate the chart for the students to place in their composition binder.

Composition Symbols Chart

Spelling errors	sp
Capitalization errors	C̳ or ₵
Comma errors	⌃
Other punctuation errors	P
Paragraph errors	¶ or no ¶
Fragment	Frag.
Run-on sentence	RO
Awkward sentence	Awk
Not clear	NC
Omission	/\
Incorrect syllable division	/
Indentation or margin error	[or]
Wrong tense	t
Agreement of subject and verb	agr

2. Taking one symbol at a time, explain its use, provide examples, and allow students to use the symbol as well as to make the necessary corrections indicated by the mark. Example:

Directions: Use the following symbol in marking the paragraph. Then rewrite the paragraph correctly.

≡ capital letter needed

dear uncle frank,

for my birthday, mom and dad's present was a day at marriott's great america parkway. when they told me about it, all I could say was, "wow! thank you!"

the demon was my favorite ride because of the upside-down turns.

however, the most exciting part of the day was meeting governor smith who was campaigning for the presidential election. his speech reminded me that i am proud to be an american. I think my mom and dad are going to vote for him this fall.

i'm looking forward to spending my summer with you.

with love,

bill

3. The paragraph with the correction symbols will look like this:

dear uncle frank,

for my birthday, mom and dad's present was a day at marriott's great america parkway. when they told me about it, all I could say was, "wow! thank you!"

the demon was my favorite ride because of the upside-down turns. however, the most exciting part of the day was meeting governor smith who was campaigning for the presidential election. his speech reminded me that i am proud to be an american. I think my mom and dad are going to vote for him this fall.

i'm looking forward to spending my summer with you.

with love,

bill

4. Repeat this process, adding a new symbol each time, until all symbols have been discussed.

Follow-up:

- When helping students with editing, use the symbols with which they are familiar.
- Have the students use these symbols in editing the work of their peers.
- Set up a learning center with the worksheet and a correction explanation on tape so that the students can self-correct and have the lesson reinforced.

TAKING DICTATION

Objectives:

Students will be able to

1. Write what the teacher dictates
2. Correct their writings

Description:

The teacher dictates goal-oriented sentences, which students write and then correct. Through these exercises, the students gain skills and practice in correcting their own writings.

Organization:

Large group, class period

Procedure:

1. Select sentences appropriate to the students' level, including elements currently being taught.
2. Establish the format.

   a. Have the students listen to the content as you say the complete sentence.
   b. The students are to repeat the sentence quietly to themselves but may not start writing. This repetition forces them to understand what the sentence is saying.
   c. After 10 seconds, have the students write each part of the sentence as you repeat a part of it at a time.
   d. Have the students point to every word with their pencil as you slowly say the complete sentence once again.
   e. After several sentences have been dictated in this fashion, give the students two minutes to correct their sentences.

Follow-up:

- Several students may write the sentence on the chalkboard. The class corrects the sentences on the board together and the students correct their own work. Repeat the process for each sentence.
- Discuss the elements that were confusing to most of the students and those concepts you intended to highlight.
- This approach can be used with weekly spelling sentences.

PROOFREADING WITH A TAPED PASSAGE

Objective:

Students will be able to make the necessary corrections in a given passage.

Description:

The students are given a written passage with omitted or repeated words and errors in capitalization and punctuation. Listening to a taped reading of the passage, which enables them to hear what the writer had intended, the students make the necessary corrections in the passage. This is another method that forces the students to focus on proofreading skills that they can utilize in their own writing.

Organization:

Class, learning center, or individuals, one-half hour

Procedure:

1. Prepare a passage including the specific concepts you desire to reinforce in the proofreading process. Elements such as omitted or repeated words, punctuation, and capitalization are especially appropriate to include in this activity. In order to avoid reinforcing errors, misspellings and improper usages should not be included in the passage.
2. Record the correct reading of the passage.
3. Have the students read through the passage making a preliminary round of corrections.
4. As they listen to the reading on the tape, they should write any corrections necessary to make the passage read as recorded on tape. Example:

the hot orange african sun rose the plain I awoke slowly hesitantly the
golden plain came alive the herd of zebras dressed as prisoners escaped to

the muddy water hole thousand yards to the east. A hungry tigress grunted

as as she came into view from behind the prickly bush. Good morning, Mt

Kilimanjaro. I cried as I bowed to the majestic mountain glisten with snow

in morning sun.

The passage should be corrected in this manner.

> The hot, orange African sun rose above the plain. I awoke slowly, hesitantly. The golden plain came alive. The herd of zebras, dressed as prisoners, escaped to the muddy water hole a thousand yards to the east. A hungry tigress grunted as she came into view from behind the prickly bush.
>
> "Good morning, Mt. Kilimanjaro!" I cried, as I bowed to the majestic mountain glistening with snow in the morning sun.

Follow-up:

- Highlight any trouble spots with discussion and examples of the concept.
- The students may rewrite the passage if they need the practice in following proofreading marks to produce a final form.
- Set up a learning center with several earphones and rotate the students through this proofreading experience.
- Type a passage from the current reading selection omitting the punctuation and capitalization. Have the students rewrite the passage adding the necessary punctuation and capitalization and check their work against the author's. Discussion of alternate methods and their inherent interpretations is important.

CORRECTING SENTENCE FRAGMENTS

Objectives:

Students will be able to

1. Correct sentence fragments by incorporating the given fragments into complete sentences
2. Apply their knowledge of correcting sentence fragments to their own writings

Description:

The students learn to recognize and rewrite sentence fragments. When they are aware of a variety of ways to rid a passage of sentence fragments, students can eliminate such errors in their own writing.

Organization:

Large group, class period

Procedure:

1. Write paragraphs containing sentence fragments or find such paragraphs in workbooks.

2. Duplicate such paragraphs and have the students rewrite the entire selection with logical complete sentences by supplying the correct subject, verb form, or punctuation mark in the appropriate place. Example:

> Finding the missing part of a sentence fragment can be a snap. When one knows what to look for. Often a fragment fails to tell *who* or what is doing something; that is, may lack a subject. On the other hand. sometimes there a subject but no verb; that is, it fails to say what that subject *does*. At other times, both a subject and a verb. Frequently, a fragment in written work is caused by a matter of incorrect punctuation. And capitalization. Once in a while a fragment has in it the *to* form or the *ing* form of a verb. Watching for this. To pay attention to these details. Can help one become a bonafide Sherlock Holmes.

3. Share the corrected paragraphs in class. Highlight the variety of ways to express the same ideas, fragment-free. Here is one approach:

> Finding the missing part of a sentence fragment can be a snap when one knows what to look for. Often a fragment fails to tell *who* or *what* is doing something; that is, it may lack a subject. On the other hand, sometimes there is a subject but no verb; that is, it fails to say what the subject *does*. At other times, both a subject and a verb are missing. Frequently, a fragment in written work is caused by a matter of incorrect punctuation and capitalization. Once in a while a fragment has in it the *to* form or the *-ing* form of a verb. Watching for this and paying attention to these details can help one become a bonafide Sherlock Holmes.

Follow-up:

- Continue to reinforce fragment-free writing in other editing exercises.
- Use student writing with sentence fragments as anonymous examples needing correction.
- Have students do this activity with paragraphs that focus on other common errors such as run-on sentences, incorrect verb tenses, and lack of subject-verb agreement.

GROUP EDITING

Group editing can occur in small groups such as established reading groups, or in half the class, or in the class as a whole. This format trains students in the editing process and in the questioning technique that they can apply in editing their own work. The use of overhead transparencies of students' work helps to show them how to look for errors, an often neglected technique. Duplicating sample compositions is also useful in giving students a sense of audience and in helping them recognize strengths, weaknesses, and methods of improvement. With the teacher and aides as leaders, the students are able to formulate a system to follow. When they have become more adept at revising and proofreading, they can work independently in small groups.

USING THE OVERHEAD PROJECTOR

Objective:

The students will be able to revise and proofread a composition.

Description:

The students revise and proofread a composition as a group, sharing ideas for improvements and making the necessary corrections.

Organization:

Small or large group, class period

Procedure:

1. Make a transparency of a composition that needs revision. Number the lines for easy reference. Example:

1 The Delayed Departure

2 We were delayed at the airport in Istanbul.
3 We found out later that it was because an alligator
4 was discovered in the luggage area. It took two
5 hours to capture it and restrain it. Minor
6 injuries due to the occurrence were reported. Ali
7 Bali who discovered the reptile said he became
8 suspicious when he noticed that the handle on a
9 passenger's alligator bag was missing.

2. With input from the students, make a list of areas needing improvement, thus:

Needs Improvement

✓ Title
✓ Topic sentence
✓ Details
✓ Sentence variety

3. Start revising the composition by treating one point at a time. As you discuss each point, have students write the improvements on the transparency. This technique helps to maintain interest. You may write some of the suggestions yourself to keep up the pace of the lesson. The revision may be written on the board if changes are extensive. Example:

a. *Title.* The title is dull and does not touch upon the key element of the alligator. Some possibilities are:

The Unexpected Alligator
Who's Been Snacking on the Alligator Bag?
Is There an Alligator in the House?
Snap! The Handle's Gone!

b. *Topic Sentence.* The topic sentence is general and uninspiring. Mention of the alligator would add spark to it.

c. *Details.* More details are needed to make the scene come alive. Description of the capture, the injuries, and the discoverer would add spice to the narration.

d. *Sentence Variety.* Although there are simple and complex sentences in the paragraph, all of the sentences begin with the subject. We can improve that aspect by starting two sentences with adverb and adjective phrases.

4. Check off each revision as it is completed.
5. Emphasize the possibility of altering a change already made.
6. Read the revised piece to culminate the activity on a positive note and to achieve a sense of completion, for example:

Who's Been Snacking on the Alligator Bag?

An alligator in the luggage area delayed our flight departure from Istanbul. Following two grueling hours of slithering and tangling with the net, the alligator was finally subdued and captured. Scratches and bruises were reported by its captors. Shaken and in disbelief, Ali Balí, who discovered the unexpected alligator, reported that he became suspicious when he noticed that the handle on a passenger's alligator bag was missing.

Follow-up:

- Upon completion of the activity, allow the students to rewrite the composition in their own way. Encourage divergent productions.
- Have the students share their rewritten compositions.
- Follow the same format with duplicated copies of a composition.
- Use both duplicated copies and the transparency technique to maintain student interest.

Objective:

The students will share their writings and comments in small groups.

Description:

The students meet in small groups to read aloud their writings and discuss the strengths and weaknesses of the compositions.

Organization:

Small groups, one class period

Procedure:

1. Organize the students into small groups of eight to ten students who get along well together or who represent different levels of writing ability. Using the established reading groups is an advantage for several reasons:

   a. Students are comfortable with each other.
   b. Writings can be related to reading selections.
   c. Many teachers have aides to assist in group discussions during the language arts period.

2. Have the writers read their compositions in turn. After each reading, the students and group leader can point out the strengths of the writing and make suggestions for improvement. A guide sheet such as the following could be used.

Small Group Editing

1. Tell one thing you especially liked about the writing.
2. Specific questions related to the type of composition:
   a. *Description.* Could you picture what was described? What senses were used? Could another sense have been used? How would you have described the scene?
   b. *Narration.* Could you follow the story line? Was there enough dialogue? Was the dialogue interesting and real? Was there a buildup in the action?
   c. *Exposition.* Was the explanation clear? If not, what part needs to be made clearer? How would you do that? Is there enough development to make the writing interesting and complete?
   d. *Persuasion.* Was the argument persuasive? Are there enough reasons to convince you? What reason would you develop further? What would you add to make the writing more persuasive?

3. The student writer notes the reactions of the group for later improvement of the piece. For younger children, the group leader can take notes for the student writer to use. It is important that each writer feel good about something in his or her writing. The group leader has the responsibility of ensuring positive feelings.

4. Group attention can then focus on the next writer.

5. Editing groups should remain stable so that trust can grow.

Follow-up:

- Students can revise and rewrite their compositions for evaluation.
- If the class is not ready to handle the interaction of a small group discussion, you will need to train the students. Meet with a small group while the rest of the class engages in a self-directed activity. Your aide should observe you in this process; he or she would then be better able to lead groups later.
- As often as possible, have the students share their writing with an audience.

CHECKING PRIMARY TRAITS

Objective:

Students will be able to

1. Edit compositions by checking for correctness of a primary trait
2. Be responsible for editing compositions in the area of their specialization

Description:

The students meet in small, predetermined groups to accomplish assigned editing tasks.

Organization:

Small groups, full class period

Procedure:

1. Decide on the task for each group: spelling, capitalization, punctuation, sentence structure, content, paragraph development, or grammar.

2. Select students for the groups. Base your initial selection on strengths and then gradually rotate the students to their areas of weakness. Another possibility is to have a strong student in each group at all times to ensure validity of editing comments.

3. At the outset explain the tasks of the various groups.

a. Use the agreed-upon symbols above the errors.
b. Use the dictionary to check spellings.

4. Give each of the groups a set of papers.

5. When the students have edited for their assigned primary trait, instruct them to pass the paper to someone in the next group. Specify the route ahead of time to avoid confusion and ensure that each paper is edited by all of the editing groups.

Follow-up:

- Return papers to the authors.
- Allow the students enough time to go over the comments and corrections.
- Encourage challenges of the editors, for this fosters healthy learning.
- Have younger students start by focusing on specific items such as punctuation marks. The groups could be: period, comma, exclamation mark, question mark, quotation mark. As they become more adept in the process, add a new item each time.
- You might have a few practice sessions to acquaint students with the process.
- Have students attach a cover sheet to their compositions. Since the groups might vary from time to time, a general format could be used.

Student Writer:____________

Editing Sheet

Specialty	Comments	Signature

All groups, especially content-related ones, should write comments on the cover sheet explaining the strengths and weaknesses of the paper and making suggestions.

PEER EDITING

Young students are generally open and earnest in their relationships. Most students will be interested in helping each other work through the editing processes to improve their writing. We can provide an open, comfortable environment that promotes growth and learning as students work together. Students will learn social skills as well as writing skills through interacting during the writing process.

A variety of peer-editing activities will stimulate a greater concern for writing well. Peer editing also plays an important role in helping students to become not only proficient self-editors, but also concerned and helpful individuals.

POLISHING WITH A PEER

Objective:

Students will be able to edit their peers' writings.

Description:

Each student gives her or his writing to a peer who marks the paper for content and mechanics.

Organization:

Changing pairs, class period

Procedure:

1. Before they begin the assignment, tell the students that they will exchange papers for editing.

2. Require the students to use predetermined symbols to mark errors in mechanics and make comments on the content.

Content Symbols

+	good
++	especially strong
?	confusing passage
✓	weak

3. The student editor circles errors, notes his or her judgment of the content, and signs the paper in a designated place. For younger students, use different colored pencils for editing. Example:

I love to walk in the rain. I reccomend it to anyone. If one wears the right clothing he can stay completely dry and comfortable. It is fascinating to see how different the world looks in the rain. Sheets of water against the window persist in trying to enter. Drops falling on the pavement seems to make music. Walking in the country along back roads is also a delight.

Anne Prentiss Merri Sampler

4. Circulate and observe the students as they edit, helping as needed. Encourage those who finish early to do more readings of student papers.

Follow-up:

- Give the students time to analyze their readers' markings.
- The students can polish their writings and submit for evaluation.
- Have the students read for one kind of error and write the focal point across the top of the paper.
- Have the younger students perform only one of the activities, either the editing or the quality comment.

USING MARGIN CORRECTIONS

Objectives:

Students will be able to

1. Assist their peers with correcting errors
2. Use peers' suggestions to improve their own papers

Description:

A peer edits the student composition and makes suggestions by placing correction symbols in the left margin. The writer makes improvements on the same sheet.

Organization:

Changing pairs, class period

Procedure:

1. Tell the students that this particular set of papers will be peer edited.
2. Have the students write on legal paper specially prepared with a three-inch lefthand margin.
3. The students, as editors, are to write the correction symbols and short comments on the appropriate line in the left margin.

Follow-up:

- Give the students time to analyze their editors' comments.
- The students can improve their writings on the same sheet without distracting symbols that get in the way.
- When corrections have been made, slice off the left margin and the student will have a tidy sheet to display.

• This technique can be used also when the teacher evaluates the students' papers.

• Primary students benefit from this approach because rewriting entire pieces is often too burdensome for young children.

IMPROVING DIALOGUE

Objective:

Students will be able to make appropriate corrections in writing that contains dialogue.

Description:

Partners edit dialogue by reading the dialogue aloud while checking direct and indirect quotations, indentations, capitalization, and punctuation.

Organization:

Pairs, class period

Procedure:

1. Following a review of the elements inherent in dialogue writing, have the students write narration that includes dialogue.
2. Instruct the students to read their dialogue with another student, each taking the part of one of the characters.
3. The student who reads character X's part must carefully edit that particular passage; the same applies to character Y.
4. The students should watch for:

    a. direct versus indirect quotations
    b. indentations
    c. capitalization
    d. punctuation

5. After the first reading, the partners switch characters and double-check the other's editing proficiency.
6. Monitor the dyads and provide help as needed.

Follow-up:

• Receiving input from the class, discuss the passages that were troublesome to the partners.

• The students can improve their papers and submit them for evaluation.

• Cartoon strips without the dialogue or a picture from a coloring book can be used to suggest dialogue for this activity.

• Allow dyads to work together in checking other specific components. For example, with a description paper, as one partner reads the composition, the other can note any words or phrases that are especially descriptive. At the end, both students can analyze how and where to improve the piece, adding more description if needed.

ORGANIZING THOUGHTS

Objectives:

Students will be able to

1. Write a sequential paragraph
2. Observe the feasibility of the written approach
3. Make any necessary corrections to improve the flow of thought

Description:

The students will write a sequence paragraph, explaining the steps to follow in accomplishing a task. A peer will read the composition and attempt to follow the procedure. Since any confusing or misplaced step will be obvious, the writer will know how to improve his or her work.

Organization:

Pairs, three class periods

Procedure:

1. Share several pieces of writing that demonstrate a logical and well-organized sequence.
2. Have students develop their own sequence paragraph on a topic of their interest.
3. Class demonstration

    a. Select a couple of products to read with the class and have the class or an individual demonstrate the process.
    b. Discuss the feasibility of the procedure as written and the ways to improve the clarity of it.

4. Pair demonstration

    a. Divide the class into pairs.
    b. Have pairs repeat the class demonstration. The writer reads the paragraph and the peer demonstrates.

Follow-up:

- Have students improve their writing before submitting it for evaluation.
- Reinforce outlining and transition strategies in this lesson.

SELF-EDITING

With group and peer editing experiences and with your guidance, students are able to become proficient self-editors. The guidelines in this section provide a concrete instrument to aid students in this process.

Conferring on a one-to-one basis is critical. The time required is often a complaint of teachers but when considered from the perspective of its value, a few minutes of personal contact is well rewarded by improved writings.

Several techniques can be taught to ensure more successful editing and therefore more concern for the enhancement of such skills:

- When writing the first draft, students should write on every other line and leave wide margins, allowing space for additions, corrections, or comments.
- When editing, students should read their papers, word-by-word, out loud to themselves. This method reveals careless errors and unclear thoughts.
- As students edit, they should feel free to ask the opinions of their teacher and peers on various items such as specific descriptions, word choices, and clarity of passages.
- When editing, they should look for one kind of error at a time. It does not matter what error they focus on first. For example, they could read through for errors in spelling, then read for complete sentences, then errors in punctuation.
- Encourage students to use the reverse-sequence method when editing their papers. In checking for spelling accuracy, the students can analyze each word individually starting from the last word in the composition and ending with the first. Sentences also can be read and checked in reverse order. Reading in reverse sequence slows down eye movement, overcoming the writer's tendency to glide over errors. Editing our own material is difficult because we read what we intended to write.

PROMOTING SENTENCE VARIETY

Objective:

Students will be able to use a flow chart to verify a variety of sentences in their writing.

Description:

The students will learn to write compositions that contain a variety of sentences by using a flow chart to check sentence structure and patterns.

Organization:

Individuals, 30 minutes

Procedure:

1. Following lessons on sentence structure and the use of sentence variety in writing, introduce the use of the flow chart.

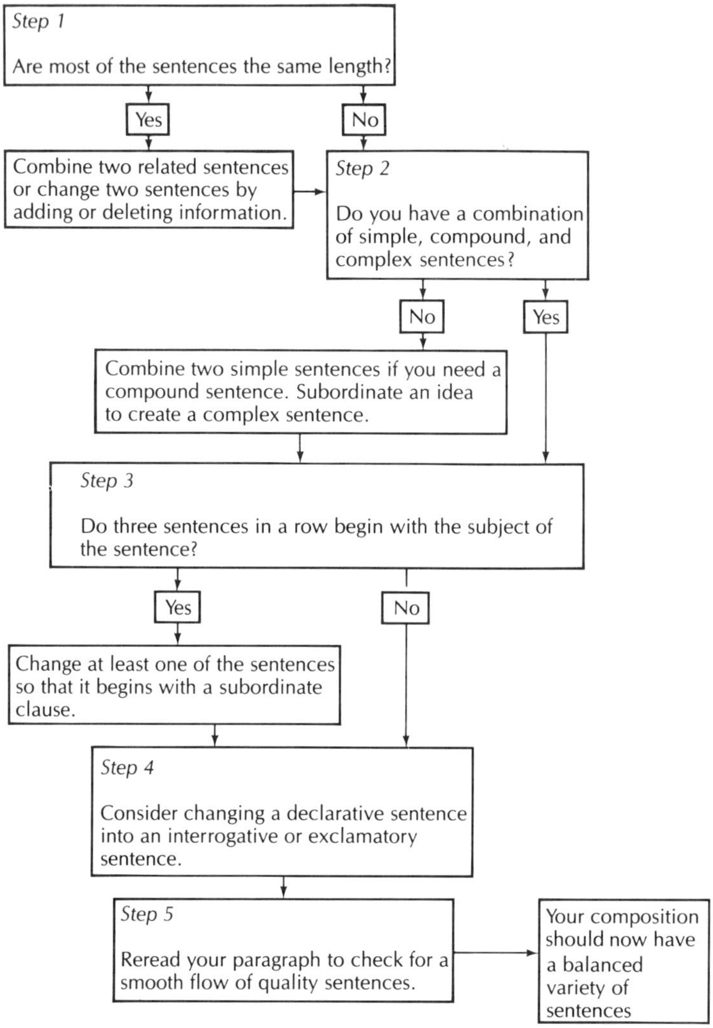

Fig. 8-1: Sentence Variety Flowchart

2. Have students keep the flow chart in their writing folder or binder so that they can refer to it whenever they edit their papers.

3. Instruct students to follow the chart and to make the necessary changes at each point.

4. Have students rewrite their compositions.

Follow-up:

• Refer students back to one of the numbered steps of the flow chart, if necessary.

• Make specific comments relating to the length, type, and structure of the sentences.

• The flow chart example is intended for upper grade students. Create one for use with younger children.

HANDWRITING CHECK

Objective:

Students will be able to

1. Evaluate their handwriting with the aid of a checklist
2. Use good handwriting consistently

Description:

After the students have completed a piece of writing, they will self-check their handwriting. They will be applying what they have learned in their handwriting practice to their writing products.

Organization:

Individuals, 15 minutes

Procedure:

1. At whatever level you are teaching, either introduce or reinforce the handwriting concepts and letter formations, building upon each lesson to the completion of the checklist.

2. Extend the lesson to students' written work. Inform the students that the application of what they have learned will be seen in their compositions.

3. To facilitate the self-check, have the students look for one quality in each line. Example:

Check the first line for uniform height.
Check the second line for spacing.
Check the third line for correct letter formations.
Check the fourth line for proper slant.
Check the fifth line for uniform alignment.

Follow-up:

• Commend the students for their effort and improvement. Positive reinforcement provides impetus for further effort and self-directed practice.

• Introduce calligraphy to the students and emphasize the same qualities stressed in the handwriting lessons. The transfer of knowledge is increased because of heightened interest.

<u>Handwriting Checklist</u>

1. *Margins* Are there margins on all sides of the writing paper?
2. *Size* Are the letters of the proper height?

   a. All capital letters are a little less than one space high.
   b. Tall loop letters are the height of capital letters.
   c. Lower loop letters extend below the base line one-half space.
   d. Small letters are one-third of a space high.
   e. Two letters *d* and *t* are intermediates two-thirds of a space high.

   To check uniform height, draw horizontal lines just touching the tops of the letters as shown below:

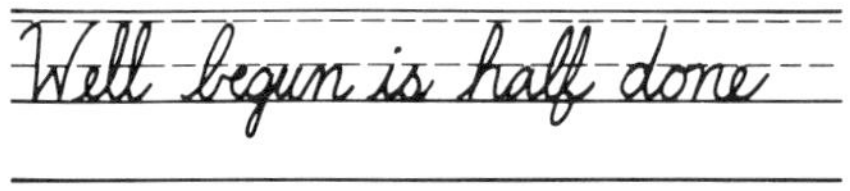

3. *Spacing* *Manuscript* Is there uniform spacing between the words? The space of the index finger is left between words.
   Cursive

   a. Is there uniform spacing between the letters in a word?
   b. Is there uniform spacing between the words? The distance between words should be the width of a small "o."

4. *Shape* Are the individual letters correctly formed and in proportion to each other?

Is there any letter that can be mistaken for another?
Example: 
This unclosed *d* with a loop looks like *cl*.

5. *Slant* *Manuscript* Are the vertical strokes straight and parallel?
Example:

Cursive Is there a consistent slant to the right? Check it by placing a slant sheet beneath your paper.
Prepare a full sheet of lines slanted at a 30° angle.

6. *Alignment* Is there uniform alignment with all of the letters in a line of writing resting on the base line?

EDITING GUIDE

Objective:

Students will be able to edit their writings with the use of a step-by-step guide sheet.

Description:

The students are introduced to a guide sheet listing considerations to be checked off when editing their writings.

Organization:

Individuals, full class period

Procedure:

1. Prepare a guide sheet with the appropriate items to be checked, based on the progress made in class. Build upon each item.

A Guide Sheet for Editing Compositions

Organization

The composition focuses on one central idea.

Grammar and Mechanics

All paragraph beginnings are indented.

Style

The sentence pattern is varied. (Self-check with the Sentence Variety Flowchart.

Format

Legible handwriting is used. (Self-check with the Handwriting Checklist.)

2. Duplicate the guide sheet for the students each time they are given a writing assignment.
3. Have the students reread their papers, check off the item(s) under "Organization," and make the necessary revisions.
4. Instruct students to proceed to the other sections, rereading the composition and making the necessary changes immediately.
5. Have the students rewrite their compositions and attach the guide sheet.

Follow-up:

- Write appropriate comments such as "good," "okay," or "needs work" next to each step as you read the compositions.
- Have students improve on at least one specific area needing work.
- The complete guide sheet can be placed in the composition folder or binder and used as a guide for all writings rather than as a checklist.
- Start a new guide sheet with one item on which to focus in each section and have the students write additional items as you present them to the class.
- Primary students can be taught to use a very simple checklist.

SELF-CHECKING POETRY

Objectives:

Students will be able to

1. Follow a prescribed pattern to write original poetry
2. Self-check their poetry following the pattern

Description:

Given a variety of poetic forms to follow, the students will write original poetry. Through self-checking, they will edit their work while also checking its format.

Organization:

Individuals, class period

Procedure:

1. Prepare information sheets with various types of poetry patterns, including an example of each. Some popular forms for young students include the haiku, cinquain, diamante, and limerick (*see* chapter 3).

2. Have each student select a form and write a piece of original poetry.

3. When the students have finished, instruct them to self-check their poem against the prescribed pattern, making any necessary changes and improvements.

Follow-up:

• Have the students share their poetry with an audience. They might read their poems to younger children, create a book, or add artwork for a display.

• To give the students a pool of words and ideas from which to select, use the fluency techniques described in chapter 3.

CONFERRING WITH STUDENTS

Objective:

Students will be able to revise their writing, following an individual conference with the teacher.

Description:

In a scheduled private conference, the teacher and the student writer will discuss the content of a composition in process.

Organization:

Individuals, flexible schedule

Procedure:

1. Allow two consecutive periods in two consecutive weeks to cover the whole class, two consecutive periods to reach half the class on one assignment, the other half to be reached on another assignment. For a self-contained class, use the staggered time or the language arts block.

2. Explain the guidelines for the conference:

a. Conferences are reserved for suitable writing assignments—revisions before making final copies, final copies before publication, selection from earlier writing assignments in the folder to be revised for evaluation.
b. There is a necessary time limit for each conference. Budgeted time should allow for skimming and traveling time.
c. A specific kind of help may be asked for. The student's questions should be thought through carefully to avoid wasting time.
d. The writers should be ready to confer; they should be prompt.
e. Each student calls the next person in line.

3. List the names for the day's conference on the chalkboard. For self-contained classrooms, the order and format may be determined according to needs.

4. Introduce the period's assignment to the whole class. Plan an activity that requires no teacher assistance. A low level of noise is preferred to total silence.

5. Begin the conference.

a. Skim the writing.
b. Ask an appropriate set of questions. Example:

- What (idea, description, phrase, opinion, event) do you like most in your writing and why do you like it?
- Is there anything you don't like? If so, what is it and why don't you like it?
- With what aspect of your writing would you like help?

c. End the conference in a pleasant way.

6. Keep a record of the conferences—date, brief comments—in your grade book or special folder.

Follow-up:

- Informal conferences can be arranged whenever a student needs help.
- Have students revise and rewrite their compositions for a specific purpose (see next section).
- After considerable experience with teacher–student conferences, students can use the approach in pairs.
- Use the conference approach in the prewriting stage. Have the students brainstorm or cluster their ideas and discuss these with you. Your guidance and encouragement at this point is valuable.

THE FOLLOW-UP

Teachers want to promote the students' sense of pride in their work and their eagerness to share, for writing becomes communication only when shared. Successful writing inspires more successful writing, and so the wheel turns.

Energy builds as students are motivated to write well and to edit proficiently so as to share proudly with an audience.

Because editing is a function performed by many people in the working world, having guests who edit speak to your class will reinforce your emphasis on the importance of editing before going public. Authors, whether renowned or not, are excellent choices as guest speakers.

The activities included in this section provide opportunities to enhance the students' editing energy and their desire to write well.

DIVERSIFIED DISPLAYS

Objective:

Students will be able to edit their work so as to display it proudly

Description:

Edited student writing is displayed throughout the classroom and school.

Organization:

Individuals, ongoing

Procedure:

1. Inform the students that their writing will be put on display. This announcement will encourage them to take the time to produce a product of which they can be proud.
2. Display student writings in a variety of ways to keep the interest alive.

Displays of Student Writing

bulletin boards (class, office, library)
class collections
newspapers
mobiles
school magazines
seasonal and other appropriate shapes
parent gifts
attached to photos, pictures, or posters
covering hanging boxes

3. Exhibit especially outstanding compositions in a special place as models for other students.

Follow-up:

- Discuss informal reactions and comments made to the students about their displayed writings.

• Create a photo-writing display.

a. Prepare an attractive exhibit space with colored butcher paper, lettering, photographs, and yarn or paper frames.
b. Encircle each photograph with related student writings. Some students might prefer to write poetry to accompany the mood of the photograph.

• Create poetry displays. Poetry written on colored index cards can hang from a tree branch ("Poet-tree"), stick out of cloth pockets ("Pockets Full of Poetry"), or be attached to the items to which they relate (bat, mitt, racket, ski, table setting, and so on).

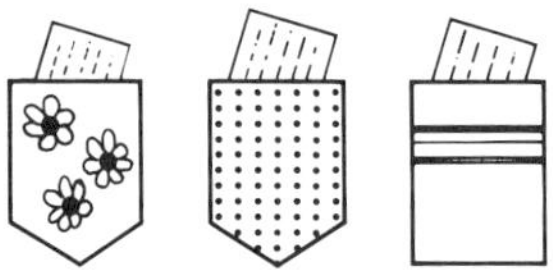

PUBLISHING STUDENT WRITING

Objective:

Students will be able to edit their work so as to produce publishable writing.

Description:

Students will edit carefully in order to publish their writing as often as possible and in as many places as possible.

Organization:

Individuals, ongoing

Procedure:

1. Student writing can be published in a variety of ways:

   a. Duplicated for the class and parents
   b. Posted throughout the school
   c. Circulated in manuscript form
   d. Submitted to school or class magazine
   e. Submitted to local or school newspaper
   f. Bound into a book for the classroom or school library
   g. Recorded on tape for a library of recorded literature
   h. Submitted to national magazines

2. Entrance into contests should be encouraged. The winners are always published.

3. These publishers specialize in printing children's original works. Refer to *Writer's Market,* available in the library, for a comprehensive listing of publishers' addresses and other specific information.

Cricket Cricket League Box 100 LaSalle, Illinois 61301	Monthly contests cover three areas: drawing, poetry, and stories in two divisions: ages 5–8 and ages 9–12.
Ebony, Jr. 820 S. Michigan Avenue Chicago, Illinois 60605	Prints letters, poetry, stories, jokes, and riddles. Annual contest in two divisions: ages 6–8 and 9–12.
Fun Publishing Company P.O. Box 40283 Indianapolis, Indiana 46240	Annually publishes children's work in paperback format in three divisions: ages 6–8, 9–12, and 13–16.
IMED 1820 Cotner Avenue Los Angeles, California 90025	Write for information on the Gotalott Awards and publication of children's books.
Jack and Jill P.O. Box 567B Indianapolis, Indiana 46206	Publishes children's letters (address to "Our Readers Write") and original poetry (address to "Poetry by Our Readers").
Kids Magazine Box 3051 Grand Central Station New York City, New York 10017	Written by and for children under 15 years of age.
Stone Soup A Journal of Children's Literature Box 83 Santa Cruz, California 95063	All writings done by children; published five times a year.

SHARING A PRODUCT

Objective:

Students will be able to edit a writing product.

Description:

The students will share a finished piece of writing with an outside reader who, in turn, will respond to it.

Organization:

Individuals, several months

Procedure:

1. Provide the necessary motivation, instruction, and activities to enable the students to create a longer, edited writing product. Examples:

   Short story with illustrations
   Patterned book
   Autobiography with photos
   Children's book
   Anthology of original poems
   Form of fictional writing (folktale, fable, tall tale, myth, fantasy, adventure)

2. Have the students consider binding their product.

Shape books with pages and soft covers stapled together or hole-punched and secured by yarn or fasteners.

Hole-punched pages and stiff covers secured by rings or ties.

Hard-cover books like a scrapbook secured with ties or fasteners—top cover is bendable because of cut at left margin, taped with binding tape.

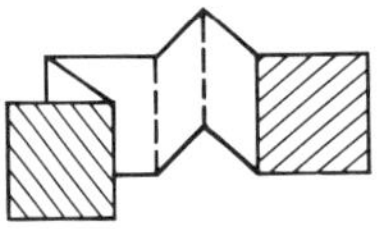

Accordion style with stiff covers at both ends.

Hard covers with pages done in pairs and machine or hand-sewn down the center.

How to Make Hard-Back Books

Lay two identical pieces of cardboard side by side, leaving a half-inch space between them.
Run five pieces of masking tape horizontally across the two pieces of cardboard to secure them.

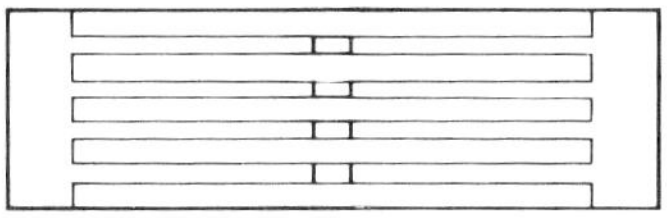

Run two long pieces of masking tape vertically between the two pieces of cardboard on the front and back.
Cut the cover material (wallpaper, cloth, contact paper, wrapping paper, or other suitable material) to cover the entire cover, with an extra inch all around.

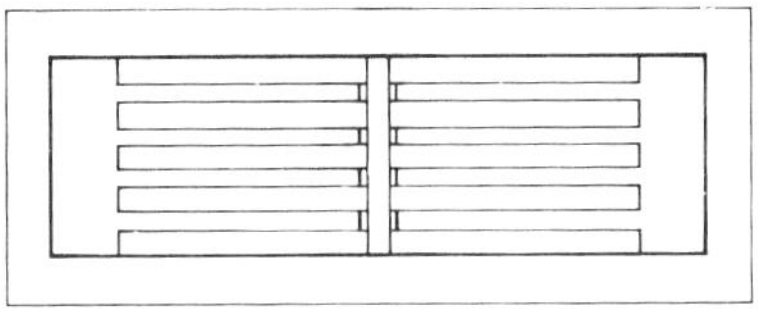

Fold the material down and paste it on all sides.

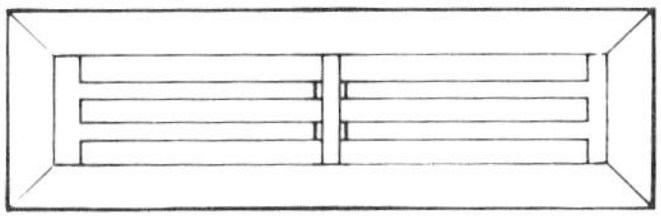

To put the leaves into the book, staple the pages. Cut two strips of paper the length of the book and four inches wide and fold them in half. Paste one-half of the folded strip on the front cover and the other half on the stapled pages. Do the same thing with the back of the book.

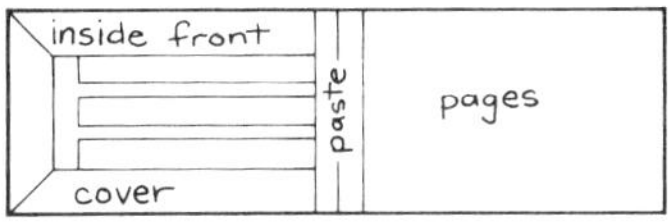

To give the inside a neat, finished look, cut two pieces of paper for the front and back inside covers about one-fourth inch smaller than the cover and paste them in place.

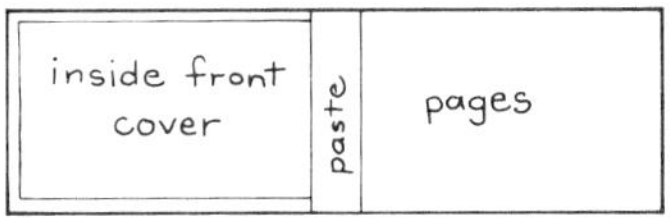

3. In planning their books, students should consider the following:

- Book cover material (fabric, gift wrapping paper, wallpaper, maps, contact paper, leather, vinyl, home designed paper with prints, rubbings, or finger painting)
- Title page
- Table of contents
- Artwork (pen and ink, felt pens, paint, water color, photographs, thumbprints, collage, tissue paper, prints, silhouettes, cotton, yarn, fabric, buttons, feathers)
- Material at end of book (glossary, information about the author)

4. Have students prepare a reaction sheet including instructions to the reader and space for comments and signature, thus:

Example: *Reaction Sheet*
Author: ____________________
Writing: ____________________
Comments:
  Style ____________________
  Content ____________________
  Presentation (appearance, evidence of editing)
  ____
  ____
Other: ____________________
  ____
Reader: ____________________
Relation/Occupation: ____________________

5. The outside readers may be parents, neighbors, relatives, older friends, librarians, or any public figure who would be interested in the piece of writing.

Follow-up:

- Have the students share the reactions of people who reviewed their writing products.
- Put the final products on display in the school or public library, district office, or other classrooms.
- For the younger students who might not be able to handle a long-term project, a class book is the answer. Each student can have a separate page for his or her original writing and artwork.

Objective:

Students will be able to discuss the total process of writing in various professions.

Description:

Guest speakers present their ideas on the importance of writing in their line of work.

Organization:

Flexible: one week per quarter; once a semester

Procedure:

1. Brainstorm a list of careers in which writing is important, and invite guest speakers from various fields. Your list might include the reporters and editors of your local newspaper, for example, and local people who have written books.

2. Have the students arrange for persons representing the selected careers to speak to the class or school. You will never run out of resource people because new students each year will bring new contacts.

3. Discuss telephone etiquette and important points to cover in a telephone invitation. The written invitation also should be covered.

4. Have the student(s) who made the contact introduce the speaker and thank the person after the talk. (Pointers on how to do this should be discussed in advance.)

Follow-up:

- Have a class discussion on the points covered by the speaker.
- Have the class write a thank-you letter.
- Extra credit can be awarded to students who perform the responsibilities.
- Invite several guests to serve on a panel to discuss the importance of writing in their professions. Other classes may share this presentation.

CHALLENGE

1. Decide on the presentation order of the correction symbols. Write lessons to accompany each set of symbols.

2. Create a large flow chart that will guide the students through the editing process. For your bulletin board display of the flow chart, have interchangeable

cards for the sections that will vary. For example, the cards for the group, peer, or self-editing section could be varied appropriately without changing the entire flow chart.

3. Prepare the passages and create a tape file for the activity entitled "Proofreading with a Taped Passage." Include those specific concepts on which students need reinforcement.

4. Prepare several books with different bindings as examples for the class. Follow the instructions in this chapter.

RECOMMENDED RESOURCES

Burrows, Alvina Treut, Doris C. Jackson, and Dorothy O. Saunders. *They All Want to Write.* New York: Holt, Rinehart, and Winston, 1964.

Shaughnessy, Mina P. *Errors and Expectations, A Guide for the Teacher of Basic Writing.* New York: Oxford University Press, 1977.

Tiedt, Iris M. *The Language Arts Handbook.* Englewood Cliffs, N.J.: Prentice-Hall, 1983.

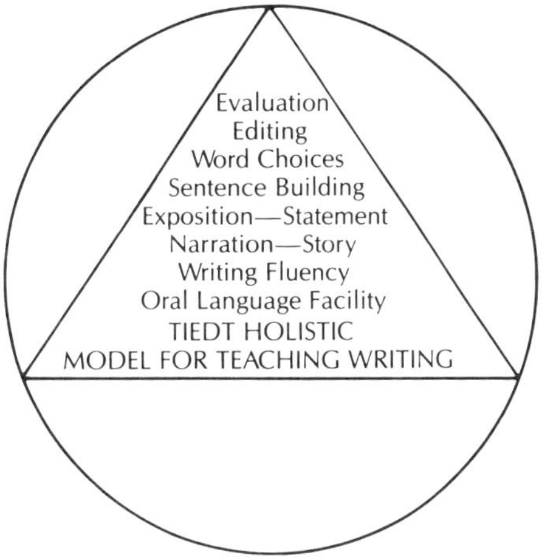

9

Evaluating Student Work

Assisting students to reach the top of the holistic model as they evaluate their writing is the climax of the adventure. At this point progress can be analyzed and the course determined for continued improvement of individual writing skills.

As we consider the purposes of evaluation, we should also look at the teacher's role as facilitator in the teaching-learning process. Because evaluation determines where students are in their growth as writers, evaluation should provide students with goals for achieving their personal writing potentials. As we guide students in overcoming their weaknesses and expanding their strengths, we need to be aware of their individual differences in maturity, knowledge, and style in writing. We can help students discover personally appropriate forms for their writing, recognizing that the creative process is uniquely individual. Evaluation teaches students to be good judges of quality and helps them to develop sound, individual standards. Evaluation should be both formative (ongoing during the writing process) and summative (judging the fully revised writing). The chief purpose of evaluation should be to help students learn.

Just as every composition will not be rewritten, every paper will not be evaluated. Students need writing experiences that allow them to experiment with alternative styles, to write freely just for themselves, and to write rough drafts for possible development later.

Evaluation should involve acceptance of the expressed thought and open-ended, searching questions rather than a final grade or a quality rating of good, fair, or poor. Hence the distinction between *grading,* a means of judging or ranking, which often finalizes an incomplete process, and *evaluating,* a positive response that assesses the individual's abilities at a specific time and provides encouragement for growth.

A positive focus is the essential element in the evaluative process. Because the goal is successful communication, the teacher's task is to help the student recognize and use the techniques of composition that are the direct means to effective communication. It is also the teacher's responsibility to ensure successful writing throughout the entire process. Positive evaluations of students' writings indicate that proper guidance has been provided along the way.

After reading this chapter, you will be able to

1. Select strategies that ensure success in writing, such as prewriting preparation, conferences, and holistic scoring assessment
2. Create activities for peer evaluation and self-evaluation
3. Use alternative methods of evaluation management
4. Organize appropriate record-keeping formats

Using a variety of evaluative measures, strategies, and activities will create a stimulating evaluation process that encourages students in their upward climb toward improved writing.

EVALUATION STRATEGIES

This section presents strategies that assure quality writing and promote growth at any level. Setting up the students for success is the key, and following through with positive responses and constructive insight brings the task full circle. Learning has occurred when students acquire a new skill and demonstrate its proper application. Evaluation fosters a sense of direction and provides evidence of measurable growth.

In allowing for feedback, conferences are an invaluable strategy. Not only do conferences make it easier for teacher and student to discuss the issues openly, they also enhance the teacher–student relationship. When student and teacher work cooperatively to evaluate progress, set up goals, and follow through on them, the essence of good teaching permeates the writing process.

ASSURING SUCCESSFUL WRITING

Objective:

The students will be able to write successfully for positive evaluation.

Description:

The students are properly prepared for the writing situation and carefully guided through the process to ensure successful writing.

Organization:

Class presentation, individual writing; class period

Procedure:

1. Suggest interesting and relevant topics for student writing. Allow the students to make suggestions or choose one of your suggestions. Spin-offs from your ideas are often appealing.
2. Explain the assignment clearly. For example, if the writing is to be in narrative form, review the elements of narration so that students will submit the correct form.
3. Share the criteria for evaluation with the students. Knowing what to include in the writing and what to edit for will guide the students appropriately.
4. Anticipate the errors and help the students avoid them. For example, a review of the use of quotation marks might be necessary before requiring conversation in a narration.
5. Use large-group cooperative prewriting activities such as brainstorming to work out a plan of attack together so that the students grasp the concept. For example, the development of a well-rounded, flowing composition can be worked on collectively to reinforce organization skills.
6. Use clustering and other fluency techniques to motivate the students and to start their ideas flowing (*see* chapter 3).
7. Monitor the students as they write. Encouragement, suggestions, and guiding questions spur students on.

8. Highlight outstanding sentences or passages during the process of development. This builds students' self-confidence, encourages further writing, and provides ideas for other students.

Follow-up:

- Accept only edited work for evaluation to encourage students to do their best.
- Analyze the errors with the students to help them understand the source of the error.
- Classify the kinds of errors a student makes most often. Realizing that five errors are due to punctuation helps the student focus on that element and regain control.
- Have ten-minute "bursts" (periods of concentrated review) on a weakness or strength prevailing in a class set of papers.

RESPONDING TO STUDENTS

Objective:

The students will be able to succeed with their writings.

Description:

The teacher responds to the students' papers, individualizing comments to help the students reflect on their presentations.

Organization:

Individuals

Procedure:

1. Your role can vary as editor, friend, advisor, and concerned person, depending on the assignment and the student's concerns.
2. Respond directly to the content and style of the writing.

> David, I felt like part of the scene because of the real-life conversation and the vivid description of the character's feelings.

3. Ask the students open-ended questions that require them to reflect on their writing.

Follow-up:

- Have the students revise their writings into a final form that satisfies them.
- When it is time for publication, work directly with the student in considering revisions that are necessary for that paper and that particular audience at that level of the student's development.

EVALUATING A PRIMARY TRAIT

Objective:

The students will be able to demonstrate application of a specific skill and be evaluated on it.

Description:

The students' compositions are evaluated on one skill taught in a recent lesson and reviewed prior to the writing session.

Organization:

Class, class period; individuals

Procedure:

1. Teach a specific skill you want students to apply in their writing.
2. Phrase the writing assignment clearly so that students' work can be evaluated in terms of the specific skill. Example:

> The paragraph should contain at least three well-explained reasons or examples.

3. At the top of the sheet, have the students write the skill being evaluated.

Follow-up:

- Evaluate the writing based on that one skill area.
- You may comment on other aspects of the writing, especially if the student has accomplished an objective on which he or she has been working.

Objectives:

The students will be able to

1. Write a composition keeping in mind the criteria by which their papers will be evaluated
2. Set individual goals for writing improvement
3. Critically review their writings in a process devoid of grades

Description:

Students understand the criteria by which their papers will be evaluated. Compositions are read for a total impression and given an appropriate score. Two evaluators read each piece. A third evaluator is the adjudicator when the two scores conflict.

Organization:

Ongoing effort

Procedure:

1. Analyze the characteristics of good writing and create a rubric for your class or grade level. The entire staff can develop a continuum of writing skills, which can be reflected in the rubric.

   a. Use guidelines such as the ones presented here.
   b. Determine a scale to be used, for example, Tiedt's nine-point scale for narrative writing or Santa Clara County's three-point scale.

Holistic Scoring Criteria: Narration

A Sample Rubric by Dr. Iris M. Tiedt

Use of this rubric assumes that writing samples will be read by at least two readers and that papers will be read as a whole without analysis. Even numbers may be used when papers seem to fall between the scores listed here. Inservice training is recommended for teachers who are collecting and scoring a writing sample.

Score	Characteristics of the Writing

1 The writer lacks understanding of the topic.

a. Little communication with the reader
b. Confused sense of audience
c. General lack of coherence or evidence of purpose
d. Weak grasp of spelling, punctuation, and syntax
e. No sense of paragraphing

3 The writer understands the topic and writes relatively clearly.

a. Lacks singleness of purpose
b. Contains some irrelevancies
c. Some attempt at organizing the materials coherently
d. Some knowledge of spelling, punctuation, and syntax
e. Frequent mechanical errors

5 The writer presents a fairly competent discussion of the topic.

a. Uses examples and/or details
b. Reasonably clear purpose
c. Evidence of adequate organization with few irrelevancies
d. Some attempt at paragraphing
e. A clear sense of conclusion
f. Occasional mechanical errors do not interfere with clarity
g. Syntax generally adequate with some fragments or run-ons

7 The writer presents a full discussion of the topic with well-chosen examples and details for support.

a. Some elaboration and refinement of ideas
b. A clear beginning, middle, and end
c. A clear sense of purpose and audience
d. Generally competent mechanically
e. Few run-ons or fragments
f. Some variety in sentence structure

9 The writer presents unusually complete and/or imaginative development of the topic.

a. Striking use of evidence, examples, details or reasoning
b. Tightly or imaginatively organized with an effective opening and conclusion
c. Clear sense of writer control of voice, purpose, and audience
d. Mature sense of sentence structure
e. Free from mechanical errors

Criteria for Evaluating Student Writing

	Grades 2,3,4	Grades 5 & 6	Grades 7 & 8
3 Superior	CONTENT Feelings attributed to self or others Writer is aware of degrees, shades, ideas, is tentative Recognizes motivation or intent ORGANIZATION Unity and cohesiveness STYLE Controlled sentences, longer than average Sentences varied in length and syntax Uses descriptive words Uses analogies or other figurative language Uses complete sentences Includes conversation MECHANICS Capitalizes and punctuates correctly Uses informal contractions Spells well and uses past tense consistently	CONTENT Understands subject Perceptions are direct and accurate details relevant Details support ideas Renders feelings well ORGANIZATION Sustained purpose Logical order Has introduction and conclusion Constantly aware of theme STYLE Uses personal voice Variety in sentence length and syntax Rich vocabulary Standard usage MECHANICS Minimal errors; neat manuscript, indent paragraphs	CONTENT Original in interpretation and viewpoint Sensitive to the reader or "audience" ORGANIZATION Consistency of voice, tense and person Consistency in point of view Well-developed sentence structure: thesis statement, support, and conclusions are present but not formulaic STYLE Vivid, accurate, and specific in direction Varied sentence structure MECHANICS Spelling and punctuation errors minimal Capitalization almost perfect
2 Typical	CONTENT Unremarkable content Uninspired ideas Some attribution of feelings Some redundancy Lack of originality ORGANIZATION Sentences tend to be isolated bits around a theme	CONTENT Overall inconsistency in skills Unsophisticated Tends toward factual Information not always pertinent Feelings mentioned adequately ORGANIZATION Some relation between ideas Lacks consistency	CONTENT Meets requirements of task General rather than specific Infrequent originality STYLE Limited in sentence variety and length Overuse of pronouns and linking verbs Dull: lack conviction and emotional tone

	STYLE Brief, unelaborated sentences: subjects and predicates Sentences begin with pronouns or "And" Many run-ons Some variation in sentence length and syntax Few, if any, transition words MECHANICS Spelling, capitalization, punctuation uncontrolled	Uncertain in paragraph development Good and weak elements side by side STYLE Matter of fact Little variation in sentence pattern Ordinary vocabulary: little vivid imagery Some personal expression, no descriptive verbs MECHANICS—Some errors in spelling, punctuation	
1 Weak	CONTENT Has meaning but lacks ideas and feelings which interest reader Some vivid supporting detail No writer's feelings; no judgments ORGANIZATION No sense of audience: of a reader's needs No direction: random writing STYLE Sentences are all simple Many fragments Frequent use of "and" MECHANICS Editing errors are frequent	CONTENT Often misses point; overly simple Serious omissions Literal: few feelings expressed ORGANIZATION No central purpose No clear direction; skips around Weak conclusion STYLE No exact verbs Dull choice of words Awkward sentences MECHANICS Many errors in spelling, punctuation, agreement and tense consistency Difficulty paragraphing; run-ons and fragments Manuscript unattractive; inconsistent slant	CONTENT Language itself seems to be a stubborn barrier to expression: most are also inarticulate in oral language Neither thought nor feeling flow easily ORGANIZATION Organization reflects neither purpose nor audience STYLE Style is non-existent MECHANICS Punctuation, spelling, handwriting are poor

Students Can Write
Santa Clara County Committee on Writing
Office of the Santa Clara County
Superintendent of Schools
Spring, 1977.

2. Select an appropriate prompt (writing stimulus) for each grade level and establish prewriting activities.

a. The prompt (a photograph, situation, title, or topic) should produce a variety of writing that can be evaluated objectively.
b. Instructions should be clear to avoid any error in content or form.
c. Prewriting activities are helpful in promoting the flow of thoughts.

3. Have the teachers who will score the papers write on the topic and follow with a discussion of the prompt, considering possible difficulties and making any improvements necessary to ensure successful writing by the student.

4. Have students write assigned code numbers on their compositions instead of their names.

5. Establish a consensus for scoring.

a. Generally you should ignore mechanics, except as it affects the overall quality of the paper.
b. Select a few papers for the readers to read, score, and compare scores. Work out discrepancies and establish anchor papers for reliability of the scoring procedure.

6. Begin scoring the set of papers.

a. The first reader puts the score and his/her initials on the back of the paper. The second reader marks the front of the paper the same way and then checks the two scores for a discrepancy. A discrepancy exists if the two scores differ by more than one point on a three- to five-point scale or by more than two points on a nine-point scale.
b. If there is a discrepancy, the paper is given to a third reader whose score is added to the next closest one to determine the final score.

7. Record the scores (the total points awarded by both readers).

Follow-up:

- Assess the student writings, noting relative strength and weakness. This process allows for goal-setting and evaluation of the writing program.
- Evaluate the holistic scoring process, noting strengths and making changes necessary for improvement of any component part.
- Have the students record their scores on individual cards.
- Hold conferences with students to discuss progress and set goals.
- This procedure may be used regularly in the classroom, periodically for a grade level, or yearly on a school-wide basis.

Objective:

The students will be able to discuss their evaluated compositions in a scheduled conference with the teacher.

Description:

Each student will have a scheduled private 15-minute conference every six weeks to discuss the evaluated compositions, determine progress to date, and set short-term goals. The students evaluate their progress over the six-week period and complete the conference guideline sheet prior to the conference.

Organization:

Five students per week for a rotating six-week period

Procedure:

1. Have the students complete a conference guideline sheet summarizing their performance during the six-week period.

Conference Guideline Sheet

Date	Composition	Evaluation done by Teacher Peer Self

1. The composition ______of which I am most proud / ______in which I put most effort / ______I found most enjoyable } is __________
   because______________________________
2. I did well on______________________________
3. I should be careful with______________________________
4. I am improving in______________________________

2. Schedule two 15-minute conferences each day or set aside two periods each week for conferences with individual students.

3. Post the schedule of conference dates so that the students will be adequately prepared for their conferences.

4. Prepare for the conference the day before by reviewing the student's folder of compositions and the student's completed conference guideline sheet. Make

note of the patterns of development to be commended, persistent shortcomings that need work, and accomplishments in relation to the goals set. You can record your notes on the "Comments" section of a conference report.

Conference Report   Name ____________________

Date: ______________
Comments: ____
____
____
____
____
Goals: ____
____
____
____
Student's Signature ________________________________

Teacher's Signature ________________________________

5. During the conference, be sure to

a. Allow the students to speak freely from their prepared guidelines
b. Have a positive focus
c. Write additional comments on the conference report and have the students write comments of their own
d. Cooperatively set up short-term goals and record them in the "Goals" section
e. Have the report signed by the student as an acknowledgment of the proceedings and a commitment to the goals.

Follow-up:

- Attach the conference sheet in the student's folder for future reference.
- At the next conference, check on the attainment of goals by referring to the "Goals" section of previous conference sheets.
- The format can be simplified for younger students.

Date	Composition Title

1. My favorite composition is ______________________________
   because ______________________________.
2. The strength in these compositions is ______________________________
   ______________________________.

PEER AND SELF EVALUATION

Studies indicate that students involved in peer evaluation do significantly better than those who are not exposed to this process. The reasons are fairly evident. When the students are aware that an audience other than the teacher exists, and that the audience is their peers whose opinions are considered important, then more concern and effort is placed on the writing act. Furthermore, evaluating the work of others helps students learn the elements of effective writing. Specific constructive comments with supportive references to the work are translated into tools with which students build their own writing skills.

From such practice, students are better able to critique their own compositions. Although self-evaluation is the most difficult of the evaluative procedures, it should be emphasized since it is this essence of writing that will accompany the students when they leave the classroom. Varied peer and self evaluation techniques enliven the writing program by motivating students to perform and to support others in their climb to the holistic pyramid's peak.

EVALUATION

Objective:

Students will be able to

1. Evaluate compositions in a variety of specialization areas
2. Accept responsibility for evaluating compositions in their designated skill areas

Description:

The students meet in small, predetermined specialty groups to evaluate the compositions in their designated skill areas.

Organization:

Specialty groups, full class period

Procedure:

1. Organize specialty groups of 5 students on designated areas of evaluation, such as organization, style, spelling, capitalization, punctuation, sentence structure, and usage.

2. Select students for the groups. To start out, you may base your selection on strengths. Gradually rotate the students to areas of their weaknesses.

3. Have the students attach a cover sheet to each composition. Since the groups will vary from one evaluation session to the next, a general format can be used.

Student Writer ____________

Evaluation Sheet

Specialty	*Comments*	*Signature*

4. Explain to the class the responsibilities of the various groups. This procedure will save time by eliminating the need to explain again later when the students rotate from group to group.

a. Use the agreed-upon symbols above the errors.
b. Use the dictionary to check spellings.
c. All evaluators, especially those in the content-related groups, should write comments on the evaluation sheet explaining the strengths and weaknesses of the paper and making suggestions.
d. Each paper will be evaluated by one member of each group.
e. Each evaluator must pass the composition to the next group in an organized fashion following a predetermined route.

5. Give each of the groups a set of papers.

Follow-up:

- Encourage the writer to discuss, challenge, defend, or agree with evaluations.
- Hold a class discussion on the findings. All students can benefit from others' mistakes and successes.
- Have the students use a code number as identification for the composition to ensure anonymity.

Objective:

The students will be able to evaluate the compositions of their peers individually and privately.

Description:

Individual students evaluate compositions, commenting on two strong points in each paper. The evaluators keep their own evaluation forms, but pass the composition along to the next evaluator. After several readings, the composition and the evaluation forms are matched and returned to the writer.

Procedure:

1. Prepare an evaluation form that will allow for comments on two strong points. You may want to highlight what the students should watch for in their evaluation.

Student Writer ____________

Strong points of ______________________________________
Composition Title

1. ______________________________________
____
____
____

2. ______________________________________
____
____
____

Evaluator ____________

2. Give each student a few evaluation forms with instructions on their use.

3. Pass out the compositions. The students may be sitting in a circle or in their regular classroom setup. Determine the route for passing the compositions.

4. After the students have completed each evaluation, they should pass the composition to the next evaluator, but keep the evaluation form.

5. After three or four readings, have the students return the compositions and the evaluation forms to their owners. If a code number system is used, each student can be responsible for collecting the evaluation forms that match the

composition he or she last evaluated. These can be stapled to the composition and submitted to the teacher for returning to the writers.

Follow-up:

• Allow students to read the comments made by their peers and to discuss the strong points in their own compositions.

• More experienced students can identify three strong points and make one suggestion for improvement. Use this more advanced technique in the self-evaluation process.

• Set up an evaluation learning center with tape recorders and sets of students' papers. Divide the class into groups. Prepare a chart so that each student knows what paper to evaluate.

Evaluator	Paper
Sue Jones	1
John Brown	2

Instead of completing a form, each student will identify him/herself on tape and tape record the information requested. After review by you, tapes can be shared, along with the writings, a few at a time throughout the week. This adaptation would be especially useful with younger students.

PARTNER EVALUATION

Objective:

The students will be able to evaluate a peer's composition on a scoring sheet.

Description:

A scoring sheet is used to rate the elements of the compositions with a score of 1, 3, or 5 for each grammatical, mechanical, and structural component and a score of 5, 10, or 15 for the qualitative analysis.

Organization:

Partners, class period

Procedure:

1. Create a scoring sheet including whatever components you feel are important. Introduce a component in each lesson and build upon it.

Composition Scoring Sheet: Expository Paragraph

	Rarely	Some Exceptions	Without Exception
Capitalization is used correctly.	1	3	5
Words are spelled correctly.	1	3	5
	NO	Usually	Yes
Paragraph has an easily recognizable topic sentence.	1	3	5
Ideas are stated clearly.	1	3	5
	Weak	Average	Strong
Qualitative analysis of content.	5	10	15
		Composition Score ☐	

Build to include elements such as sentence structure, subject-verb agreement, verb tenses, pronoun case, paragraph development, diction, and style.

2. Have the students work in pairs to evaluate each other's papers.

3. Allow students to use the scoring sheet in the editing process.

4. Instruct students to evaluate the compositions by circling the appropriate number for each component on the scoring sheet and computing the total score.

Follow-up:

- Encourage students to discuss the various component scores with their partners.
- Check through the compositions and the evaluation sheets. Discuss any discrepancies with the partners.
- Allow students to rewrite their compositions.
- If the students are advanced, have them mark their partner's compositions using correction symbols.
- Have the students evaluate their own compositions using the scoring sheet.

HOLISTIC SCORING

Objective:

Students will be able to

1. Remember the rubric (criteria) by which their papers will be evaluated
2. Use the criteria in preparing their compositions

Description:

Given the rubric by which their papers will be evaluated, the students write their compositions. Several student evaluators read each piece for a total impression and give an appropriate score.

Organization:

Class, individuals, small groups, three class periods

Procedure:

1. With student input, set up the criteria by which the papers will be evaluated and determine a scale to be used.
2. Select an appropriate topic and establish prewriting activities.

   a. The prompt or stimulus for the writing can be a picture, situation, title, or topic and should produce a variety of writing that can be scored objectively.
   b. Instructions should be clear enough to avoid errors in form or content.
   c. Prewriting activities such as brainstorming, having discussions, sharing books, and doing artwork are helpful in promoting fluency of ideas.

3. Have the students identify their compositions by writing their assigned numbers in place of their names. They should be given the opportunity to write a final draft and told that their peers will be evaluating their papers.
4. Conduct a holistic scoring session with the class to acquaint them with the process.

   a. Read, score, and discuss the compositions with the class.
   b. During the scoring session, the students must decide on a score, record it, and provide reasons for their given score, referring to the rubric and the composition.
   c. A score sheet can be used.

Evaluator ____________

Code Number	Score
1. ____________	____________
2. ____________	____________

5. When they can handle this sytem, divide the class into groups of five or six students and give each group a set of compositions to be evaluated holistically.

a. Each paper should be individually read by at least five different students; this can be assured by having the students put a check in the upper left-hand corner of the composition after it has been read.
b. Monitor the process and help students who consistently score differently from the others.
c. After the compositions have been evaluated, allow the group to discuss the discrepancies in scores.

Follow-up:

- Have a class discussion on the prompt, the rubric, and the strengths and weaknesses of the compositions.
- A group recorder should record the scores for each composition.

Code Number	Scores					Average

- Hold formal or informal conferences with the students regarding their compositions and scores.
- Have the students use the rubric to evaluate their own writing.

MANAGEMENT SYSTEM

Time management and record keeping are two concerns of teaching writing. This section considers record-keeping formats and alternative methods for handling the paper load. Record-keeping sheets that help students to recognize their strengths and weaknesses are assets in a conference. Kept in a folder, student writings accompanied by record-keeping sheets provide a running record of writing development. These record-keeping sheets can include conference notes, critique sheets, scale forms, records of strengths and weaknesses, and self-evaluation forms. Periodic assessment sheets reflecting growth over a period of time also are valuable. Samples of these forms can be found in this book. Modifications adapted to the individual student's needs can make writing a more enjoyable experience for the student and the follow-up a more rewarding opportunity for the teacher.

Some alternative ways of handling the paper load are:

• Skim papers to pick out frequently made errors and teach to the common problems, using examples from various students' works. Have the students evaluate their own work in relation to the points discussed.

• Write comments in responding to student writings, for example, in journals.

• Focus on one element and read for that limited purpose.

• Once a week, review the students' writings for the week and then evaluate one paper that the student has chosen to rewrite.

• Evaluate the student-selected rewritten composition from the set of three peer-evaluated compositions.

• Be selective about the assignments that you evaluate analytically.

• Analytically evaluate only half the class at one time.

• Use holistic scoring instead of letter grading.

Followup:

Follow through on a complete revision process for evaluated papers.

• Have the students skip lines as they write their compositions. Analytically score the paper on first reading. The students will make a correction in the blank space above each error. On second reading, focus only on those corrections. Circle with a different color those items that are still a problem. Continue this procedure until the correction process is complete.

Find the personally adapted system that leaves you content in the profession while effectively teaching students to write. This is the key to good evaluation.

TEACHER RECORD KEEPING

Objectives:

Students will be able to "write" stories by dictating them to the teacher, so that the teacher can keep a record of each student's progress.

Description:

The students "write" stories even if they don't have the command of writing by dictating directly to someone who prints what is dictated. The teacher keeps a record of the students' progress in language development.

Organization:

Ongoing

Procedure:

1. Prepare a record sheet with the objectives you feel are important in a dictated language experience story.
2. Provide opportunities for the students to relate their stories to you, to an aide, or into a tape recorder.
3. Evaluate the students' progress each time or on a weekly or monthly basis. Immediate feedback by you or your aide will suffice between more formal evaluations.
4. Evaluate the class periodically by using the record sheet as a tally of class performance.

Follow-up:

- Teach to the concepts needed, either individually, in small groups, or with the class.

Dictated Language Experience Story

Student ______
Date ______

Does the student's story . . .

	Yes	*No*
• "stick" to the assigned topic?	____	____
• develop the topic beyond listing (add details, examples, reasons)?	____	____
• have a clear plan of organization (beginning, middle, and end)?	____	____
• show creativity and originality?	____	____

Does the student's story contain . . .

	Frequently	*Sometimes*	*Never*
• complete sentences?	____	____	____
• adjectives?	____	____	____
• adverbs?	____	____	____
• prepositional phrases?	____	____	____
• subordinate clauses?	____	____	____
• correct verb forms?	____	____	____
• correct pronoun case?	____	____	____
• correct usage?	____	____	____

Objective:

Students will be able to keep a record of their progress in writing development.

Description:

The students keep a record sheet to note both strong and weak points of their compositions. Students learn to evaluate their progress so as to improve with each successive piece of writing.

Organization:

Ongoing

Procedure:

1. Decide on the format you would like your students to use and duplicate a chart, such as the one below.

Date	Composition	Score/ Grade	Strengths	Areas for Improvement

2. For more proficient writers, start with a few specific items and add more expectations as writing improves.

Assignments				
Grade or Score				
Spelling error(s) (sp)				
Capitalization error(s) (C or ¢)				
Punctuation error (P)				

On this chart, students can tally the number of errors made for any particular element and, at a glance, determine areas needing improvement.

Follow-up:

- Make the evaluation chart an integral part of the evaluation process.
- At conferences, review the students' progress as shown on such charts.

WRITING ASSESSMENT

Objective:

Students will be able to demonstrate progress for assessment on a quarterly basis.

Description:

Each quarter the teacher will perform a writing assessment of each student to evaluate progress and suggest future goals.

Organization:

Ongoing

Procedure:

1. Prepare a writing assessment sheet listing the concepts you feel are important for your students to master.
2. Assess the students' last assignment of the quarter or use several of the quarter's assignments in the students' writing binder.
3. Evaluate the class by using the assessment sheet as a tally sheet of class performance.

Follow-up:

- Teach the needed concepts listed, either individually, in small groups, or with the class as a whole.
- Once a semester, select the outstanding and the very weak papers to assess. This information on the strengths and weaknesses in student writing abilities helps you to plan lessons.

Writing Assessment

	Strength	Weakness
Content		
Develops the topic		
• details	______	______
• examples	______	______
• reasons	______	______
Ingenuity, creativity, originality	______	______
Individual style	______	______
Organization		
Clear plan of organization		
• beginning	______	______
• middle	______	______
• end	______	______
Addresses all sections of prompt	______	______
Stays on the topic	______	______
Maintains order	______	______
Clear transitions	______	______
Vocabulary		
Precise word choice	______	______
Clear, accurate usage	______	______
Vivid, concrete language	______	______
Mechanics		
Sentence structure		
• complete sentences	______	______
• clear, logical sentences	______	______
• variety of sentence structure	______	______
Paragraphing	______	______
Punctuation	______	______
• appropriate end punctuation	______	______
• dialogue punctuation	______	______
• internal punctuation	______	______
Spelling	______	______
Usage	______	______
• pronoun forms	______	______
• verb forms	______	______
Other		
____________	______	______
____________	______	______
____________	______	______

CHALLENGE

1. Create a quarter's management system schedule that incorporates a variety of the alternatives listed in this chapter as well as your own alternatives.
2. Conduct a holistic scoring assessment with a class.

   a. Create a rubric covering the elements you feel are critical in the evaluation of a paper.
   b. Write a prompt for a composition assignment.
   c. Evaluate the compositions using holistic scoring methods.
   d. Evaluate the procedure.

3. Create the evaluation sheets, grading sheets, conference forms, assessment sheets, and charts described in this chapter.
4. Plan a workable management system for conferring with students so that the conference is the focal point around which other writing activities are scheduled.

RECOMMENDED RESOURCES

Fagan, William T., Charles R. Cooper, and Julie M. Jensen. *Measures for Research and Evaluation in the English Language Arts.* Urbana, Ill.: ERIC/NCTE, 1975.

Hawley, Isabel L. *Common Sense Composition.* Boston, Mass.: Education Research Associates Press, 1977.

Koch, Carl, and James M. Brazil. *Strategies for Teaching the Composition Process.* Urbana, Ill.: National Council of Teachers of English, 1978.

Stanford, Gene, and the Committee on Classroom Practices. *Classroom Practices, 1979–80: How to Handle the Paper Load.* Urbana, Ill.: National Council of Teachers of English, 1979.

APPENDIX
Resources

This book helps the teacher to create a more comprehensive writing program. To complement this book, this chapter directs you to additional resources, books for both teachers and students. A recommended reading list for students, offered at the end of this chapter, is divided into two grade levels: lower elementary (K-3) and middle school (4-8). Resources are presented in the following categories:

Alphabet Books
Books about Language*
Films
Multicultural Books*
Picture Books
Poetry
Self-Awareness*
Stimulating Writing
Themes for Children
Wordless Books
Writing across the Curriculum
The Writing Process

*Separate lists are provided for teachers and children.

ALPHABET BOOKS

Alphabet books are not merely a means to teach alphabetical order or recognition of letter symbols. Instead, they represent a pleasurable way of organizing a variety of information for the child. Since there is no meaningful story involved, the alphabet book is a unique picture book that elicits oral responses from the reader. The alphabet books listed here present excellent illustrations and concepts for the young child.

Charlip, Remy, and others. *Handtalk: An ABC of Finger Spelling and Sign Language.* Parents, 1974.
An attractive explanation of sign language for upper elementary or middle grade students.

Farber, Norma. *I Found Them in the Yellow Pages.* Little, Brown, 1973.
Would interest fourth graders who are studying the community.

Gasiorowicz, Nina, and Cathy Gasiorowicz. *The Mime Alphabet Book.* Lerner, 1974.
Mime figures enact words suggested for each letter (such as *i—icky*).

McGinley, Phyllis. *All Around the Town.* Lippincott, 1948.
Concepts are presented alphabetically by a poet.

Smith, William Jay. *Puptents and Pebbles.* Little, Brown, 1959.
A poet's use of alphabet books to present concepts.

Wildsmith, Brian. *ABC.* Watts, 1963.
A well-known artist uses the alphabet book as a framework for his art.

BOOKS ABOUT LANGUAGE

Playing with language is both enjoyable and stimulating. Springing into idioms, dialects, similes, metaphors, origins, and vocabulary development turns the classroom into a place of discovery. The following list provides ample resources to share a world of words with students.

Children's Books

Cole, William, ed. *A Case of the Giggles.* World, 1967; *Oh, How Silly!* Viking, 1970; and *Oh, What Nonsense!* Viking, 1966.
Great nonsense guaranteed to cause giggles.

DeRegniers, Beatrice Schenck. *It Does Not Say Meow and Other Animal Riddle Rhymes.* Seabury, 1972.
Rhymed riddle provides clues that enable reader to identify the animals on the next page.

Epstein, Samuel, and Beryl Epstein. *The First Book of Codes and Ciphers.* Franklin Watts, 1956.
For upper-level students, this book gives explanations and illustrations of codes and ciphers.

Greene, Ellin, ed. *Clever Cooks: A Concoction of Stories, Charms, Recipes, and Riddles.* Lothrop, Lee, & Shepard, 1973.
A fascinating mixture of stories, recipes, riddles and charms. Stories are written by master chefs.

Gwynne, Fred. *A Chocolate Moose for Dinner.* Windmill, 1976.
Plenty of laughter that starts children imagining about our English language.

Gwynne, Fred. *The King Who Rained.* Windmill, 1970.
A story of a child's imagination of the spoken language; fun with idioms.

Hoban, Tana. *Push, Pull, Empty, Full: A Book of Opposites.* Macmillan, 1972.
Black and white photographs and single words per page help young children understand word opposites.

Kohn, Bernice. *What a Funny Thing to Say!* Dial Press, 1974.
Shows the history, development, and diffusion of language.

Krauss, Ruth. *A Hole Is to Dig.* Harper & Row, Pub. 1952.
A childlike classic of first definitions offered by nursery and kindergarten children.

Kuskin, Karla. *Roar and More.* Harper & Row, Pub. 1956.
Appealing drawings related to the sounds of animals.

Longman, Harold. *What's Behind the Word!* Coward, McCann & Goeghegan, 1968.
Gives the story of the origins of 40 common words, such as *pretzel* and *sandwich.*

O'Neill, Mary. *Fingers Are Always Bringing Me News.* Doubleday, 1969.
Words that illustrate the adventures of fingers—tapping, gripping, grabbing, opening, and whistling.

O'Neill, Mary. *What Is That Sound?* Atheneum, 1966.
Explores words which label diverse sounds around us; looks at onomatopoeia, beat, and rhyme.

Parish, Peggy. *Amelia Bedelia.* Harper & Row, Pub. 1963.
A hilarious book that shows how Amelia takes words literally, for example, by serving cookies on home plate.

Prelutsky, Jack. *Circus.* Macmillan, 1974.
Tongues trip through this book of alliteration and rhythmic verses.

Schwartz, Alvin, ed. *A Twister of Twists, a Tangler of Tongues.* Lippincott, 1972.
A fun book filled with tongue twisters.

Silverstein, Sheldon. *Where the Sidewalk Ends.* Harper & Row, Pub. 1974.
Silverstein's clever nonsense is sharpened by pen and ink drawings.

Spier, Peter. *Crash, Bang, Boom.* Doubleday, 1972; and *Gobble, Growl, Grunt.* Doubleday, 1971.
Illustrations are accompanied by onomatopoetic sounds of the kitchen, bathroom, holiday, classroom, and animals.

Wiesner, William, ed. *The Riddle Pot.* Dutton, 1973.
Suitable for primary grades because the riddles are short and the clues are simple.

Teacher Resources

Briggs, F. Allen. *The Play of Words.* Harcourt Brace Jovanovich, Inc., 1972.
Activities that will make students word conscious.

Doty, Roy. *Gunga, Your Din-Din Is Ready.* Doubleday, 1976.
A book filled with charmingly illustrated puns, riddles, gags, and quips.

Emrich, Duncan. *Riddles, Jokes and Foolish Facts.* Scholastic, 1970.
A paperback collection of word plays, riddles, and silly advice.

Farb, Peter. *Word Play.* Bantam, 1973.
Of exceptional value, this book provides exciting background information in language acquisition; it explores both the beginning of language and current theory.

Holmes, Stewart. *Meaning in Language.* Harcourt Brace Jovanovich, Inc., 1972.
Playfully examines the meanings behind our words.

Hunt, Bernice. *Your Ant Is a Which.* Harcourt Brace Jovanovich, Inc., 1968.
A beginner's book of homophones—written in verse.

McKenzie, Harry, and Issy Tindimsuebwa. *Names from East Africa.* Harry McKenzie, Pub., 1980.
Examines interesting derivatives from the East African culture.

Platts, Mary. *Anchor.* The Spice Series. Educational Services, 1970.
A book filled with interesting and relevant classroom language arts activities.

Reid, Alastair. *Ounce, Dice, Trice.* Little, Brown, 1958.
A good stimulator for word collecting; words for grumbling, singing, counting, and more.

Tiedt, Iris M. *Reading Games.* Contemporary Press, 1976.
Activities to interest students in reading and spelling.

Tremain, Ruthven. *Fooling Around with Words.* Greenwillow Books, New York, 1976.
An interesting book filled with many ideas for word play.

The pleasure of watching a film stimulates creative writing in the classroom by igniting visual images and recalling experiences of the viewer. Films motivate students to relate personal experiences on paper. The following film list provides superb entertainment as well as motivation for writing in your classroom.

Adventures of an Asterisk. Guggenheim Museum. 11 min.
Film describes pressures of conformity on children; artfully filmed in color.

Begone, Dull Care. International Film Bureau. 11 min.
Work of artist Norman McLaren and musician Oscar Petersen; imaginative use of sight and sound.

A Child's Christmas in Wales. Marvin Lichtner. 11 min.
Reading of "A Child's Christmas in Wales" by Dylan Thomas (from Caedmon Records); effective pictorial presentation.

Dream of Wild Horses. 11 min.
Dramatic color film of horses playing in the surf.

Finish the Story. Easton Films. 16 min.
A black-and-white series of eight two-minute story starters.

Hailstones and Halibut Bones. Sterling Films. 11 min.
Wonderful presentation of the book by Mary O'Neill (Doubleday); motivates poetry writing.

Hunter in the Forest. Britannica Films. 10 min.
Wordless black-and-white film about a hunter's experience.

The Lively Art of the Picture Book. Weston Woods. 1 hour.
Includes two short films, *Snowy Day* and *A Time of Wonder.*

The Loon's Necklace. Britannica Films. 10 min.
Tells a legend through the filming of authentic Indian masks; film relates social studies and literature.

A Lover's Quarrel with the World. Holt. 30 min.
Story of Robert Frost told in the poet's own words; black and white.

Moonbird. San Jose State Film-A 494. 11 min.
A sensitive color film that tells the story of a midnight hunt for the moonbird; told in children's voices.

Rainshower. Dimension Films. 30 min.
Lovely color film without words pictures the effects of a rainshower in rural and urban settings.

The Red Balloon. Albert La Morrisse. 30 min.
Sensitive story of a French boy and his magical balloon, based on the book by Albert La Morrissee; black and white.

Story of a Book. Churchill Films. 10 min.
Holling C. Holling, the author of *Pagoo* (Houghton Mifflin), tells how he and his wife wrote and illustrated this story about a hermit crab; color.

The use of multicultural books in the language arts classroom is imperative because students should be exposed to many different races and cultures. The following list will help you incorporate multicultural literature into your lessons to stimulate writing.

American Indians

Bierhorst, John, ed. *In the Trail of the Wind; American Indian Poems and Ritual Orations.* Farrar, Straus & Giroux, 1971.
An excellent collection of Indian poetry, songs, chants, prayers, and orations.

Clark, Ann Nolan. *Circle of Seasons.* Farrar, Straus & Giroux, 1970.
Describes the Pueblo Indians who live in New Mexico as they observe the seasons and perform their ceremonies.

Forman, James. *The Life and Death of Yellow Bird.* Farrar, Straus & Giroux, 1973.
Relates the story of a young Cheyenne, Yellow Bird, who struggles to survive the battles of Little Big Horn and Wounded Knee.

Goble, Paul, and Dorothy Goble. *Lone Bull's Horse Raid.* Bradbury, 1973.
A historically accurate and well-illustrated account of 14-year-old Lone Bull's first raid against the Crow Indians.

Gridley, Marion E. *American Indian Women.* Hawthorne, 1974.
A collection of biographies that focus on American women and the study of Indians.

Hofsinde, Robert. *Indians on the Move.* Morrow, 1970.
A nonfiction book about American Indians; other titles by this author are: *Indian Arts,* Morrow, 1971; *The Indian Medicine Man,* Morrow, 1966; and *Indian Music Makers,* Morrow, 1967.

Houston, James. *Ghost Paddle.* Harcourt Brace Jovanovich, Inc., 1972.
Hooits, an adolescent boy, hopes for peace between the Inland River people and his people.

Houston, James. *Songs of the Dream People.* Atheneum, 1972.
A collection of chants and songs from Indian lore.

Kroeber, Theodora. *Ishi.* Parnassus, 1964.
Anthropologists discover a lone Indian, the last of his tribe, in California.

Matson, Emerson. *Legends of the Great Chiefs.* Nelson, 1972.
Provides information about customs and taboos of Pacific Coast tribal cultures and tells of the lives of Sitting Bull, Crazy Horse, and others.

McDermott, Gerald. *Arrow to the Sun.* Viking, 1974.
Winner of the Caldecott Award; a Pueblo tale that describes a boy growing up.

O'Dell, Scott. *Island of the Blue Dolphins.* Hougton Mifflin, 1960.
Winner of the Newbery Award, this story tells of Karana, a young Indian girl who is left alone on an island and manages to exist for years.

Mexican Americans

Franchere, Ruth. *Cesar Chavez.* Crowell, 1970.
A biography of the background of the Chicano leader who became head of the National Farm Workers and led a strike in the California vineyards.

de Gerez, Toni. *2-Rabbit, 7-Wind.* Viking, 1971.
Adapted from Nahuatl Indian texts, this collection of poems reflects Mexico.

Hall, Marie, ed. *Bad Boy, Good Boy.* Crowell, 1967.
A sympathetic story of a little boy who gets into trouble because he doesn't understand English.

Hitte, Kathryn, and William B. Hayes. *Mexicali Soup.* Parents, 1970.
Moving to a new city causes problems for a Chicano family.

Jackson, Robert B. *The Lee Treviño Story.* Walck, 1973.
Story of a well-known golfer.

Lampman, Evelyn S. *Go up the Road.* Atheneum, 1972.
Yolanda, child of a migrant family, is trying to finish the fifth grade.

Molnar, Joe. *Graciela: A Mexican-American Child Tells Her Story.* Franklin Watts, 1972.
Graciela, 12-year-old daughter of a migrant family, tells of her struggles to cope with problems of getting an education.

Todd, Barbara. *Juan Patricio.* Putnam, 1972.
Juan wants a job; story uses Spanish words in context.

Others

Baron, Virginia Olsen, ed. *Here I Am.* Dutton, 1969.
Anthology of poems by young people in American minority groups—Black, Eskimo, Puerto Rican, Navajo, and Aleut.

Bloch, Marie. *Ivanko and the Dragon.* Atheneum, 1969.
A translation of a Ukrainian folktale about an old man and woman who didn't have any children; the old man makes a cradle that turns into a little boy.

Bloch, Marie. *Ukrainian Folk Tales.* Coward, McCann & Geoghegan, 1964.
A dozen animal tales that the author first heard from her grandmother.

Carey, Bonnie. *Baba Yaga's Geese and Other Russian Stories.* Indiana University Press, 1973.
An excellent collection of Russian folktales.

Haviland, Virginia. *Told in Japan.* Little, Brown, 1967.
Part of the Favorite Fairy Tales Series; Japanese folktales retold.

Hodges, Margaret. *The Wave.* Houghton Mifflin, 1964.
A Japanese folktale that lends itself to reading aloud; shares the feelings of an old man who sets fire to his rice fields in an effort to warn villagers of a tidal wave.

Hopkins, Lee Bennett, ed. *City Talk.* Knopf, 1970.
Urban area children write cinquain poetry of the city's seasons. Sensitive photographs by Roy Arenella create poem-pictures.

Jordan, June, and Terri Bush, eds. *Voice of the Children.* Holt, Rinehart and Winston, 1970.
Peace, love, hope, courage, and misery are captured in the prose and poetry of 26 Black and Puerto Rican children in Brooklyn.

Lewis, Richard, ed. *Miracles.* Simon & Schuster, 1966.
Poetry of children from all over the world.

Lourie, Richard. *Soldier and Tsar in the Forest.* Farrar, Straus & Giroux, 1972.
Translation of a Russian story in which a simple soldier, mistreated by his brother, manages to save the Tsar from robbers.

Newman, Shirlee. *Folk Tales of Japan.* Bobbs-Merrill, 1963.
An adapted version of Japanese folk literature.

Uchida, Yoshiko. *The Dancing Kettle and Other Japanese Folktales.* Harcourt Brace Jovanovich, Inc., 1949.
A collection of Japanese tales, including the famous folktale about Momotaro, who was brought to his foster parents in a giant peach.

Teacher Resources

Broderick, Dorothy M. *Images of Blacks in Children's Fiction.* Bowker, 1973.
Many examples of the Black culture.

Goodykoontz, William, ed. *Prejudice: The Invisible Wall.* Scholastic, 1968.
An excellent treatment of prejudice.

Harmin, Merrill, Howard Kirschenbaum, and Sidney Simon. *Clarifying Values through Subject Matter: Applications for the Classroom.* Winston, 1973.
A very good sourcebook for the study of multicultural implications.

Keating, Charlotte Matthews. *Building Bridges of Understanding between Cultures.* Palo Verde, 1971.
Helps students see the need to bridge the gap between cultures.

Landeck, Beatrice. *Learn to Read, Read to Learn.* McKay, 1975.
Shows how Afro-rooted folk songs can improve oral language and increase word fluency.

Tiedt, Iris M., and Pamela Tiedt. *Multicultural Teaching: Activities, Information and Resources.* Allyn and Bacon, 1979.
An excellent source for the classroom teacher because it supplies ample activities and examples for multicultural teaching.

PICTURE BOOKS

Colorful illustrations stimulate the creativity and interest of young readers. The picture books on this list will promote discussion and writing in the classroom.

Brown, Margaret Wise. *The City Noisy Book.* Harper, 1939.
Shares the noise of the city with the young reader.

Leaf, Munro. *The Story of Ferdinand.* Viking, 1939.
A well-told story of a bull who would rather smell flowers than fight; exceptional black and white drawings.

Lexau, Joan. *Benji.* Dial Press, 1964.
Portrays with sensitivity the feelings of young children.

Lionni, Leo. *Swimmy.* Pantheon, 1963.
Many fish unite to protect themselves against the big fish. The story shows how cooperation leads to a solution.

Miles, Miska. *Eddie's Bear.* Little, Brown, 1970.
An interesting animal story.

Piatti, Celestino. *The Happy Owls.* Atheneum, 1963.
Beautiful poster art illustrates this animal story of owls who enumerate the happy things that happen each season.

Steptoe, John. *Stevie.* Harper & Row, Pub., 1969.
A young black author portrays black children realistically.

Williams, Jay. *Petronella.* Parents, 1973.
The third prince turns out to be a princess with a mind of her own, who sets out to make her fortune.

Yashima, Taro. *Crow Boy.* Viking, 1955.
A silent little boy is encouraged to speak by the new teacher.

POETRY RESOURCES FOR TEACHERS

Arnstein, Flora. *Poetry and the Child.* Dover, 1970.
Awakening a child's ability to write a poem.

Buscaglia, Leo. *Because I Am Human.* Charles B. Slack, 1972.
A book-length poem about the beauty of being human.

Dunning, Stephen, Andrew Carrigan, and Ruth Clay. *Poetry.* Scholastic, 1970.
Collection of poems that serve as excellent models.

Hopkins, Lee Bennett. *Pass the Poetry, Please.* Citation, 1972.
Stimulating ideas about teaching poetry.

Koch, Kenneth. *Rose, Where Did You Get That Red?* Random House, 1973.
Teaching classic poems as models for student writing.

Koch, Kenneth. *Wishes, Lies, and Dreams.* Vintage, 1970.
Many suggestions for teaching students to write poetry.

Kushin, Karla. *Roar and More.* Harper & Row, Pub., 1956.
Verses about the sounds of animals; when the book is read aloud, students can join in to make the sounds.

Miller, Albert G. *Backward Beasts.* Bowmar, 1974.
An animal's name is turned backward and made into a new animal on each page; animal collage illustrations.

Morrison, Bill. *Squeeze a Sneeze.* Houghton Mifflin, 1971.
Sensible nonsense that inspires students to write rhyme.

Petty, Walter. *Slithery Snakes and Other Aids to Student Writing.* Meredith, 1967.
Stimulates creative writing of poetry.

Wolsch, Robert. *Poetic Composition Through the Grades: A Language-Sensitivity Program.* Teachers College Press, 1970.
Helping students express themselves through writing.

SELF-AWARENESS

Helping young people find themselves and develop self-esteem is one of the most stimulating aspects of teaching. By using books that model self-awareness, you are guiding your students toward a pleasurable journey of self-discovery. This list of resource books will help you achieve that goal.

Books for Children

Bach, Alice. *Meat in the Sandwich.* Harper & Row, Pub., 1975.
A ten-year-old boy creates a fantasy world to deal with the problems of being a middle child.

Ho, Minfong. *Sing to the Dawn.* Lothrop, 1972.
A 14-year-old girl is determined to get an education.

Jarrell, Mary. *The Knee-Baby.* Farrar, Straus & Giroux, 1973.
Deals with Alan's feelings as he waits for a chance to sit on his Mom's knee, as he did before the baby came.

Levy, Elizabeth. *Lizzie Lies a Lot.* Delacorte, 1976.
A heartwarming story of a girl who habitually embroiders the truth.

Miles, Betty. *Around and Around Love.* Knopf, 1975.
A warmly exuberant book that stresses the importance of caring.

Rice, Eve. *Ebbie.* Morrow, 1975.
A picture book that tells the story of a boy who couldn't pronounce his own name.

Scott, Ann. *Sam.* McGraw-Hill, 1967.
The story of a boy who needs to feel success.

Schlein, Miriam. *The Girl Who Would Rather Climb Trees.* Harcourt Brace Jovanovich, Inc., 1975.

An excellent book for primary grades because it portrays a six-year-old who would rather play with her boy cousin than with other girls.

Wilkinson, Brenda. *Ludell.* Harper & Row, Pub., 1975.
Ludell, the child of an unwed mother and unknown father, copes with the experiences of racism, selfishness, love, and friendship.

Williams, Barbara. *The Secret Name.* Harcourt Brace Jovanovich, Inc., 1972.
A book for middle grades that shows the difficulty of a Navaho girl adjusting to a strange new life.

Williams, Jeanne. *Winter Wheat.* Putnam's, 1975.
The story of a Mennonite family that fled Czarist Russia and a 17-year-old girl who is determined to help her immigrant family succeed.

Zindel, Paul. *I Love My Mother.* Harper & Row, Pub., 1975.
A very positive book that depicts the open, warm, loving relationship between a mother and her son.

Teacher Resources

Canfield, Jack, and Harold C. Wells. *100 Ways to Enhance Self Concept in the Classroom: A Handbook for Teachers and Parents.* Prentice-Hall, 1976.
A wide variety of self-awareness activities.

Harmon, Merrill. *People Projects.* Addison-Wesley, 1975.
Ready-to-use activities for the classroom.

Hopkins, Lee Bennett. *Let Them Be Themselves.* Scholastic, 1969.
A book of activities that have been used effectively in inner-city language arts classes.

Satir, Virginia. *Self-Esteem.* Celestial Arts, 1978.
An excellent book of introspection to help writers overcome the "blank page syndrome."

Simon, Sidney, Leland W. Howe, and Howard Kirschenbaum. *Values Clarification: A Handbook of Practical Strategies for Teachers and Students.* Hart, 1972.
An outstanding collection of activities that help children become aware of values and attitudes.

STIMULATING WRITING

Adler, John. *Inventions.* Harcourt Brace Jovanovich, Inc., 1972.
Gives literary models and stimulating questions that motivate student writing.

Anglund, Joan Walsh. *Christmas Is a Time of Giving.* Harcourt Brace, 1961.
Each of her warm, poetic little books shares honest, universal feelings that serve as starters for student writing.

Barrett, Judith. *Animals Should Definitely Not Wear Clothes.* Atheneum, 1970.
A projection of what might happen if every animal wore clothes.

Baylor, Byrd. *Everybody Needs a Rock.* Scribner's, 1974.
A rock-lover tells ten rules for finding and loving a special rock; a good writing stimulator.

Baylor, Byrd. *Sometimes I Dance Mountains.* Scribner's, 1973.
Unusual illustrations and a few words show a child using creative movement, which also leads to writing activities.

Burrows, Alvina Treut, Doris C. Jackson, and Dorothy O. Saunders. *They All Want to Write.* Holt, Rinehart & Winston, 1964.
An old favorite with good ideas for writing in the elementary school.

Carlson, Ruth K. *Writing Aids through the Grades.* Teachers College Press, 1975.
A variety of ways to stimulate student writing.

Daigon, Arthur. *Write On.* Harcourt Brace Jovanovich, Inc., 1972.
Contains short excerpts from literary models and motivating questions to accompany these models.

Deen, Beverly, and Frank Deen. *Writing Ideas.* Contemporary Press, 1975.
Many writing activities for the students; great for learning centers.

DeMille, Richard. *Put Your Mother on the Ceiling.* Viking, 1973.
A series of activities designed to stretch student imaginations; can be a motivator for writing fantasies.

Forte, Imogene, and Joy MacKenzie. *Try Squiggles and Squirms and Wiggly Worms.* Incentive, 1978.
A book that gets kids moving, feeling, and pretending; recommended for very young children through grades 1 and 2.

Forte, Imogene, Marjorie Frank, and Joy MacKenzie. *Kid's Stuff.* Incentive, 1973.
Contains many "ready-to-use" writing activities.

Grimm, Gary, and others. *Imaginations and Me.* Good Apple, 1976.
Two records, with accompanying activity books, that are filled with songs and questions to prod imaginative thinking.

Hennings, Dorothy G. *Smiles, Nods, and Pauses.* Citation Press, 1974.
Techniques for developing nonverbal language as well as spoken and written language. The activities get steadily more difficult. Exceptional value.

Hoban, Tana. *Look Again!* Macmillan, 1971.
A no-word book of surprises. It gives the writer a chance to look at ordinary things in an extraordinary way.

Pied Piper Materials. Verdugo City, CA.
Great for grades four through eight; has excellent filmstrips for the teaching of writing.

Tiedt, Iris, and Sidney Tiedt. *Creative Writing Ideas.* Contemporary Press, 1975.
A variety of provocative ideas for stimulating student writing.

Tiedt, Iris M. *The Language Arts Handbook.* Prentice-Hall, 1983.
Contains excellent materials for letter writing, technical writing, journal writing, and creative writing.

Tiedt, Iris, and Sidney Tiedt. *The Elementary Teacher's Ideas and Materials Handbook.* Prentice-Hall, 1980.
A comprehensive collection of ideas for every subject in the curriculum.

CHILDREN'S BOOKS WITH THEMES

Through books that present a new perspective on their problems, children learn to cope with the realities of life. Teachers can facilitate understanding by choosing books that deal with a variety of realistic themes. The lists in this section help you to prepare children for life crises, such as death and divorce, and to understand people unlike themselves, such as the aging and the handicapped.

The Aged

Bartoli, Jennifer. *Nonna.* Harvey House, 1975.
Family members share a great love for their grandmother.

Byars, Betsy C. *House of Wings.* Viking, 1972.
The doors of understanding open between a man and his grandson as the boy begins to understand the man's love for animals.

Jansson, Tove. *The Summer Book.* Pantheon, 1975.
Though 70 years separate a girl and her grandmother, they are very much alike and able to talk about important subjects such as God, Heaven, and Hell.

Konigsburg, E. L. *Altogether, One at a Time.* Atheneum, 1971.
An excellent collection of four short stories that deal with problems of age, obesity, mental retardation, and being black in a white world.

Krumgold, Joe. *Onion John.* Thomas Y. Crowell, 1959.
A young boy forms a relationship with an old hobo.

Kruss, James. *My Great Grandfather, the Heroes and I.* Antheneum, 1973.
A 14-year-old boy spends a week with his grandfather, who has just had a stroke. Though a common interest in heroes in literature, they gain insights about each other.

LaFarge, Phyllis. *Granny's Fish Story.* Parents, 1975.
This book challenges the age stereotype because Granny wears blue jeans and knows all about animals.

Mathis, Sharon Bell. *The Hundred Penny Box.* Viking, 1975.
An excellent story of the love between a little black boy and Aunt Dew who is 100 years old. Only the boy knows the importance of the 100 pennies in the box.

Taylor, Theodore. *The Cay.* Doubleday, 1969.
Timothy, a 70-year-old black man, helps Phillip learn to live with blindness.

Birth and Death

Brown, Margaret Wise. *The Dead Bird.* Scott, Foresman, 1965.
One of the first children's books that dealt with death.

Clifton, Lucille. *Good Times.* Random House, 1969.
A realistic portrait of a girl's grief as she accepts the fact that her dad died in the midst of good times.

DePaolo, Tomie. *Nana Upstairs and Nana Downstairs.* Putnam's, 1973.
A four-year-old boy is helped to deal with his grandmother's death.

Gruenberg, Sidonie. *The Wonderful Story of How You Were Born.* Doubleday, 1955.
A book that describes the birth process.

Joseph, Stephen M. *Children in Fear.* Holt, 1974.
This book shows that "shutting children out" from the experience of death can cause many fears.

May, Julian. *A New Baby Comes.* Creative Education, 1970.
Includes pictures of the embryo developing in the womb; written for sixth-graders and older students.

Sheffield, Mary. *Where Do Babies Come From?* Knopf, 1973.
A good treatment of the birth process through the actual delivery as the baby leaves the mother's body.

Slote, Alfred. *Hang Tough, Paul Mather.* Lippincott, 1973.
Story of a boy who is dying of leukemia.

Smith, Doris. *A Taste of Blackberries.* Thomas Y. Crowell, 1973.
A boy's feeling when his friend dies of bee stings.

Talbot, Toby. *Away Is so Far.* Four Winds, 1974.
Pedro and his father move out of the home when Pedro's mother dies. They soon realize that they cannot run away from death.

Viorst, Judith. *The Tenth Good Thing about Barney.* Atheneum, 1971.
A child remembers the good times he had with his cat before it died.

Warburg, Sandol Stoddard. *Growing Time.* Houghton Mifflin, 1969.
A story about the death of a dog.

Zolotow, Charlotte. *My Grandson Lew,* Harper & Row, Pub., 1974.
A sensitive treatment of the feelings of a six-year-old who misses his Grandpa.

Divorce

Anker, Charlotte. *Last Night I Saw Andromeda.* Walck, 1975.
An exceptional book that deals with both sexism and racism. An 11-year-old girl is determined to pursue her father's interests so that he will visit her after her parents' divorce.

Blue, Rose. *A Month of Sundays.* Watts, 1972.
After a divorce, a boy and his mother move to a big city, where he experiences loneliness.

Blume, Judy. *It's Not the End of the World.* Bradbury, 1972.
A 12-year-old girl attempts to bring about a reconciliation between her parents, then realizes that if they are not together, it is not the end of the world.

Greene, Constance. *I Know You, Al.* Viking, 1975.
A girl questions herself when she thinks that her divorced mother's boyfriend may ask her for permission to marry her mother.

Goff, Beth. *Where's Daddy?* Beacon Press, 1969.
More appropriate for adults who are having problems talking about divorce with children.

Heide, Florence. *When the Sad One Comes to Stay.* Lippincott, 1975.
Story of a contemporary divorced woman who never talks to her daughter about the girl's father.

Lexau, Joan. *Me Day.* Dial Press, 1971.
Book about divorce, recommended for primary grade students.

Family Ties

Baldwin, Anne Norris. *Jenny's Revenge.* Four Winds, 1974.
A mother has to work to support the family, consisting of mother, daughter, and babysitter; but the daughter feels that the mother should stay home.

Blaine, Marge. *The Terrible Thing That Happened at Our House.* Parents, 1975.
A mother returns to work, and the family has to adjust to new family roles.

Coatsworth, Elizabeth. *Houseboat Summer.* Macmillan, 1942.
Bill, who has been fatherless since he was small, spends the summer with his aunt and uncle. He discovers that he needs a father and his uncle becomes the substitute.

Lawson, Robert. *They Were Strong and Good.* Viking, 1940.
A sense of pride in family and ancestors is portrayed excellently.

Morgan, Alison. *Pete.* Harper & Row, Pub., 1973.
An adolescent boy seldom sees his father, who travels to construction sites to work. He visits his father and sees him as a real person.

Neville, Emily. *Garden of Broken Glass.* Delacorte, 1975.
Thirteen-year-old Brian deals with a broken home, an alcoholic mother, and welfare.

Snyder, Zilpha. *Witches of Worm.* Atheneum, 1972.
A lonely 12-year-old turns her attention to a strange cat.

Storey, Margaret. *The Family Tree.* Nelson, 1973.
Ten-year-old Kate discovers her family through family possessions and old photographs.

Tobias, Toby. *The Quitting Deal.* Viking, 1975.
A seven-year-old daughter who wants to stop sucking her thumb, helps her mother who wants to stop smoking. An unusual relationship between mother and daughter.

Friendship

Anglund, Joan. *A Friend Is Someone Who Likes You.* Harcourt Brace Jovanovich, Inc., 1958.
A small book that shows friendship with a boy, a dog, a white mouse, and the wind.

Burch, Robert. *Queenie Peavy.* Viking, 1966.
An eighth grade girl in rural Georgia faces real problems, such as a father who is in jail and kids who tease her; an interesting character study.

Clifton, Lucille. *The Times That Used to Be.* Holt, Rinehart & Winston, 1974.
A delightful, realistic tale of best friends.

Myers, Walter Dean. *Fast Sam, Cool Clyde, and Stuff.* Viking, 1975.
A moving novel about black and Puerto Rican friends.

Rockwell, Thomas. *How to Eat Fried Worms.* Watts, 1973.
Billy accepts a $50 bet to eat fried worms, and begins to like them.

Schultz, Charles. *I Need All the Friends I Can Get.* Determined Publications, 1964.
Presents important concepts for both adults and young people about friendship.

Stolz, Mary. *The Noonday Friends.* Harper & Row, Pub., 1965.
Shows the relationship between an 11-year-old girl and her younger brother.

Warburg, Sandol Stoddard. *I Like You.* Houghton Mifflin, 1970.
A delightful small book that describes friendship in an exuberant tone.

Positive Images of Women

Behn, Harry. *Faraway Lurs.* World, 1963.
Heather is portrayed as a strong female character; for adolescent readers.

Bemelmans, Ludwig. *Madeline.* Viking, 1939.
Popular series about a lovable girl with many friends of both sexes.

Byars, Betsy. *Summer of the Swans.* Viking, 1970.
Portrays a retarded child within a family setting.

George, Jean Craighead. *Julie of the Wolves.* Harper & Row, Pub., 1972.
Winner of the Newbery Award, this book is about a 13-year-old Eskimo girl who imitates wolf behavior.

Klein, Norma. *Mom, the Wolfman and Me.* Avon, 1974.
The story of an 11-year-old girl who lives with her unmarried mother; she's not sure she wants her mother to get married.

Lindgren, Astrid. *Pippi Longstocking.* Viking, 1950.
A delightful tale about a lovable girl who enjoys life.

Merriam, Eve. *Boys and Girls; Girls and Boys.* Avon, 1974.
Children are shown choosing roles other than the traditional sex roles.

Steig, William. *Sylvester and the Magic Pebble.* Simon & Schuster, 1969.
One of the best examples of a stereotyped image of a woman and the police. A Caldecott winner, the book portrays a female donkey who wears an apron and who needs the support of a strong male. Good for teaching.

Special Children

Cleaver, Vera, and Bill Cleaver. *Me Too.* Lippincott, 1973.
Lydia tries to help her identical twin sister, who is severely retarded. After many frustrations, Lydia realizes that her sister needs to remain in a special school.

Heide, Florence. *Sound of Sunshine, Sound of Rain.* Parents, 1970.
Young people and adults can gain insight into the world of a blind boy; an excellent book.

Hickok, Lorena. *The Story of Helen Keller.* Grosset and Dunlap, 1958.
An inspiration for all ages, Helen, who had been deaf, mute, and blind since age two, overcomes her handicaps.

Klein, Gerda. *The Blue Rose.* Lawrence Hall, 1974.
A sensitive story of a girl who is mentally retarded.

Spence, Eleanor. *The Nothing Place.* Harper & Row, Pub., 1973.
Glen becomes deaf after an illness but refuses to tell anyone. He attempts to lip-read and has difficulty because no one can understand his unusual behavior.

Wolf, Bernard. *Don't Feel Sorry for Paul.* Lippincott, 1974.
Paul was born with deformed hands and feet but he deals with his handicap. Wolf portrays Paul with sympathy but without sentimentality.

WORDLESS BOOKS

Wordless books are books that tell a story through pictures. These books are especially effective in stimulating oral language since they encourage the students to react. The following list can be of exceptional value in the classroom.*

Alexander, Martha. *Bobo's Dream.* Dial Press, 1970.
A dachshund dreams he returns his master's football after big boys take it.

*Recommended source for an even more complete list of wordless books is: Tiedt, Iris M. *Exploring Books with Children.* Houghton Mifflin, 1979.

Aruego, Jose. *Look What I Can Do.* Scribner's, 1971.
Two water buffalo get into unusual predicaments as they challenge each other to "Anything you can do . . ."

Barton, Byron. *Elephant.* Seabury, 1971.
A girl sees elephants on TV, in books, as toys, and in dreams until her parents show her a real one.

Baum, Willi. *Birds of a Feather.* Addison-Wesley, 1969.
A bird decides to leave the flock and enhance his plumage with feathers from a lady's hat.

Bollinger-Savelli, Antonella. *The Knitted Cat.* Macmillan, 1971.
A knitted cat is almost completed when a mouse unravels its unfinished tail. The cat walks outside and an owl ties up the unraveling tail.

Carl, Eric. *Do You Want to Be My Friend?* Thomas Y. Crowell, 1971.
Little mouse, who wants to find a friend, finds a tail on each page; the owner of the tail is revealed.

Carroll, Ruth. *The Christmas Kitten.* Walck, 1970.
A little kitten is finally allowed to stay with a family.

Goodall, John. *The Adventures of Paddy Pork.* Harcourt Brace Jovanovich, Inc., 1968.
Paddy, a pig, leaves home to join the circus but returns when he has problems.

Goshorn, Elizabeth. *Shoestrings.* Carolrhoda, 1975.
A humorous account of a girl trying to tie her shoestrings.

Hoban, Tina. *Look Again!* Macmillan, 1971.
The book shows the beauty of simple things and our disregard for detail as the reader looks through a two-inch-square peephole at a black-and-white photograph.

Hutchins, Pat. *Changes, Changes.* Macmillan, 1971.
Play blocks are used to tell the story of a fire engine putting out a fire and causing a flood. Building a new house is the answer.

Krahn, Fernando. *A Flying Saucer Full of Spaghetti.* Dutton, 1970.
Unwanted spaghetti is flown across town to a hungry girl.

Mayer, Mercer and Marianna. *A Frog and a Friend.* Dial Press, 1967.
One of a fascinating series of the adventures of the frog.

Mayer, Mercer. *A Boy, a Dog, and a Frog.* Dial Press, 1967.
The author–illustrator portrays a series of hilarious events as a small boy and his dog attempt to catch a frog. One in a series of wordless books on the adventures of the frog.

Meyer, Renate. *Hide-and-Seek.* Bradbury, 1969.
A game of hide and seek occurs as a girl in pink chases a boy in blue.

Mordillo, Guillermo. *The Damp and Daffy Doings of a Daring Pirate Ship.* Harlin Quist, 1971.

A light-hearted account of daffy little characters who build and launch their own pirate ship.

Schick, Eleanor. *Making Friends.* Macmillan, 1969.
A shopping trip with Mother shows the little girl noticing many things along the way . . . things that Mother had not noticed before.

Wezel, Peter. *The Good Bird.* Harper, 1964.
This book can be used with a large group of students since it has large pictures. A bird catches a worm to share with a goldfish, and both are contented.

WRITING ACROSS THE CURRICULUM

Writing is a process that should not be isolated in the English classroom. Students need help with writing in all subject areas. The following lists provide excellent examples of good writing across the curriculum.

Animal Life

Corcoran, Barbara. *Sasha, My Friend.* Atheneum, 1969.
After moving to Montana, a girl makes friends with a wolf, an old Indian, and a crippled girl.

George, Jean Craighead. *Julie and the Wolves.* G. K. Hall, 1973.
A Newbery Award-winning book; an Eskimo girl's account of the wolves who saved her life.

Kipling, Rudyard. *Mowgli and His Brothers.* Watts, 1900.
A haunting story that tells of a young boy who lives happily with wolves.

Lampman, Evelyn Sibley. *The City under the Back Steps.* Doubleday, 1960.
A fictional but informational explanation of ant life.

Mason, Herbert Molloy. *The Fantastic World of Ants: A Microview of Earth's Most Ingenious Insect.* D. McKay, 1974.
A nonfiction account written in clear, readable style, and accompanied with diagrams and photographs.

Mowat, Failey. *Never Cry Wolf.* Little, Brown, 1963.
An informative story of wolves, including a map of where they live.

Math

Branley, Franklyn M. *Think Metric!* Thomas Y. Crowell, 1972.
Shows an overview of the metric system and helps intermediate grade students translate from one system to another.

Hirsch, S. Carl. *Meter Means Measure.* Viking, 1973.
Discusses the politics involved with making the change to the metric system.

Science

Benchley, Nathaniel. *Deep Dives of Stanley Whale.* Harper & Row, Pub., 1973.
A playful story about a whale.

Carson, Rachel. *The Sea around Us.* Adapted by Anne Terry White. Golden Press, 1958.
An oversize book that contains many fine colored photographs.

Cook, Joseph, and William Wisner. *Killer Whale.* Dodd, Mead, 1963.
A short book for middle graders; exciting nonfiction.

Coombs, Charles. *Deep Sea World: The Story of Oceanography.* Morrow, 1966.
An overview of the study of oceanography.

Fisher, Leonard. *Diary of a Young New England Whaler.* Doubleday, 1972.
A well-researched documentary based on the diary of a cabin boy; tale about power of supernatural forces.

McCloskey, Robert. *Burt Dow, Deep-Water Man.* Viking, 1963.
A charming whale story for primary grades.

Stephens, William. *Come with Me to the Edge of the Sea.* Messner, 1972.
An attractive book that invites children to explore the ocean.

Social Studies

Berry, Brick. *Hay-Foot, Straw-Foot.* Viking, 1954.
A story about a drummer boy and the origins of "Yankee Doodle."

Blassingame, Wyatt. *The Story of the United States Flag.* Garrard, 1969.
The history of the United States flag is revealed with diagrams and illustrations in color.

Bourne, Miriam Anne. *Nabby Adam's Diary.* Coward, McCann, Geoghegan, 1975.
Nabby's diary tells of events preceding the American Revolution and her experiences as the daughter of John Adams.

Colver, Anne. *Bread and Butter Indian.* Holt, Rinehart & Winston, 1964.
During the Revolutionary period, Barbara develops a friendship with an Indian by sharing bread and butter with him.

DeAngeli, Marguerite. *Ellin's Amerika.* Doubleday, 1941.
Ellin and her Swedish family have moved to the "new world." Ellin's experiences as the only girl in her community provide a good look at pre–Revolutionary life.

Epstein, Samuel, and Beryl Epstein. *Young Paul Revere's Boston.* Garrard, 1966.
The illustration, diagrams, and maps show what Boston was like when Revere was a boy.

Fritz, Jean. *And Then What Happened, Paul Revere?* Coward, McCann & Geoghegan, 1973.
A humorous and interesting story that reveals many little-known aspects of Revere's life.

Lawson, Robert. *Ben and Me.* Little, Brown, 1951.
An amusing fantasy, illustrated by the author, about the genius mouse who "helps" a famous inventor of Revolutionary times.

Loeper, John L. *Going to School in 1776.* Atheneum, 1973.
Describes the children, teachers, and schools, and tells what after-school life was like in 1776.

Longfellow, Henry Wadsworth. *Paul Revere's Ride.* Thomas Y. Crowell, 1963.
Could be presented as a choral reading.

McGovern, Ann. *The Secret Soldier.* Scholastic, 1975.
A true story about Deborrah Samson, a Revolutionary soldier, who disguised her identity.

Millender, Dharathuia, H. *Crispus Attucks, Boy of Valor.* Bobbs-Merrill, 1965.
A story of a Black hero of the Revolution.

Monjo, F. N. *King George's Head Was Made of Lead.* Coward, McCann & Geoghegan, 1974.
The head of the statue of King George explains the British view of the war.

Yates, Elizabeth. *Amos Fortune: Free Man.* Dutton, 1950.
A Black born in 1766, Mr. Fortune worked hard for the cause of freedom long after the Revolutionary War had ended.

THE WRITING PROCESS

The resources provided on this list give you both a theoretical examination of the teaching of writing and a pragmatic approach. You'll enjoy comparing various philosophies and finding additional activities that can be used to strengthen writing instruction. Additional recommended resources are listed at the end of chapter 1.

Barzun, Jacques. *Simple and Direct: A Rhetoric for Writers.* Harper & Row, Pub., 1975.
Excellent book with many examples for writers who would like to edit their own work.

Brown, George Isaac. *Human Teaching for Human Learning.* Viking, 1971.
Creative ideas for all areas of the curriculum.

Flesch, Rudolf. *The Art of Readable Writing.* Harper & Row, Pub., 1949.
An exceptional analysis of the writing process. Provides a formula to measure readability.

Johnson, Edna, Evelyn Sickels, Frances Clarke Sayers, and Carolyn Horowitz. *Anthology of Children's Literature.* Houghton Mifflin, 1977.
Excellent anthology of children's literature, including fables, poetry, picture books, folk tales, biographies, and much more.

Moffet, James, and Betty Wagner. *Student-Centered Language Arts and Reading.* Houghton Mifflin, 1976.
An integrated approach to the teaching of language arts.

Schrank, Jeffrey. *Teaching Human Beings: 101 Subversive Activities for the Classroom.* Beacon Press, 1972.
As the title suggests, this book offers many unique, "subversive" suggestions for using a change in methods and media in the classroom.

Tiedt, Iris M. *Exploring Books with Children.* Houghton Mifflin, 1979.
An excellent source that helps you explore a wide variety of books, enjoy children's literature, and share what you discover with young children.

Tiedt, Iris M., and Sidney Tiedt. *Elementary Teacher's Ideas and Materials Handbook.* Prentice-Hall, 1980.
A comprehensive study of ideas for every subject in the classroom.

Tiedt, Iris M., and Sidney Tiedt. *Language Arts Activities for the Classroom.* Allyn and Bacon, 1978.
Hundreds of exciting ideas and activities for teaching listening, speaking, reading, and writing.

Smith, James. *Creative Teaching of the Language Arts in the Elementary School.* Allyn and Bacon, 1975.

Van Allen, Roach and Claryce Allen. *Language Experience Activities.* Houghton Mifflin, 1963.
Resources for creating learning centers.

RECOMMENDED READING LIST FOR STUDENTS

The following books for literature study are divided into two levels, lower elementary (K–3) and middle school (4–8). Since many of these books are mentioned in other sections of this resource chapter, this section is not annotated. These books provide an excellent reading list and are models for students engaged in independent writing, for good readers usually make good writers.

Lower Elementary (K–3)

Andersen, Hans Christian. *The Emperor's New Clothes.* Houghton Mifflin, 1949.

Bailey, Carolyn S. *The Little Rabbit Who Wanted Red Wings.* Platt and Munk, 1931.

Bemelmans, Ludwig. *Madeline.* Viking, 1939.

DuBois, William Pene. *Three Little Pigs.* Viking, 1962.

Edmonds, Walter D. *The Matchlock Gun.* Dodd, Mead, 1941.

Fatio, Louise. *The Happy Lion.* Whittlesey, 1954.

Flack, Marjorie. *Ask Mr. Bear.* Macmillan, 1932.

Hawthorne, Nathaniel. *The Golden Touch.* McGraw-Hill, 1959.
Hunter, Edith Fisher. *Child of the Silent Night.* Houghton Mifflin, 1968.
Keats, Ezra Jack. *The Snowy Day.* Viking, 1962.
LaFontaine. *The North Wind and the Sun.* Watts, 1964.
Minarik, Else H. *Little Bear.* Harper & Row, Pub., 1957.
Potter, Beatrix. *The Tale of Peter Rabbit.* Warne, 1903.
Seuss, Dr. *And to Think That I Saw It on Mulberry Street.* Vanguard, 1937.
Thurber, James. *Many Moons.* Harcourt, 1943.
Tresselt, Alvin. *Hide and Seek Fog.* Lothrop, 1965.
Wersba, Barbara. *Land of the Forgotten Beasts.* Atheneum, 1964.
Yates, Elizabeth. *Carolina's Courage.* Dutton, 1964.

Middle School (4–8)

Anderson, Hans Christian. *The Nightingale.* Eva Le Gallienne, trans. Harper & Row, Pub., 1965.
Blume, Judy. *Are You There God? It's Me, Margaret.* Bradbury, 1970.
Brink, Carol Ryric. *Caddie Woodlawn.* Macmillan, 1935.
Brooks, Jerome. *Uncle Mike's Boy.* Harper & Row, Pub., 1973.
Byars, Betsy. *Summer of the Swans.* Viking, 1970.
Carlson, Natalie. *Ann Aurelia and Dorothy.* Harper & Row, Pub., 1968.
Cleaver, Vera, and Bill Cleaver. *Where the Lilies Bloom.* Lippincott, 1969.
Clymer, Eleanor. *Luke Was There.* Holt, Rinehart & Winston, 1973.
Cohen, Barbara. *Thank You, Jackie Robinson.* Lothrop, 1974.
Colum, Padraic. *Children of Odin.* Macmillan, 1920.
Conford, Ellen. *The Luck of Pokey Bloom.* Little, Brown, 1975.
Corcoran, Barbara. *A Dance to Still Music.* Atheneum, 1974.
DuBois, William Pene. *The Twenty-One Balloons.* Viking, 1947.
Farley, Carol. *The Garden is Doing Fine.* Atheneum, 1975.
Fenton, Edward. *Duffy's Rocks.* Dutton, 1974.
Fitzhugh, Louise. *Harriet the Spy.* Harper & Row, Pub., 1964.
Fox, Paula. *How Many Miles to Babylon?* White, 1967.
Fritz, Jean. *The Cabin Faced West.* Coward, McCann & Geoghegan, 1958.
George, Jean. *Julie of the Wolves.* Harper & Row, Pub., 1971.
Grahame, Kenneth. *The Wind in the Willows.* Scribner's, 1908.
Greene, Bette. *Philip Hall Likes Me. I Reckon, Maybe.* Dial Press, 1974.
Greene, Constance. *A Girl Called Al.* Viking, 1969.
Hamilton, Virginia. *The Planet of Junior Brown.* Macmillan, 1971.

Henry, Marguerite. *King of the Wind.* Rand McNally, 1947.

Hentoff, Nat. *This School Is Driving Me Crazy.* Delacorte, 1975.

Hinton, Susan. *RumbleFish.* Delacorte, 1975.

Holman, Felice. *Slake's Limbo.* Scribner's, 1974.

Ish-Kishor, Sulamith. *Our Eddie.* Pantheon, 1969.

Klein, Norma. *Confessions of an Only Child.* Pantheon, 1974.

Konigsburg, Elaine. *About the B'Nai Bagels.* Atheneum, 1969.

Krumgold, Joseph. *And Now Miguel.* Thomas Y. Crowell, 1953.

Lampman, Evelyn. *The Year of Small Shadow.* Harcourt Brace Jovanovich, Inc., 1971.

Lewis, C. S. *The Lion, the Witch, and the Wardrobe.* Macmillan, 1950.

Little, Jean. *Look Through My Window.* Harper & Row, Pub., 1970

Miles, Betty. *The Real Me.* Knopf, 1974.

Murray, Michele. *Nellie Cameron.* Seabury, 1971.

Paterson, Katherine. *Bridge to Teriabithia.* Thomas Y. Crowell, 1977.

Sachs, Marilyn. *The Bear's House.* Doubleday, 1971.

Sandburg, Carl. *Abraham Lincoln Grows Up.* Harcourt Brace, 1923.

Smith, Doris. *A Taste of Blackberries.* Thomas Y. Crowell, 1973.

Sorensen, Virginia. *Around the Corner.* Harcourt Brace Jovanovich, Inc., 1971.

Sowthall, Ivan. *Let the Balloon Go.* St. Martin, 1967.

Speare, Elizabeth George. *The Bronze Bow.* Houghton Mifflin, 1961.

Stolz, Mary. *The Noonday Friends.* Harper & Row, Pub., 1965.

Ter Haar, Jaar. *Boris.* Delacorte, 1970.

Tolkien, J. R. R. *The Hobbit.* Houghton Mifflin, n.d.

Weik, Mary. *The Jazz Man.* Atheneum, 1968.

White, E. B. *Charlotte's Web.* Harper & Row, Pub., 1952.

Wrightson, Patricia. *A Race Course for Andy.* Harcourt Brace Jovanovich, Inc., 1968.

Yates, Elizabeth. *Amos Fortune: Free Man.* Dutton, 1950.

Index

A

Acrostics, 43–44
Adjectives, 130–31
Advertising, 160–61
Aesop, 77–78
Alexander's Terrible, Horrible No-good, Very Bad Day, 24, 62
All about Letters, 121
Alphabet books, 229
American Indians, 233
Anastasiow, Nicholas, 38
Another Way Out, 121
Assessment, 17, 225–26
Assumptions, 9, 20
Attitudes, 18–19

B

Baby talk, 123–25
Bennett Cerf's Book of Laughs, 76
Bertman, Floyd, 121
Biggest Bear, The, 60
Bookbinding, 198–200
Book lists
  aged in children's books, 240
  birth and death, 241
  divorce, 241
  family ties, 242–43
  friendship, 243
  special children, 244
  women, positive images of, 243–44
Books
  multicultural, 233–35
  picture, 236
  stimulus for writing, 238–40
Brain, 4–5
Brooks, Cleanth, 90
Brown, Rosellen, 73
Browne, Margaret W., 63
Burrows, Alvin T., 202

C

Capitalization, 172–74
Carlson, Ruth, 99
Carroll, Lewis, 41
Categorizing, 102–3

Characterization, 84–85
Charlip, Remy, 24, 63
Charlotte's Web, 142
Cheyney, Arnold, 73
Child, 3–4
Choral speaking, 26–27
Christmas, 98
Christmas Carol, A, 149
Cinco de Mayo, 98
Cinderella, 79–80
Cinquain, 64–65
Clapp, Ouida, 20
Classroom Practices, 1979–80: How to Handle the Paper Load, 227
Clown, 15
Clustering, 14–15, 42
Color poems, 53
Common Sense Composition, 227
Composing: The 1979 Yearbook of the Michigan Council of Teachers of English, 21
Compounding, 134–35
Concepts, 18
Conversation, 125–26
Correction symbols, 172–74
Curriculum, 8, 17–18

D

Dayrell, Elphinstone, 29
Definitions, 49–50
Description, 34–35
  sensory, 96
Dialogue, 58–60, 88–89, 185–86
Diamante, 69–70
Diary of a Young Girl, The, 52
Dickens, Charles, 149
Dictation, 15–17, 138–39, 174–75, 222–23
Directions, 34
Displays, 195–96
Dodd, Anne W., 73, 99
Don't Tell the Scarecrow, 68
Do You Know What I'll Do?, 24, 59
Dragonwings, 16, 142
Drama, 28

E

"Ear for language," 1, 6
Editing, 8, 12, 14, 18, 167–202
  group, 177–78, 180–81
  peer, 182–87
Elliott, Susan, 73
English as a Second Language, 16
English Teacher's Activity Book, The, 121
Errors and Expectations, 202
Essay, five-paragraph, 113–16
Evaluation, 8, 13, 18, 203–27
Expanding sentences, 123–25, 130–33
Exploring Books with Children, 21
Expository writing, 8, 11, 100–121

F

Fables, 77–79
Fagan, William, 227
Fairy tales, 79–80
Figurative language, 162–66. *See also* Metaphor; Simile
Films, 15, 90, 232
Finlay, Ian H., 47
Five-paragraph essay, 113–16
Fluency, 8, 10–11, 39–72
Folktales, 28, 233–35
Fortunately, Unfortunately, 24, 63
Fourth of July, 98
Fragments, 176–77
Freeman, Gwen, 19
Froman, Robert, 47
Funk, Wilfred, 166

G

Gibbs, Ruth, 19
Gingerbread Boy, The, 87
Giving Tree, The, 26
Gonzales, Linda, 19–20
Grammar, 122–42
Grammar for Teachers: Perspectives and Definitions, 142
Grandpa Grig Had a Pig, 60
Grant, Barbara M., 21
Great Big Ugly Man Came up and Tied His Horse to Me, A, 60
Group editing, 177–78, 180–81

H

Haiku, 67–68
Hailey, Jack, 21
Hailstones and Halibut Bones, 97
Handwriting, 2, 189–91
Hansel and Gretel, 79–80
Hanukkah, 98
Harold and the Purple Crayon, 41
Hawley, Isabel, 227
Heide, Florence, 16, 63
Help for the Teacher of Written Composition, 21
Hennings, Dorothy G., 21
Hole Is to Dig, A, 49
Holistic scoring, 208–12, 219–20
Homonyms, 150–52
Hopkins, Lee B., 72, 73
How and why stories, 81–82

Hunter in the Forest, 90
Hyperbole, 82

I

Ideas for Teaching English, 121
Idioms, 155–56
If It Weren't for You, 25
I Love My Mother, 24–25
Imagination and Language, 99
In a Spring Garden, 68
Individualization, 13–14
Inference, 106–7
I Remember, 55–57
I-search paper, 116–17

J

Johnson, Crockett, 41
Jokes, 75–77
Journal, 3, 51–52
Judy, Stephen, 21
Juncture, 30
Just-so Stories, 81

K

Kipling, Rudyard, 81
Klein, Marvin L., 38
Koch, Carl, 227
Koch, Kenneth, 72
Krauss, Ruth, 49

L

Laird, Charlton, 166
Language, books about, 229–31
Language Arts Activities for the Classroom, 21, 38, 166
Language Arts Handbook, The, 5, 7, 21, 115, 142, 166, 202
Language development, 6–10
Language Play: An Introduction to Linguistics, 21, 142, 166
Lantern poems, 66–67
Lear, Edward, 41, 71
Letter writing, 118–21
Lewis, Richard, 68, 72
Library skills, 110–17
Limerick, 70–72
Listening, 33–37, 157–58
Literature, 23–28
Little Red Riding Hood, 80, 87, 90, 114–15
Long, Bob, 19
Love, 25–26
Lundsteen, Sara W., 21

M

McCord, David, 41
McGraw Hill Elementary Science Study Kit, 105
Magazines, 197
Malapropism, 159–60
Mapping, 92–93, 114
Maxwell, Rhoda J., 21
Measure for Research and Evaluation in the English Language Arts, 227
Memory writing, 55–57
Messick, Elaine, 19
Metaphor, 53–55, 96–98
Mexican Americans, 234
Michel, Lois A., 121
Miracle of Language, The, 166
Miracles, 72
Modeling, 138–40
Moffett, James, 2–3, 4, 21
Mother Goose, 28, 60–61
Multicultural books, 233–35

N

Narrative writing, 8, 11, 74–99
Neakrans, Roberta, 19
Neman, Beth, 21
Newspaper headlines, 126–28
Nilsen, Alleen Pace, 21, 142, 166
Nilsen, Don L. F., 21, 142, 166
Nobody is Perfick, 52
Notebook, writing, 169–70
Notetaking, 112–13
Nursery rhymes, 27–28, 60–61

O

Observation, 95–96, 105–9
"Old Mother Hubbard," 28
O'Neill, Mary, 49, 97
Oral language, 8, 10, 22–38
Oral Language: Expression of Thought, 38
Outlining. *See* Clustering; Mapping
Overhead projector, 178–79

P

Padgett, Rod, 99
Paperload. *See* Editing; Evaluation
Paragraph, 91–95, 103–4, 112–13, 115, 219–20
Parallel stories, 63
Paraphrasing, 2
Parody, 60–61
Pass the Poetry, 73
Patterned writing, 23, 53–63
Paul Bunyan, 82–83
Peer editing, 182–87

Peer evaluation, 215–21
Personification, 164–66
Philosophy, 2–6, 9
Picture books, 236
Pitch, 30
Plan Write, 8
Poems to Hear and See, 47
Poetry, 45–48, 53, 59, 60–61, 73
  editing, 192–93
  forms, 63
  resources for teachers, 236–37
Point of view, 90–91
Pooley, Robert, 166
"Poor Old Lady," 26–27
Porter, Robert, 99
Pourquoi tales, 81–82
Prefixes, 146–47
Prewriting, 14–15
Primary traits, 181–82, 207
Prompts, 17
Proofreading, 172–74, 175–76
Proverbs, 8
Publishing writing, 196–200
Punctuation, 140–42
Puppetry, 28–30

R

Readers' theater, 31–33
Reading aloud, 18
Reading list, 249–51
Real Mother Goose, The, 60
Record keeping, 222–26
Reeves, Ruth, 121
Reports, 109–17
Research, 110–17
Resources, 228–51
Response groups, 14, 17
Revising, 3
Role playing, 31
Rubrics for scoring, 208–11

S

Schwartz, Alvin, 76
Scope of Fiction, 90
Scoring, holistic, 208–12, 219–20
Self-awareness, 237–38
Self-editing, 187–93
Self-esteem, 3
Self-evaluation, 215–21
Sentence combining, 135–38
Sentence expanding, 123–25, 130–33
Sentences, 8, 12, 35–36, 122–42
Sentence variety, 187–89
Sequencing, 37
Setting, 85–86, 106–7
Shaughnessy, Mina, 202
Silverstein, Shel, 26, 41
Simile, 53–55, 63, 96–98, 162–64
Sleeping Beauty, 114
Some Things Are Scary, 63
Sound of Sunshine, Sound of Rain, 16
South Bay Writing Project, 8–9, 20
Sparkling Words, 99
Speakers, guest, 201
Spelling, 17, 170–71
Stanford, Gene, 227
Stories, 8, 11, 74–99
Story, elements of, 83–99
Strategies for Teaching the Composition Process, 227
Stream of consciousness, 50–51
Street poems, 47
Stress, 30
Student-centered Language Arts and Reading, K–13, 4
Student-teacher conferences, 193–94, 213–15
Syllables, 144–46
Synonyms, 153–54

T

Talk in the Language Arts Classroom, 38
Tall tales, 82–83
Teacher responses, 206–7
Teachers, 19–20
Teaching of English Usage, The, 166
Teaching Students to Write, 21
Teaching the Basics—Really!, 20
Teaching Writing, 21
Telegrams, 128–29
Telephone, 125–26
Television, 108–9
Tenth Good Thing about Barney, The, 26
"There Was an Old Woman," 61
They All Want to Write, 202
Thinking, 4–5
Thought & Language/Language & Reading, 21
Three Billy Goats Gruff, 87
Three Pigs, The, 79, 80, 87
Thurber, James, 77
Tiedt, Iris M., 5, 7, 21, 32–33, 38, 69, 115, 142, 166, 202
Tiedt holistic model for teaching writing, 8
Time management, 221–26
Tom Sawyer, 86
Tom Swifties, 158–59
Tovey, Duane, 121
Transcribing, 2, 123–25
Tripp, Wallace, 41, 60–61

V

Velveteen Rabbit, The, 26
Verbs, 133–34
Viorst, Judith, 24, 26, 62
Vocabulary, 149–53

W

Waber, Bernard, 52
Wagner, Betty Jane, 4, 21
Ward, Lynd, 60
Warren, Robert P., 90
Way, Sandra, 19
Weaver, Constance, 142
Welech, David, 73
Wermuth, Linda, 99
Where Have You Been?, 63
White, E. B., 142
Whole Word Catalogue, The, 73
Why the Sun and the Moon Live in the Sky, 29
Wierville, Cheryl, 19
Williams, Margery, 26
Wind Is from the North, The, 32–33
Witcracks: Jokes and Jests from American Folklore, 76
Wizard of Oz, 86
Wolf, Maryanne, 21
Word choices, 143–66
Wordless books, 244–46
Word order, 131
Word origins, 148–49
Word Origins and Their Romantic Stories, 166
Word play, 40–51, 154–61
Words
  meanings of, 147–54
  precise, 8, 12
Words, Words, Words, 49
Wright, Blanche F., 60
Write Now, 73, 99
Writing
  defined, 2–3
  memory, 55–57
  narrative, 8, 11, 74–99
  patterned, 23, 53–63
  program, 17–18
  publishing, 196–200
  success in, 205–6
Writing across the curriculum
  animal life, 246
  math, 246–47
  science, 247
  social studies, 247–48
Writing Centers in the Elementary School, 121
Writing Corner, The, 73
Writing notebook, 169–70
Writing process, 1–21, 248–49
Writing Sense, 99
Written Expression in the Language Arts, 21

Y

Year of Writing Activities, A, 73
Yep, Laurence, 16, 142

Z

Zavatsky, Bill, 99
Zindel, Paul, 24–25
Zolotow, Charlotte, 24, 25, 59